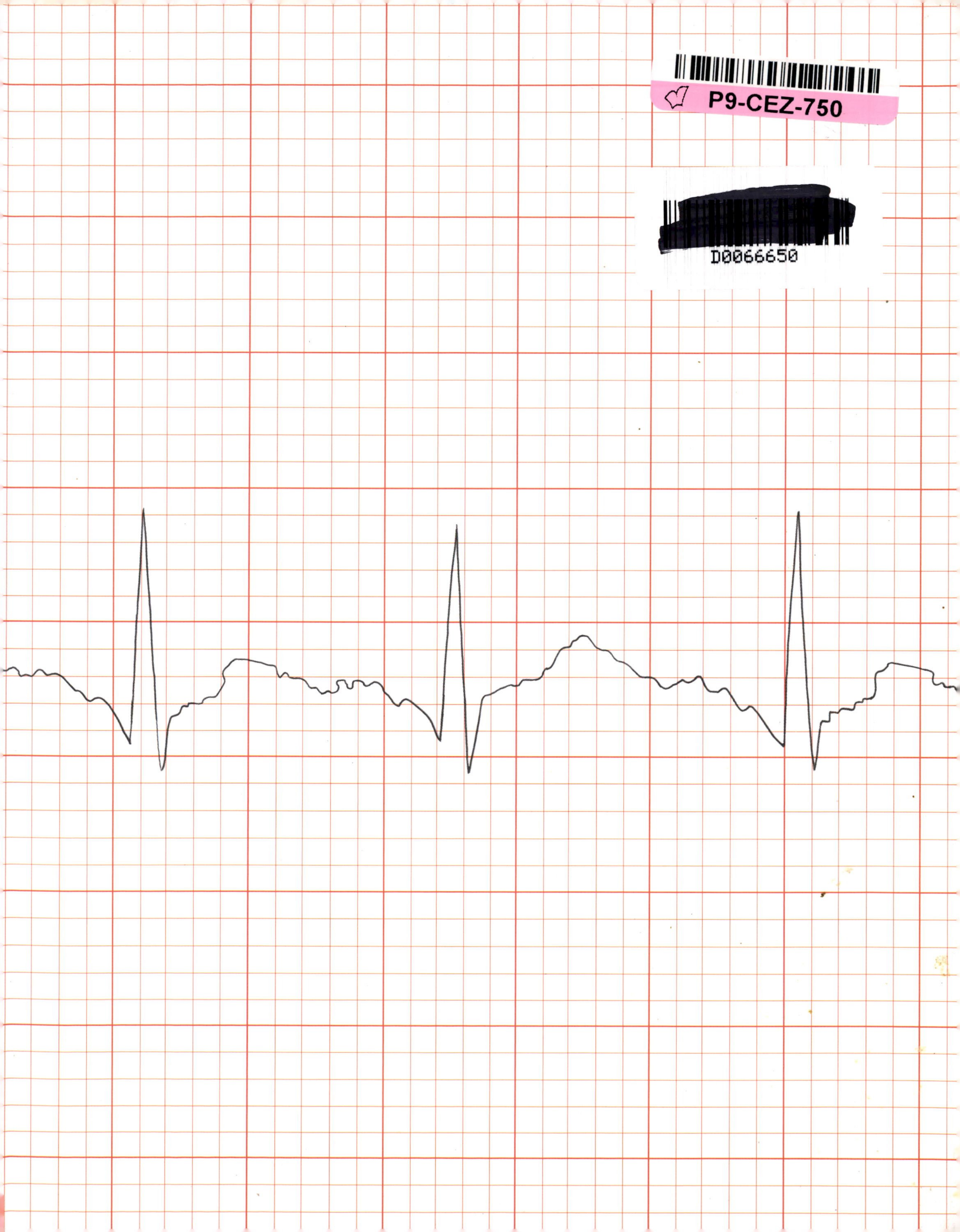

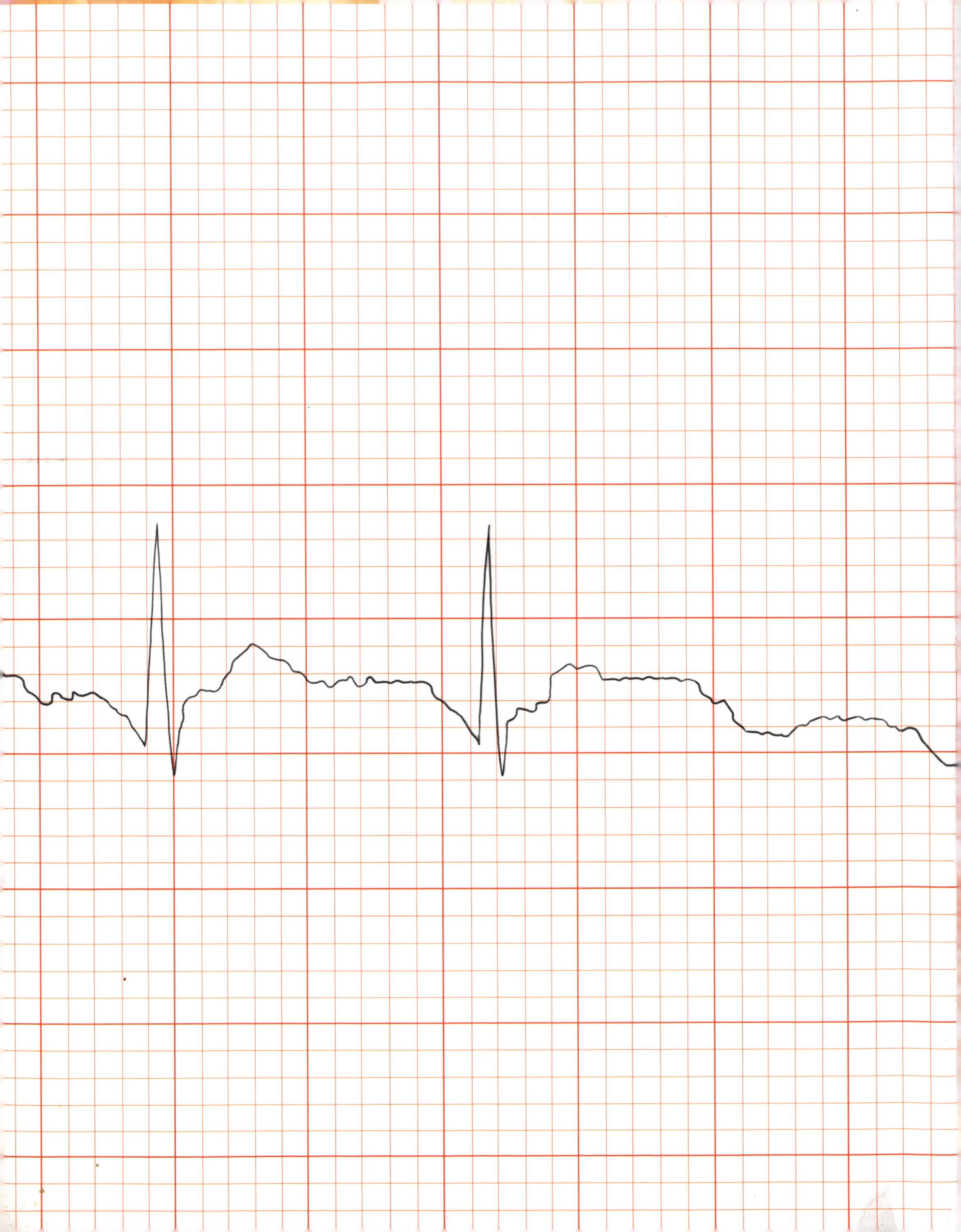

THE COMPLETE MANUAL OF THINGS THAT MIGHT KILL YOU

THE COMPLETE MANUAL OF THINGS THAT MIGHT KILL YOU

A Guide to Self-Diagnosis for Hypochondriacs

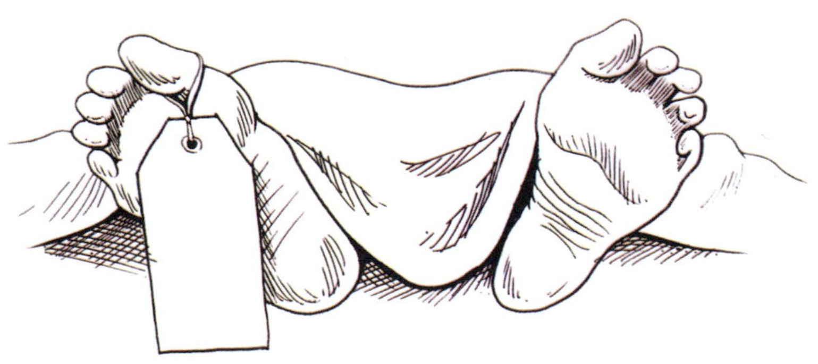

VENICE, CALIFORNIA

Created and published by Knock Knock
Distributed by Who's There, Inc.
Venice, CA 90291
knockknockstuff.com

Illustrated by Megan E. Bluhm Foldenauer

This book is a work of humor meant solely for entertainment purposes. It is not intended to recommend or advise regarding the prevention, diagnosis, or treatment of any medical condition. The advice contained in this book is intended as a parody of family medical guides; actually following the advice contained herein may be harmful to your health. In no event will Knock Knock be liable to any reader for any damages, including direct, indirect, incidental, special, consequential, or punitive damages, arising out of or in connection with the use of the information contained in this book. If you're sick, see a doctor. If you're dead, call the morgue. If you're a hypochondriac, read on. So there.

ISBN: 978-160106035-8
UPC: 8-25703-50001-1

20 19 18 17 16 15 14 13 12 11 10

Contents

FIGURES

SPOTLIGHTS

Introduction

THE NOBLE HYPOCHONDRIAC

Welcome, hypochondriac—you're about to explore the only book written just for you and your needs.

Of course you already know that intellectually traversing the vast array of human medical conditions is an exhilarating adventure inside your own mind, like riding a roller coaster or screaming through a good horror movie. In the mindset of a health detective, you can explore each and every symptom, fantasizing that it may be an indication of a debilitating—or possibility fatal—disorder.

Hypochondria boasts a long and esteemed legacy of followers because, as you know, it brings so many benefits. You're hypervigilant about your own health. You can speak to doctors in their language (and with the glossary of medical terminology at the end of this book, you'll even be able to make up your own ailments!). You've got a great imagination. You're a fascinating conversationalist at dinner parties, full of stories about rashes and infections. You frequently get to feel relieved that you're not, in fact, dying.

Until *The Complete Manual of Things that Might Kill You*, however, you've had to satisfy your need for self-diagnosis with medical reference materials written for the masses. Now, for the first time, you can indulge your hypochondria to your cardiac content with information that's been assembled expressly for your unique outlook on health.

While hypochondria is largely harmless, in some extreme cases it can intensify and begin interfering with your life and well-being. If this happens to you, and you come to the conclusion that you'd like to leave your hypochondria behind, we'll show you how to do that as well.

Whether for the "worried well" or the neurotic who's looking to make a life change, *The Complete Manual of Things that Might Kill You* is one-stop reading for all your phobic needs. Our guarantee to you? You'll come away from this book suspecting that you're terminally ill, suffering from multiple exotic ailments—or at the very least, feeling a bit itchy.

WHAT IS HYPOCHONDRIA?

Also called "health anxiety" or "hypochondriasis," hypochondria is chronic, abnormal concern for one's health, characterized by the interpretion of normal bodily functions or minor symptoms as indications of serious health problems. Some physical symptoms are imagined while others may be real but exaggerated. In the hypochondriac's mind, however, the symptoms always feel real, and it's generally difficult to reassure hypochondriacs that their fears may be unfounded. Of course, the stress over health concerns is a slippery slope, because the worrying itself can exacerbate existing symptoms and even create new ones.

THE HISTORY OF HYPOCHONDRIA

First used by Hippocrates in the 4th century BCE, the word *hypochondria* derives from *hypo-* (under) and *chondros* (cartilage), meaning "under the rib cage." The term did not, however, refer to disproportionate health fears; instead, it identified digestive disorders of the liver, spleen, and gallbladder. It was believed that humors (bodily fluids determining a person's temperament and psychological states) emanating from the hypochondrium caused both physical and emotional problems. Excessive health preoccupation was characterized by the Roman physician Galen in the 2nd century CE as a digestive disorder associated with melancholia (a medical condition resulting from an overabundance of the "black bile" humor) and distinguished by a fear of illness.

In *The Anatomy of Melancholy*, 16th-century scholar and lifelong depressive Robert Burton described the symptoms of "hypochondriacal melancholy" as "Fearful, sad, suspicious, discontent, anxiety, etc. Lascivious by reason of much wind, troublesome dreams, affected by fits, etc." In the late 17th century, Molière penned *The Imaginary Invalid*, a play about a hypochondriacal man who wants his daughter to marry a doctor so that he can receive the medical attention he desires. Molière, himself a hypochondriac, had been suffering from chronic pulmonary infection for years; by the time he wrote the play, he knew he was dying. Though his friends urged him to rest, he assumed the starring role—and collapsed and died during the fourth performance.

Through the 18th century, due to a belief that low spirits originated in the abdomen, *hypochondria* referred generally to depression. Samuel Johnson, the original author of *A Dictionary of the English Language*, defined *hypochondria* as "that which produces melancholy." In 1766, the term was used by John Hill in his "Hypochondriasis, A Practical Treatise on the Nature and Cure of that Disorder; Commonly Called *the Hyp* and *Hypo*" to characterize a vague ailment of indigestion and aches and pains. "*The hyp*" became so common in 18th-century England that it was known as the "English malady," the male counterpart to hysteria (also a depressive ailment, thought to be caused by a wandering uterus) among women.

In the 19th century, hypochondria began to acquire the meaning it carries today and was classified as a mental disorder. Marcel Proust, another great hypochondriac, wrote in *Remembrance of Things Past*, "For each ailment that doctors cure with medications (as I am told they do occasionally succeed in doing) they produce 10 others in healthy individuals by inoculating them with that pathogenic agent one thousand times more virulent than all the microbes—the idea that they are ill."

Hypochondria received little medical attention in the 20th century. Sigmund Freud viewed the condition as a neurosis resulting from blocked libido, leading to the libido being redirected into the part of the body that was imagined to be diseased. Freud also wondered about the connections between hypochondria and paranoia. In 1980, hypochondria finally got its full due and was added to the American Psychological Association's *Diagnostic and Statistical Manual of Mental Disorders*, under "Somatoform Disorder," comprising ailments for which "there is no diagnosable general medical condition to fully account for the physical symptoms."

WHO IS THE HYPOCHONDRIAC?

Studies reveal that approximately 5 percent of us are severe hypochondriacs, equally male and female, while many more are casually ailment-obsessed. Some characteristics predispose individuals to the condition:

- A serious childhood illness
- A serious illness in a family member during childhood
- Parental overprotectiveness around health during childhood
- Childhood trauma such as physical or sexual abuse
- Depression
- Anxiety
- Possibly more frequent in artists (especially actors and musicians) and medical professionals

Most hypochondriacs come into their condition in their twenties and thirties, sometimes triggered by the illness or death of a close friend or family member.

Disease-specific hypochondria can be driven by an individual's experience of a certain disease—perhaps a parent or sibling suffered from it, for example, or they have a higher statistical chance of contracting the ailment. Or, if family members died at a certain age, hypochondria can be instigated as an individual nears that birthday.

Jobs that entail overexposure to sickness can lead to unfounded health fears. Because it's often spotted in beginning medical students, their hypochondria has been variously named "medical student's disease," "nosophobia," and "medical studentitis." Directly connected to the temporary area of study (such as a particular disease or part of the body), these concerns usually pass and are a testament to the powers of suggestion.

ARE YOU A HYPOCHONDRIAC?

The term *hypochondriac* is used colloquially to describe people who frequently worry about their health, but that doesn't mean they're in the 5 percent who are actually afflicted with the clinical disorder. True hypochondriacs tend to exhibit certain behaviors:

- *Fear of serious illness*: The most common symptom of hypochondria is the conviction that you're suffering from a life-threatening or life-altering illness without medical proof. Also prevalent is the certainty that a minor symptom is evidence of a more serious illness—when hypochodriacs hear hooves, they think zebras, not horses.
- *Preoccupation with the body*: Hypochondriacs are intimately attuned to their body and its rhythms, whether heart rate, stomach rumblings, or quality of breathing.
- *Self-diagnosis*: The drive to self-diagnose through medical manuals or Internet health sites is a prominent marker of hypochondria.
- *Extreme behavior toward medical care*: While some hypochondriacs are constant visitors to the emergency room and doctor's office, others avoid medical care altogether for fear of a terrible diagnosis—and instead wind up neglecting their health.
- *Distrust or disbelief in diagnosis*: Many hypochondriacs distrust their doctors' diagnoses, feeling they are incorrect or don't take into consideration all the exhibiting symptoms and potential diseases. This distrust often leads to doctor shopping.
- *Doctor shopping*: Unsatisfied with your doctor's diagnosis and seeking a second, third, fourth, or even fifth opinion? When their fears aren't confirmed, hypochondriacs feel they aren't receiving proper care or attention from their doctors, who can grow weary of constant complaints and begin to dismiss concerns.
- *The need for reassurance*: Asking family members, friends, doctors, and other medical professionals to soothe concerns is common among hypochondriacs. Unlike those who are merely fearful about their health, the hypochondriac cannot be reassured.

The Whiteley Index

Since 1967, the gold-standard for hypochondria diagnosis has been the Whiteley Index, developed by Dr. Issy Pilowsky and first published in the *British Journal of Psychiatry*.

	Question	Yes	No
1	Do you often worry about the possibility that you have got a serious illness?		
2	Are you bothered by many pains and aches?		
3	Do you find that you are often aware of various things happening in your body?		
4	Do you worry a lot about your health?		
5	Do you often have the symptoms of very serious illness?		
6	If a disease is brought to your attention (through the radio, television, newspapers, or someone you know) do you worry about getting it yourself?		
7	If you feel ill and someone tells you that you are looking better, do you become annoyed?		

	Question	Yes	No
8	Do you find that you are bothered by many different symptoms?		
9	Is it easy for you to forget about yourself, and think about all sorts of other things?		
10	Is it hard for you to believe the doctor when he or she tells you there is nothing for you to worry about?		
11	Do you get the feeling that people are not taking your illness seriously enough?		
12	Do you think that you worry about your health more than most people?		
13	Do you think there is something seriously wrong with your body?		
14	Are you afraid of illness?		

SCORING: Give yourself a point for every "yes" response to all questions except number 9, for which you get a point if you checked "no." This should produce a score between 0 and 14. Higher scores indicate higher levels of health anxiety. A score of 8 or more usually indicates a high probability of a health-anxiety disorder.

THE CONTEMPORARY HYPOCHONDRIAC

There's never been a better time to be a hypochondriac. Thanks to today's proliferation of media, especially self-diagnosis and self-help materials, the contemporary world is practically custom-made to stimulate the hypochondriac's fantasy life. It's perfectly reasonable to feel like you're dying—if you didn't, you'd be crazy.

Print and broadcast news has increased its coverage of health issues including obesity, diabetes, cancer, Alzheimer's disease, and autism over the past few years. Potential pandemics such as avian flu or health threats like mad-cow disease get exponentially more airtime than warranted by the actual impact of the maladies. Even though the number of flu cases has been stable in recent years, for example, publicity has led to a mounting demand for vaccinations. Every newspaper now has a weekly health section, and news programs and channels employ dedicated health reporters. Talk shows feature people suffering from devastating diseases. The boom in advertising for prescription medication punctuates television hospital dramas, and if you flip the channel, you can find reality programming set in emergency rooms.

Not only does this groundswell make it appear that disease is more prevalent and common than it actually is, the coverage tends to focus on hot-button diseases, such as cancer, obesity, and AIDS, or the rarest of the rare. They prompt increased awareness and personal scrutiny while conferring social acceptability to constant health self-analysis, bringing the rest of America right in step with the hypochondriac.

The Internet, however, is the mother lode for the contemporary hypochondriac—never before has it been possible to browse so many terrifying diseases at any time, day or night. With their own high-tech condition, *cyberchondria* (using the Internet to indulge hypochondria), the worried well are on the cutting edge of technological advances. Users "symptom surf," typing their disturbing sensations into a search engine to pull up any diseases they might have. One medical website lists over 500 different diseases associated with headaches, ranging from a hangover to the bubonic plague. But users beware, according to a *Consumer Reports* study,

41 percent of doctors said patients received incorrect information online.

Add to this media climate the growth of alternative medicine and you have the perfect breeding ground for society-wide hypochondria. We're more "in tune" with our bodies, and our health conversations no longer require Western medical doctors—who are likely to assert that the hypochondriac suffers from no physiological disease. Alternative therapies provide the hypochondriac with a support system that allopathic care often doesn't. Everything is an imbalance or disease, and all maladies can be chalked up to the toxic world in which we live. Alternative medicine is strongly correlated with doctor shopping, self-diagnosis, and self-treatments ranging from dietary supplements to detoxification to enemas.

HYPOCHONDRIA: CULTIVATE OR CURE IT?

While hypochondria is an engaging source of mental stimulation for some, others find it disabling. As a hypochondriac, you'll want to search deep within to determine whether your neurosis works for you.

THE BENEFITS OF HYPOCHONDRIA

Like all forms of unique awareness, hypochondria supports creative development. Among its many benefits are:

- *Increased attention to health*: Hypochondriacs are more sensitive to their own bodies than the average person, able to note even the most minor of symptoms, making them more likely to be treated promptly. Some hypochondriacs even keep health diaries to help doctors find out what might be wrong.
- *In-depth knowledge of health-related issues*: As a result of their diligent research, hypochondriacs are extremely well informed about health and medicine.
- *Conversation booster*: Hypochondriacs always have something to talk about, whether their own health, horror stories about others, or helpful diagnoses for friends.
- *Social networking*: Not only do hypochondriacs get to meet new doctors, they will encounter potential (and possibly like-minded) friends in the waiting room or at the pharmacy. Health-related online forums expand their circle of friends even more.
- *Vivid imagination*: The hypochondriac is blessed with a powerful fantasy life, keeping those all-important mental muscles in shape with frequent exercise.

THE DRAWBACKS OF HYPOCHONDRIA

If your hypochondria is getting you down, there's no question—seek treatment. For most of us, our mild hypochondria hovers at the periphery, allowing us to function happily in daily life. However, even with all its benefits, for some people hypochondria can prove mentally, physically, and financially devastating. Negative effects include:

- *Missed school or work*: Hypochondriacs often miss school or work because they are at the doctor's office or home suffering from an ailment. Hypochondria can thus damage a career or report card.
- *Unnecessary medical procedures*: Medical testing, exploratory surgery, and unwarranted treatment can result in damaging physical complications. Even something as innocuous as repeated blood work can lead to broken blood vessels and nerve damage. And given the prevalence of nosocomial infections, the more time spent in the doctor's office or hospital, the more likely they are to actually contract something.
- *Isolation from friends and family*: In extreme manifestations of the neurosis, hypochondriacs can focus so intently and exclusively on their health that they isolate from family and friends, who tire of continually hearing about health concerns.
- *Missed diseases or conditions*: Focusing too much on diseases they *could* have means they might miss a disease they *do* have. Because hypochondriacs cry wolf, doctors and caregivers may neglect to investigate legitimate claims.
- *Unhealthy coping mechanisms*: It's not uncommon for hypochondriacs to feel angry or depressed because doctors don't believe they're actually ill, leading to damaging coping mechanisms such as the overuse of sedatives, pain relievers, alcohol, and sleep aids—even drug dependency. Because severe hypochondria is associated with depression and anxiety disorders, these palliatives tend to be mere Band-Aids.
- *Financial outlay*: Whether or not you have insurance, excessive medical care isn't cheap. Co-pays add up, as does medication. Many plans will not cover certain procedures and place limits on expenditures. If care is paid out-of-pocket, hypochondria can quickly decimate a bank account.
- *Living in a constant state of fear*: Real fear is no fun. Constantly anticipating the worst not only takes a mental

and emotional toll but also burdens the body with stress.

TREATMENT OPTIONS FOR HYPOCHONDRIA

If you find that you're falling into column B rather than A and you want to alleviate your suffering, there are a few ways to go. We've yet to discover the "cure" for hypochondria, and medical opinions differ on the best approach. Hypochondria is often considered to be a secondary manifestation of an underlying condition such as anxiety or depression, so doctors attempt to treat the primary ailment in conjunction with the hypochondria. In its link to anxiety disorders, hypochondria is characterized as an excessive preoccupation. Given that hypochondriacs are obsessive about their health and have difficulty managing their thoughts and fears, it's connected to obsessive-compulsive disorder. In addition to coinciding with clinical depression, hypochondria appears to worsen with life stress and situational depression. Professionals currently treat hypochondria in the following ways:

- *Psychotherapy*: Considered the primary treatment for hypochondria, psychotherapy views the condition as transference of non-health fears or traumas into health concerns or symptoms, and thus aims to discover and work through those underlying motivations. Additionally, it addresses the obsessive actions and anxiety associated with the hypochondria itself. Many consider cognitive behavioral therapy to work best among the psychotherapeutic regimens, as it provides the hypochondriac with alternate thought and behavior patterns as well as exploring underlying emotional causes.
- *Medication*: For many hypochondriacs, drug treatment for depression and anxiety significantly alleviates symptoms, helping to treat the primary ailment and chemically softening repetitive thought.
- *Hypnosis*: An increasingly frequent treatment, hypnosis places individuals in a trance-like state to increase receptivity to suggestions aimed at alleviating hypochondriacal behavior. Hypnosis is sometimes used in conjunction with psychotherapy.
- *Single-doctor care*: Association with a single physician who knows the patient's dynamics is found to be effective for hypochondriacs, who

tend not to trust doctors and to shop around for medical care. Within a long-term, trusted association, hypochondriacs can learn to manage their fears. This works best when the doctor is sympathetic to and knowledgeable about hypochondria. Rather than dismissing the patient by saying "it's all in your head," the doctor is firm but understanding, and helps the patient by pacing medical appointments and reassuring the patient in ways that directly address the hypochondria. Without the resonating voices of multiple doctors, the hypochondriac is able to normalize medical treatment to some extent.

If indeed you decide to seek treatment, talk to your primary care physician, therapist, or a friend who might be able to recommend either. For those whose hypochondria is not crippling, however, there is one more potential therapeutic tool:

- *This book*: Yes, *The Complete Manual of Things that Might Kill You* can result in counter-conditioning, a behavioral-therapy technique whereby the reader is systematically desensitized to the feared element. Also called "exposure therapy," facing fears in a repeated and extreme way can defuse them. Or, of course, you can use this book to continue stoking your paranoia fires—it's your call!

GO FORTH AND AIL!

Now that you're an expert on hypochondria, you're ready to delve into the wide world of affliction. Diagnose yourself, diagnose your friends, or just revel in the diversity of everything that can go wrong. With your hypochondria, you're in the company of such geniuses as Charles Darwin, Howard Hughes, Leo Tolstoy, Molière, Leonard Bernstein, Igor Stravinsky, Marcel Proust—and the mother of all nurses, Florence Nightingale! Even if you don't write a novel or compose a symphony in your lifetime, with the help of this book, hypochondriacal greatness is within your grasp.

How to Use this Book

It couldn't be easier, because this book has been organized for the knowledge-seeking hypochondriac. Whether you choose to read the book from front to back, consult it only when you feel under the weather, or keep it in the bathroom for random perusing, there's no wrong way to enjoy it. And of course, unlike the Internet, this book is eminently portable, so once you've landed on a self-diagnosis, bring it with you to the doctor's office to state your case.

- Symptoms are sequenced by body part, from head to toe, with systemic and mental conditions last. Within each physical region, common symptoms are listed. Identify yours and read on to self-diagnose from among the potential ailments.
- The individual disease profiles include an overall description ("What It Is"), specialists to consult, other symptoms to verify or rule out your self-diagnosis, and what you can expect by way of progression and treatment.
- Throughout the book, spotlights on topics of interest offer in-depth explorations of terrifying trends in the world of health.
- The glossary translates the medical prefixes and suffixes that comprise disease names and terminology. Not only will you be able to understand medical-speak, you can invent diseases of your own and make them sound legitimate!
- If you're looking for a particular ailment, consult the alphabetical disease index.

Each disease is rated according to various scales from 1 to 4, with 1 being the least and 4 being the most, as follows:

Contagion: Assessed only according to person-to-person contagion, without referencing such vectors and vehicles as insects and infected water.

Pain: Assesses degree of physical pain and whether the pain is acute or long-lasting.

Suffering: Includes debilitation, disability, and length of ailment, as well as whether the illness is chronic and compromises a healthy, active lifestyle.

Fatal: "No" indicates that the illness rarely or never causes death, while "yes" characterizes an illness that is almost always or invariably fatal; "maybe" defines those in between.

Not only are these ratings somewhat subjective, individual cases can vary significantly, causing extreme pain and suffering in some instances and mild discomfort in others. Please note that the ratings may not reflect all individuals' experiences of the characterized ailments.

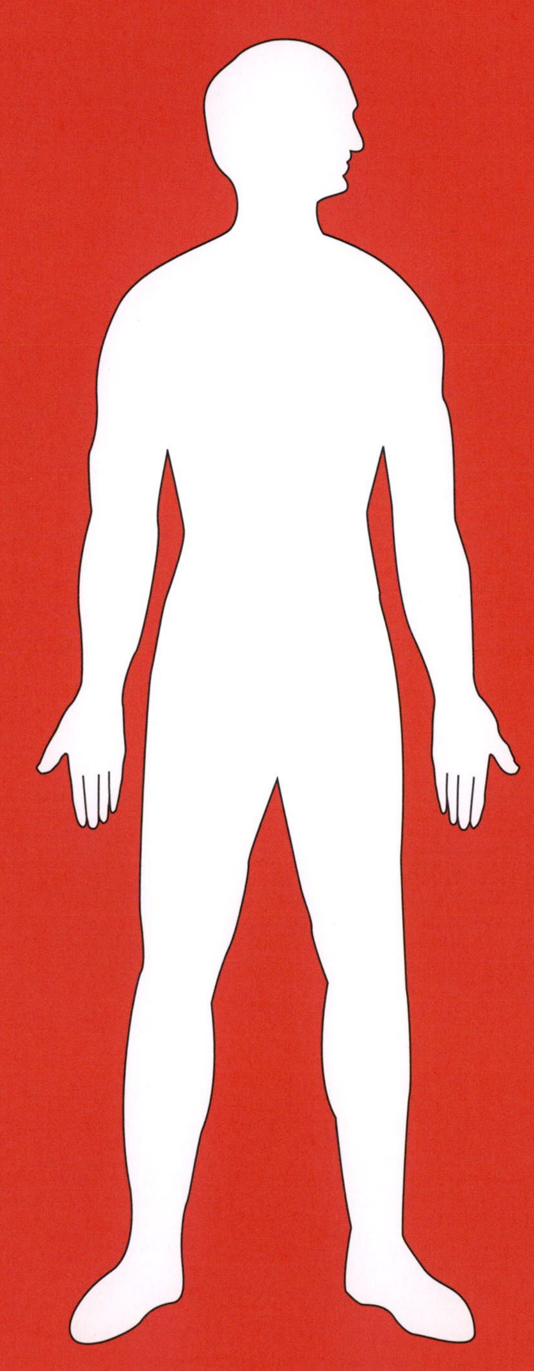

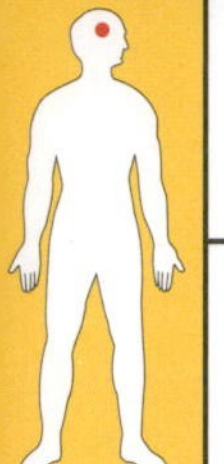

FACT | 700 million people are inhabited by blood-sucking hookworms.

If you have a headache...

...you might have

BRAIN TUMOR

WHAT IT IS: Abnormal growth of cells in brain. Underlying cause is generally unknown. May be malignant or benign. Can originate in brain or consist of cancer that has metastasized from elsewhere. Often rapidly invades surrounding brain tissue.

SPECIALIST TO SEE: Neurologist, Oncologist

OTHER SYMPTOMS:

- Vomiting
- Loss of vision, speech, or hearing
- Difficulty walking or balancing
- Memory loss
- Seizures

PROGRESSION: Initially, symptoms may be nonexistent or intermittent. As tumor grows, pressure and swelling increase and symptoms worsen. Permanent brain damage, and eventually death, may occur.

TREATMENT: Steroids to shrink tumor. Surgery, radiation, or chemotherapy. Anticonvulsants.

CONTAGION:	**1**	2	3	4
PAIN:	1	2	**3**	4
SUFFERING:	1	2	**3**	4
FATAL:	Yes	No	**Maybe**	

...or you might have

ENCEPHALITIS

WHAT IT IS: Viral infection that causes brain inflammation. Transmitted directly between humans or through blood-sucking insects such as ticks or mosquitoes. Can be caused by complications from other diseases, such as rabies or syphilis.

SPECIALIST TO SEE: Neurologist, Infectious Disease Specialist

OTHER SYMPTOMS:

- Sensitivity to light
- Drowsiness
- Fever
- Confusion
- Stiff neck
- Convulsions
- Nausea or vomiting

PROGRESSION: Symptoms may not develop for up to 30 days after infection. Can invade brain and spinal cord, causing headache, irritability, seizures, and disorientation. In severe cases, permanent brain damage, stroke, seizures, or death can occur.

TREATMENT: Antiviral medication. Pain relievers. Physical therapy and rehabilitation to treat neurological damage.

CONTAGION:	1	2	3	**4**
PAIN:	1	2	3	**4**
SUFFERING:	1	2	**3**	4
FATAL:	Yes	No	**Maybe**	

...or you might have

HIV/AIDS

WHAT IT IS: Immune system disorder that diminishes body's ability to fight infection. Mainly spread through sexual contact, infected blood products, or contaminated needles. As immune system is destroyed, other illnesses such as cancer and viral or bacterial infections invade body.

SPECIALIST TO SEE: Infectious Disease Specialist

OTHER SYMPTOMS:

- Swollen lymph nodes
- Fever or chills
- Unintended weight loss
- Diarrhea
- Skin sores
- Coughing

PROGRESSION: When first contracted, may be asymptomatic or present as mild flu. As virus multiplies, frequent infections and chronic symptoms develop. Death likely once immune system is significantly impaired.

TREATMENT: No known cure. Antiretroviral medication to delay symptoms.

CONTAGION:	1	2	**3**	4
PAIN:	1	2	3	**4**
SUFFERING:	1	2	**3**	4
FATAL:	Yes	No	**Maybe**	

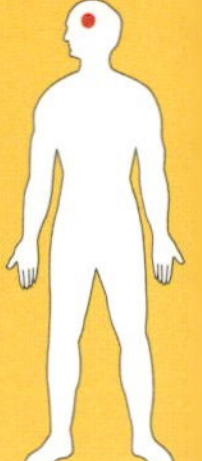

...or you might have
MUCORMYCOSIS

WHAT IT IS: Aggressive and life-threatening disease caused by common fungi found in soil. Eats away at blood vessels, bones, and tissue of face and head, including roof of mouth, nostrils, eye sockets, and brain. Those with underlying immune system disorders, cancer, or uncontrolled diabetes primarily at risk. Even with treatment, up to 80 percent mortality rate.

SPECIALIST TO SEE: Infectious Disease Specialist, Neurologist, Otolaryngologist

OTHER SYMPTOMS:

- Face or eye pain
- Bulging eyes
- Black nasal discharge
- Bloody cough
- Vision loss

PROGRESSION: Commonly starts with pain, fever, and headache. Then, quickly spreads to face, lungs, skin, and gastrointestinal system. Urgent diagnosis and aggressive treatment required. Often, severe disfigurement results from treatment. Death likely.

TREATMENT: Surgical debridement (removal) of dead or infected tissue. Intravenous antifungal medication.

CONTAGION:	1	**2**	3	4
PAIN:	1	2	3	**4**
SUFFERING:	1	2	3	**4**
FATAL:	**Yes**	No	Maybe	

If your hair is falling out...

...you might have
TINEA CAPITIS

WHAT IT IS: Fungal infection that causes ring-shaped patches of baldness and itchy, crusty, scaly scalp. Highly contagious and easily spread through

FACT | A sneeze can travel 100 MPH.

Health Makes You Sick

It's been formulated that happiness is the gap between expectations and reality. According to Richard Layard in *Happiness: Lessons from a New Science*, this results in the "hedonic treadmill, where you have to keep running in order that your happiness stand still." We quickly become accustomed to what we have, and then we want more. This equation doesn't stop at medicine: the healthier we get, the more we complain about our health.

Rapidly inflating expectations for longevity, physical fitness at older ages, illness prevention, and the curative power of science don't appear to result in greater contentment. In fact, it's precisely the opposite. A 2002 study by Amartya Sen, reported in the *British Medical Journal,* compares health perceptions in 2 states in India: Kerala and Bihar. Kerala has the highest literacy levels in India and a life expectancy of 74 years. Bihar is poor, lacking in medical care and education, and has a lifespan 15 years less than Kerala's and much lower than India overall. Yet Bihar's "self-reported morbidity," the perceived prevalence of disease, is only a tiny fraction of Kerala's—and Kerala's self-reported morbidity is less than the United States, despite Americans' greater longevity.

The unfortunate conclusion? "The more people are exposed to contemporary health care," states Dr. Iona Heath, also in the *British Medical Journal*, "the sicker they feel."

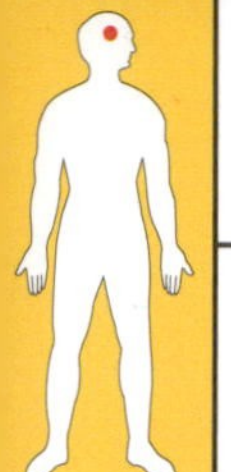

contact with infected brushes, combs, pillows, and bath towels. Can transmit through contact with cats or dogs. Also known as scalp ringworm.

SPECIALIST TO SEE: Dermatologist

OTHER SYMPTOMS:
- Flaking skin
- Brittle hair
- Swollen, oozing masses on scalp

PROGRESSION: First, hair loss and flaking skin appear. If untreated, can lead to permanent scarring and balding. Secondary bacterial infections, fever, and painful, pus-filled boils may occur.

TREATMENT: Antifungal medication.

CONTAGION: 1 2 3 **4**

PAIN: 1 **2** 3 4

SUFFERING: **1** 2 3 4

FATAL: Yes **No** Maybe

...or you might have
WERNER SYNDROME

WHAT IT IS: Genetic condition that causes body to age prematurely because cells in sufferers have shorter life span than healthy cells. Eventually leads to appearance of advanced age in physical features, such as wrinkly skin, birdlike nose, and graying hair, and diseases associated with elderly, such as cataracts and osteoporosis. Thought to be more common in Japan.

SPECIALIST TO SEE: Geneticist, Geriatrician

OTHER SYMPTOMS:
- Hoarse, high-pitched voice
- Thin arms and legs
- Thick trunk
- Muscle atrophy
- Skin ulcers

PROGRESSION: Commonly starts in late adolescence or early adulthood. Appearance of older age presents before disease and ill health emerge. Typical life span between 40 and 50 years.

TREATMENT: No known cure. Treatment of resulting afflictions.

CONTAGION: **1** 2 3 4

PAIN: 1 **2** 3 4

SUFFERING: 1 2 3 **4**

FATAL: **Yes** No Maybe

If your face is flushed...

...you might have
POLYCYTHEMIA

WHAT IT IS: Rare, chronic disease in which blood is thicker than normal due to excess red blood cells. Results from abnormality in bone marrow; underlying cause unclear. Increases risk for deadly blood clots, strokes, and heart attacks.

SPECIALIST TO SEE: Hematologist

OTHER SYMPTOMS:
- Headache
- Itchy skin
- Shortness of breath
- Chest pain
- Redness in eyes

PROGRESSION: For years, advances slowly with no symptoms. Often detected during blood tests administered for other reasons. Blood marrow cells grow out of control, leading to leukemia. Potentially fatal.

TREATMENT: No known cure. Phlebotomy (draining of blood) to control number of blood cells and reduce total blood volume.

CONTAGION: **1** 2 3 4

PAIN: 1 **2** 3 4

SUFFERING: 1 2 **3** 4

FATAL: Yes No **Maybe**

...or you might have
YELLOW FEVER

WHAT IT IS: Life-threatening viral disease transmitted by mosquitoes. Starts with flu-like symptoms such as fever, chills, and head and body aches. Can proceed to organ failure and hemorrhaging from eyes, nose, and gums. "Yellow" refers to jaundice caused by liver failure.

SPECIALIST TO SEE: Infectious Disease Specialist

Brain Tumor

[Fig. 101]

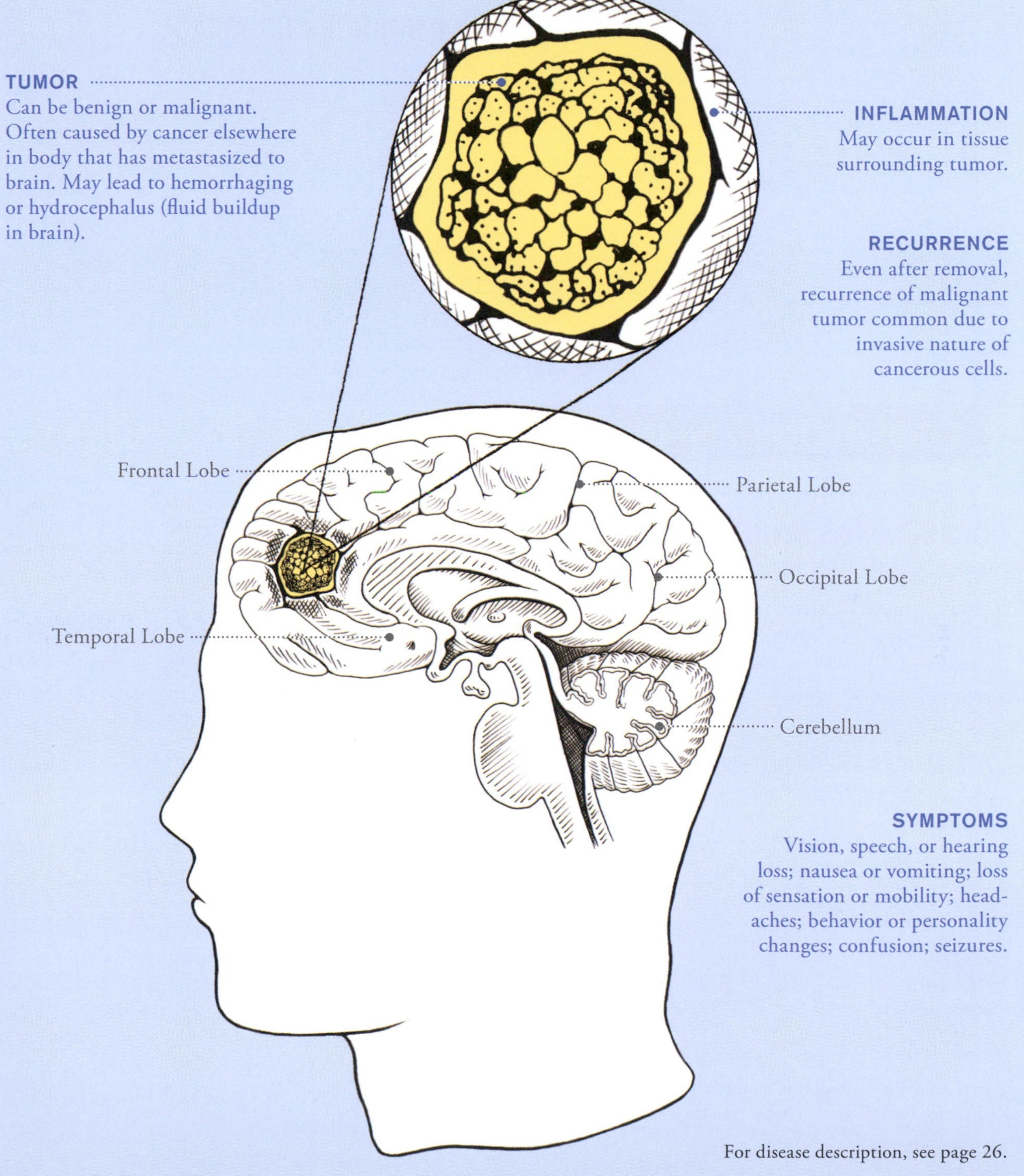

For disease description, see page 26.

FACT | Flushing a toilet can expel a 6-foot-wide plume of bacteria.

OTHER SYMPTOMS:

- Fever or chills
- Back pain
- Headache
- Black vomit
- Bleeding from gums, eyes, or nose

PROGRESSION: First symptoms develop 3 to 6 days after infection. Often self-limiting, but may be followed by "toxic phase," which results in kidney and multi-organ failure. Can lead to death within 10 to 14 days.

TREATMENT: No known cure. During toxic phase, sponge baths, dialysis, and blood transfusions to increase comfort.

CONTAGION: 1 2 3 **4**

PAIN: 1 2 3 **4**

SUFFERING: 1 2 **3** 4

FATAL: Yes No **Maybe**

If your face is twitching...

...you might have
OPSOCLONUS MYOCLONUS SYNDROME

WHAT IT IS: Rare neurological disorder characterized by sudden, brief, shock-like muscle spasms or involuntary eye movement. Usually caused by cancerous tumor or viral infection. Removal of tumor or treatment of infection may relieve symptoms but often does not.

SPECIALIST TO SEE: Neurologist

OTHER SYMPTOMS:

- Loss of speech
- Poor muscle tone
- Difficulty walking or sitting
- Lethargy
- Irritability
- General discomfort

PROGRESSION: Symptoms appear suddenly, worsen with movement, and may also occur at rest. During illness peak, sitting and standing are difficult or impossible. Long-term neurological damage may persist after treatment.

TREATMENT: Depends on underlying cause. Steroids, surgery, radiation, or chemotherapy.

CONTAGION: **1** 2 3 4

PAIN: 1 2 3 **4**

SUFFERING: 1 2 **3** 4

FATAL: Yes No **Maybe**

...or you might have
PARKINSON'S DISEASE

WHAT IT IS: Degenerative disorder of central nervous system that impairs speech and motor skills. Characterized by tremors, slowed movement, and muscle rigidity. May lead to complete loss of motor ability. Caused by decreased stimulation of area of brain that controls motor functions due to insufficient production of dopamine.

SPECIALIST TO SEE: Neurologist

OTHER SYMPTOMS:

- Shuffling walk
- Loss of balance
- Small, cramped handwriting
- Difficulty speaking or swallowing
- Soft or unintelligible speech
- Fatigue

PROGRESSION: Typically presents around age 60. First, muscle tremors, twitching, and stiffness appear, usually on one side of body. Later, both sides of body affected. Symptoms worsen with time.

TREATMENT: Medication to increase production of dopamine. Surgical destruction of damaged brain tissue.

CONTAGION: **1** 2 3 4

PAIN: 1 **2** 3 4

SUFFERING: 1 2 **3** 4

FATAL: Yes No **Maybe**

...or you might have
TOURETTE'S SYNDROME

WHAT IT IS: Neurological disorder that causes uncontrollable vocal and physical tics. Vocal tics may involve blurting out obscenities or repeating words and phrases. Physical tics may include grimacing, shrugging, or jerking movements in head and neck. More common in men. Cause unknown; likely inherited.

SPECIALIST TO SEE: Neurologist

OTHER SYMPTOMS:

- Exaggerated blinking
- Excessive throat-clearing
- Humming
- Inappropriate speech

PROGRESSION: Commonly starts with tics, which vary in severity over time. May worsen in periods of stress or excitement or during illness. Other complications often develop, including attention-deficit disorder, obsessive-compulsive disorder, anxiety, and depression.

TREATMENT: Antidepressants and antipsychotics to control tics. Surgical removal of affected brain tissue.

CONTAGION: **1** 2 3 4

PAIN: 1 **2** 3 4

SUFFERING: 1 2 **3** 4

FATAL: Yes **No** Maybe

...or you might have

TRIGEMINAL NEURALGIA

WHAT IT IS: Facial nerve damage that causes intense sensation of painful stabbing in face. Pressure on trigeminal nerve in face deteriorates nerve's protective covering, leaving it raw and exposed. Resulting pain can be incapacitating, lasting from seconds to several minutes. Affects more women than men. Often called "suicide disease"; high suicide rate due to untreatable pain.

SPECIALIST TO SEE: Neurologist

OTHER SYMPTOMS:

- Headache
- Sensitivity to chewing, swallowing, or brushing teeth

PROGRESSION: Agonizing pain can be triggered by light touch or breeze. Initially brief and mild. Later, attacks last longer and become more severe.

TREATMENT: No known cure. Anticonvulsants or antidepressants to limit pain. Surgery to damage or destroy nerve tissue or relieve pressure on nerve.

CONTAGION: **1** 2 3 4

PAIN: 1 2 3 **4**

SUFFERING: 1 2 **3** 4

FATAL: Yes **No** Maybe

If your vision is obstructed...

...you might have

LOIASIS

WHAT IT IS: Skin and eye disease caused by bite from *Chrysops* fly, which harbors parasitic *Loa loa* worm. Adult worms migrate through body and bloodstream, and settle in conjunctiva and cornea. Painless but sometimes fatal. Often referred to as "African eye worm."

SPECIALIST TO SEE: Ophthalmologist

OTHER SYMPTOMS:

- Worms in fingers and tongue
- Redness and swelling in legs
- Fever
- Watery eyes

PROGRESSION: Initial symptoms may not appear for months or years after bite. Presents as dry, itchy skin; excessive scratching can form skin lesions. Tiny, thread-like worms may enter brain, invariably leading to fatal encephalitis (brain inflammation).

TREATMENT: Antiparasitic medication to expel worms. Antihistamines or corticosteroids to relieve itching.

CONTAGION: **1** 2 3 4

PAIN: **1** 2 3 4

SUFFERING: 1 **2** 3 4

FATAL: Yes No **Maybe**

...or you might have

MACULAR DEGENERATION

WHAT IT IS: Chronic eye disease. Results from deterioration of retinal tissue (responsible for central vision). Leads to blurred vision or blind spots. Exact cause unknown. Typically presents after age 60; more common in women. No harm to peripheral vision or danger of total blindness though severe vision loss possible.

SPECIALIST TO SEE: Ophthalmologist

OTHER SYMPTOMS:

- Distorted vision
- Difficulty recognizing faces

PROGRESSION: Blurred central vision worsens over time. Rapid progression from dry (loss of pigment in

FACT | 70 percent of the dust in our homes is shed human skin.

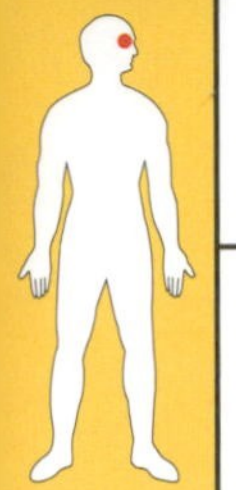

retina) to wet (blood vessels hemorrhage under retina) varieties can lead to severe vision impairment in one or both eyes. In rare cases, hallucinations called Charles Bonnet syndrome develop.

TREATMENT: No treatment to reverse damage. Surgery, therapy, and medication to prevent further damage.

CONTAGION: **1** 2 3 4

PAIN: **1** 2 3 4

SUFFERING: 1 **2** 3 4

FATAL: Yes **No** Maybe

...or you might have RETINITIS PIGMENTOSA

WHAT IT IS: Damage to retina causes degeneration and death of photoreceptor cells (neurons in retina responsible for processing light). Usually inherited genetic defect. Symptoms progress slowly through midlife. Severe vision loss likely.

SPECIALIST TO SEE: Ophthalmologist

OTHER SYMPTOMS:

- Distorted color perception
- Inability to see in low light
- Loss of peripheral vision

PROGRESSION: Commonly starts with irreparable loss of central vision. As disease worsens, peripheral vision decreases and "tunnel vision" develops. Complete blindness is rare, although many individuals are eventually classified as legally blind.

TREATMENT: None. Sunglasses for eye protection.

CONTAGION: **1** 2 3 4

PAIN: **1** 2 3 4

SUFFERING: 1 **2** 3 4

FATAL: Yes **No** Maybe

Loiasis

[Fig. 102]

SYMPTOMS
Dry, itchy skin; redness and swelling in limbs; excessive tearing; worm in fingers, tongue, or eye.

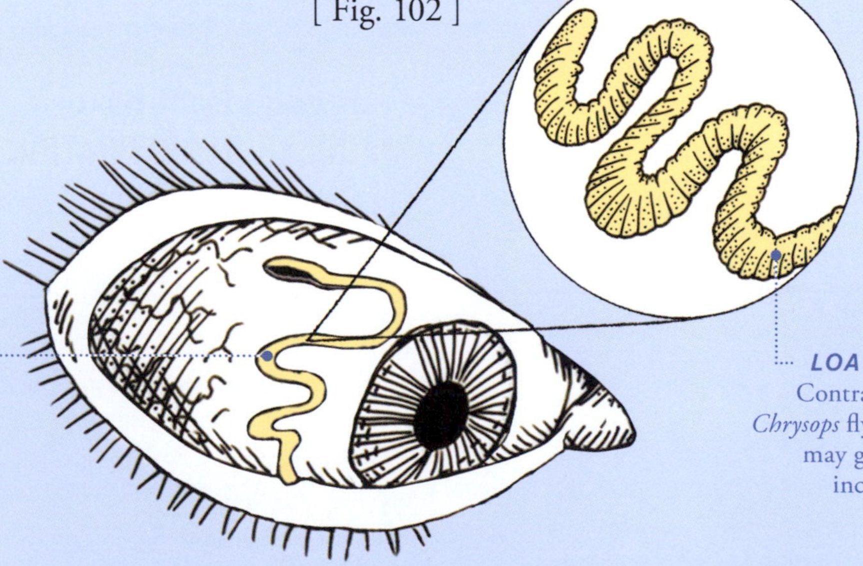

PARASITIC INFECTION
Ailment often first noticed when worm passes into eye, allowing brief opportunity for surgical removal.

***LOA LOA* WORM**
Contracted through *Chrysops* fly bite. Worms may grow up to 2.5 inches in length.

For disease description, see page 31.

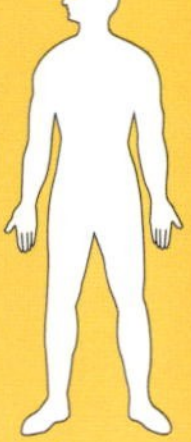

If you have blurred vision…

…you might have
CEREBRAL HEMORRHAGE

WHAT IT IS: Ruptured blood vessel leads to bleeding in brain and surrounding tissue. No specific cause. Traumatic brain injury, aneurysm, high blood pressure, or excessive use of aspirin and blood thinners could increase risk.

SPECIALIST TO SEE: Neurologist

OTHER SYMPTOMS:
- Severe headache
- Lethargy
- Rapid, involuntary eye movement
- Difficulty speaking or swallowing
- Impaired reflexes

PROGRESSION: Sudden onset of various symptoms depending on affected area of brain. May begin with blurred vision or headache, but quickly progresses to impaired speech, vision loss, and facial paralysis. Without prompt treatment, death is possible.

TREATMENT: Brain surgery to control bleeding. Medication to reduce swelling, minimize pain, and limit seizures.

CONTAGION: **1** 2 3 4

PAIN: 1 **2** 3 4

SUFFERING: 1 2 **3** 4

FATAL: Yes No **Maybe**

…or you might have
ENCEPHALOCELE

WHAT IT IS: Rare neural-tube defect. Brain tissue and membranes protrude through skull openings in sac-like formations. Often associated with neurological disorders. Exact cause unknown. Prevalent in families with history of spina bifida.

SPECIALIST TO SEE: Neurologist

OTHER SYMPTOMS:
- Poor coordination
- Vision impairment
- Mental or physical retardation

PROGRESSION: Often accompanied by craniofacial abnormalities, brain malformations, and excessive accumulation of fluid in brain. Can degenerate to paralysis of arms and legs, followed by seizures and, rarely, death.

TREATMENT: Surgery to place protruding tissue back into skull, remove sacs, and correct accompanying abnormalities.

CONTAGION: **1** 2 3 4

PAIN: 1 2 **3** 4

SUFFERING: 1 2 **3** 4

FATAL: Yes No **Maybe**

…or you might have
GALACTOSEMIA

WHAT IT IS: Genetic disorder that prevents metabolism of galactose (sugar in lactose). Sometimes confused with lactose intolerance, but symptoms are more severe. Characterized by total inability to digest any milk product. Failure to avoid certain foods can lead to permanent organ damage or death.

SPECIALIST TO SEE: Endocrinologist, Dietitian

OTHER SYMPTOMS:
- Jaundice
- Vomiting
- Lethargy
- Irritability

PROGRESSION: Toxic levels of sugar accumulate in blood. May result in poor cognitive and physical growth, ovarian failure, kidney problems, convulsions, enlarged liver, and brain damage.

TREATMENT: Avoidance of food containing galactose.

CONTAGION: **1** 2 3 4

PAIN: 1 2 **3** 4

SUFFERING: 1 **2** 3 4

FATAL: Yes No **Maybe**

If you have double vision…

…you might have
BOTULISM

WHAT IT IS: Rare paralytic illness. Caused by nerve toxins produced by *Clostridium botulinum* bacteria. May be foodborne (especially from home-canned

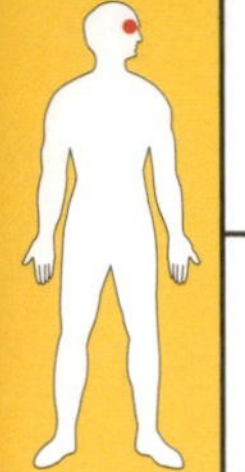

foods) or contracted via open wound. All forms potentially fatal.

SPECIALIST TO SEE: Primary Care Physician

OTHER SYMPTOMS:

- Blurred vision
- Drooping eyelids
- Slurred speech
- Vomiting or diarrhea
- Paralysis

PROGRESSION: Early symptoms appear 18 to 36 hours after exposure. Untreated, spreads rapidly, causing full paralysis, acute respiratory failure, and, ultimately, death.

TREATMENT: Antitoxin medication. Ventilator in case of paralysis. Long-term intensive care followed by physical therapy.

CONTAGION: **1** 2 3 4

PAIN: 1 2 3 **4**

SUFFERING: 1 2 **3** 4

FATAL: Yes No **Maybe**

...or you might have

PARANASAL SINUS CANCER

WHAT IT IS: Malignant cells accumulate in paranasal sinuses (air-filled spaces within facial bones connected to nasal cavity). Exact cause unknown. May be linked to tobacco use or exposure to wood dust, certain heavy metals (e.g., chromium and nickel), and some organic chemicals (including mustard gas). Not infectious or hereditary.

SPECIALIST TO SEE: Otolaryngologist, Oncologist

OTHER SYMPTOMS:

- Headaches
- Swollen eyes
- Sinus pain, blockage, and frequent infection
- Bloody nose
- Tooth pain
- Persistent lump or sore in nose

PROGRESSION: Commonly starts with cheek bulge or numbness, excessive tearing, speech changes, and hearing loss. Fatal in nearly 80 percent of cases.

TREATMENT: Surgery. Skin graft. Facial prosthesis.

CONTAGION: **1** 2 3 4

PAIN: 1 2 **3** 4

SUFFERING: 1 2 3 **4**

FATAL: **Yes** No Maybe

If you see floating spots or halos...

...you might have

AUTOIMMUNE UVEITIS

WHAT IT IS: Inflammation of uvea (portion of eye between outermost and innermost layers). Autoimmune disorder causes immune system to attack healthy tissue. Characterized by hazy vision and eye discomfort. While serious, not known to be fatal.

SPECIALIST TO SEE: Ophthalmologist

OTHER SYMPTOMS:

- Headache
- Redness in eyes
- Eyebrow pain
- Small or oddly shaped pupils

PROGRESSION: Begins with floating, flashing spots or rings, and blurred vision. Head and eye pain and sensitivity to light ensue. Untreated, retinal scarring may occur, leading to permanent vision loss.

TREATMENT: Anti-inflammatory medication. Corticosteroids. Antibiotics to prevent further damage.

CONTAGION: **1** 2 3 4

PAIN: 1 **2** 3 4

SUFFERING: **1** 2 3 4

FATAL: Yes **No** Maybe

...or you might have

CATARACTS

WHAT IT IS: Eye lens becomes cloudy due to clumping of protein fibers, resulting in problems with distance vision and glare. Very common; more than one-half of adults will eventually be affected. May be caused by exposure to ultraviolet light, diabetes, or use of steroids, diuretics, or tranquilizers.

SPECIALIST TO SEE: Ophthalmologist

Nosocomials
Medical-Facility Contagion

You go into the hospital for surgery or to your doctor's office hoping to be cured of an illness. Your treatment is successful and your original illness is gone—but now you have pneumonia! Contracted in hospitals or doctors' offices, nosocomial infections afflict 5 percent of those hospitalized every year in the United States, causing about 90,000 deaths.

Nosocomial infections are common for three reasons: one, sick patients mean a high level of pathogens in hospitals and doctors' offices; two, patients may already be in a weakened condition and thus prone to catching something else; and three, medical personnel carry germs from patient to patient. The most common nosocomials are pneumonia and urinary-tract infections, while others affect the respiratory or gastrointestinal tracts, the central nervous system, and the skin and bloodstream. Pathogens can also enter via surgical wounds and burns.

While aseptic techniques, frequent hand-washing by medical personnel and patients, and patient isolation can cut down on nosocomials, the infections are becoming ever more alarming and prevalent as antibiotic resistance increases.

Clostridium difficile

C. difficile causes symptoms ranging from diarrhea to life-threatening colon inflammation. With the French word for "difficult" in its name, this bacteria is hard to eradicate.

Staphylococcus aureus

Well known as the agent for strep throat, *S. aureus* can also cause skin infections, pneumonia, meningitis, endocarditis, toxic shock syndrome, and septicemia.

Pseudomonas aeruginosa

Easily infecting immunocompromised individuals, *P. aeruginosa* targets the bloodstream, pulmonary and urinary tracts, and burns and wounds. It also causes ventilator-associated pneumonia.

Escherichia coli

E. coli causes urinary-tract infections, meningitis, peritonitis, mastitis, septicemia, and pneumonia.

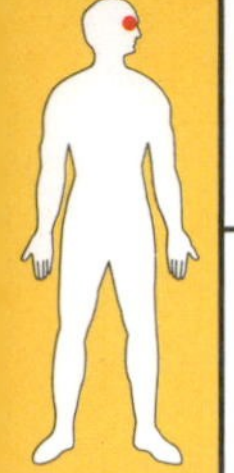

FACT | There are 60,000 miles of blood vessels in the human body.

OTHER SYMPTOMS:

- Blurred or double vision
- Sensitivity to light
- Distorted color perception
- Poor night vision

PROGRESSION: Initially lens cloudiness presents slowly and is unobtrusive. May occur in one or both eyes, but cannot spread from one eye to the other. Over time, cloudiness increases. Reading becomes difficult.

TREATMENT: Frequent eyeglass and contact lens prescription changes. Surgery to remove cataracts and restore vision.

CONTAGION: **1** 2 3 4

PAIN: **1** 2 3 4

SUFFERING: 1 **2** 3 4

FATAL: Yes **No** Maybe

...or you might have
CLOSED-ANGLE GLAUCOMA

WHAT IT IS: Acute form of glaucoma (optic-nerve disease) in which normal fluid exchange between iris and eye lens is blocked. Exact cause unknown. Commonly affects families of Asian descent. Cases of open-angle glaucoma (chronic, common form in which fluid channel gradually narrows) increase risk. Can lead to optic nerve damage and vision loss.

SPECIALIST TO SEE: Ophthalmologist

OTHER SYMPTOMS:

- Headache
- Sudden blurred vision
- Eye pain
- Redness in eyes

PROGRESSION: Increased eye pressure, followed by nausea and vomiting, rainbow-colored halos around lights, and sudden vision loss. Eyesight can be lost within 2 to 3 hours after onset of primary symptoms.

TREATMENT: Medication to lower eye pressure. Surgery to allow fluid to flow.

CONTAGION: **1** 2 3 4

PAIN: 1 **2** 3 4

SUFFERING: 1 **2** 3 4

FATAL: Yes **No** Maybe

...or you might have
RETINAL DETACHMENT

WHAT IT IS: Sensory and pigment layers of retina separate. Results in scar tissue and fluid beneath retina, leading to separation from back wall of eye. Typically occurs in middle age or later. Nearsightedness, diabetes, or other eye injury increase risk. Without prompt treatment, may cause permanent vision loss.

SPECIALIST TO SEE: Ophthalmologist

OTHER SYMPTOMS:

- Sudden vision loss or obstruction
- Heavy sensation in eye
- Straight lines appear curved

PROGRESSION: Initially painless. Identified by floating spots or halos, flashes of light, or blurred vision. Requires immediate medical attention at early onset of symptoms.

TREATMENT: Silicone oil to push retina into place; surgery to reattach retina.

CONTAGION: **1** 2 3 4

PAIN: 1 **2** 3 4

SUFFERING: 1 **2** 3 4

FATAL: Yes **No** Maybe

If your pupil size changes...

...you might have
ISCHEMIC OPTIC NEUROPATHY

WHAT IT IS: Rare form of damage to optic nerve due to blockage of blood supply. Two forms: arteritic (caused by inflammation of arteries) and non-arteritic (resulting from cardiovascular conditions like high blood pressure and elevated cholesterol). More common over age 50. History of severe migraines also increases risk.

SPECIALIST TO SEE: Ophthalmologist

OTHER SYMPTOMS:

- Jaw pain while chewing
- Tenderness in temples
- Reduced appetite
- Fatigue

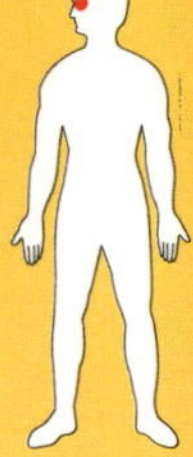

PROGRESSION: Often vision is reduced but stable. May lead to loss of peripheral or central vision. Permanent blindness can occur within minutes or hours, or develop gradually over 2 to 7 days. With nonarteritic form may experience spontaneous improvement.

TREATMENT: No known cure. Treatment of factors limiting blood supply to optic nerve.

CONTAGION: 1 2 3 4

PAIN: 1 2 3 4

SUFFERING: 1 2 3 4

FATAL: Yes No Maybe

If your eyeball is discolored...

...you might have
LEPTOSPIROSIS

WHAT IT IS: Rare bacterial disease also known as swamp fever. Caused by contact with water or soil contaminated with urine of infected animals such as cattle, pigs, horses, dogs, and rodents. Once in bloodstream, bacteria spreads throughout body, creating flu-like symptoms. Not known to transmit from person to person.

SPECIALIST TO SEE: Infectious Disease Specialist, Nephrologist, Hepatologist

OTHER SYMPTOMS:

- Fever or chills
- Headache
- Rash
- Muscle pain
- Vomiting or diarrhea
- Jaundice

PROGRESSION: Symptoms appear 2 days to 4 weeks after exposure. Untreated, Weil's syndrome (severe form of disease) develops. Leads to kidney damage, meningitis, liver failure, and respiratory distress.

TREATMENT: Antibiotics.

CONTAGION: 1 2 3 4

PAIN: 1 2 3 4

SUFFERING: 1 2 3 4

FATAL: Yes No Maybe

...or you might have
MEASLES

WHAT IT IS: Also known as rubeola. Highly contagious respiratory, skin, and eye infection. Transmitted through respiratory tract moisture. Characteristic rash spreads over entire body. For unvaccinated individuals, near-certain acquisition when in close contact with infected person (contagious 4 days before and after rash presents).

SPECIALIST TO SEE: Primary Care Physician

OTHER SYMPTOMS:

- Runny or stuffy nose
- Sneezing
- Dry cough
- Fever
- Watery or inflamed eyes
- Sensitivity to light

PROGRESSION: Initial coldlike symptoms typically resolve within one week. Koplik's spots (tiny red and blue spots inside mouth) appear 10 to 12 days after exposure. Rarely, pneumonia and brain inflammation occur. Swelling of lymph nodes in neck can prolong course of illness.

TREATMENT: Previously established cases cannot be treated. Palliative care for itching.

CONTAGION: 1 2 3 4

PAIN: 1 2 3 4

SUFFERING: 1 2 3 4

FATAL: Yes No Maybe

If you have bulging eyes...

...you might have
GRAVES' DISEASE

WHAT IT IS: Most common form of hyperthyroidism. Immune system attacks thyroid gland, producing excessive amounts of hormone thyroxine. In opthalmopathy condition, tissue behind eye swells, causing eyeball to move forward. Rapidly increases metabolism rate, leading to irregular heartbeat and anxiety. Develops at any age and in both sexes; more common in women over age 20.

FACT | Office desks contain almost 400 times more bacteria than a public toilet seat, and phones contain 700 times more.

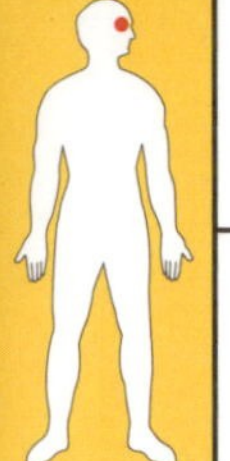

SPECIALIST TO SEE: Ophthalmologist, Endocrinologist

OTHER SYMPTOMS:

- Redness in eyes
- Swelling in eyelids and surrounding tissue
- Sensitivity to heat and light
- Goiter
- Brittle hair
- Weight loss

PROGRESSION: Advanced cases produce exophthalmos (protruding eyeballs); blurred, double, or reduced vision; corneal ulcers; and limited eye movement. Complications may weaken heart muscles (leading to heart failure), cause osteoporosis, and incite severe emotional disorders, including depression.

TREATMENT: No known cure. Beta-blockers, antithyroid medication, and radioactive iodine to decrease thyroxine production.

CONTAGION: **1** 2 3 4

PAIN: 1 **2** 3 4

SUFFERING: 1 **2** 3 4

FATAL: Yes **No** Maybe

...or you might have

MALIGNANT HYPERTENSION

WHAT IT IS: Hypertensive emergency that results in damage to eyes, brain, lungs, or kidneys. Caused by very high blood pressure accompanied by papilledema (optic nerve swelling). More common in younger adults. History of renal disorders increases risk.

SPECIALIST TO SEE: Cardiologist

OTHER SYMPTOMS:

- Headache
- Blurred vision
- Anxiety
- Delirium
- Crushing chest pressure
- Shortness of breath

PROGRESSION: Uncontrolled, runs rapid course with heart failure, encephalopathy (brain disease), and damage to inner lining of blood vessels and spleen. Retinal bleeding may develop. Death possible.

TREATMENT: Intravenous nitroglycerin to reduce blood pressure. Antihypertensive medication.

CONTAGION: **1** 2 3 4

PAIN: 1 **2** 3 4

SUFFERING: 1 2 **3** 4

FATAL: Yes No **Maybe**

If you have itchy eyes...

...you might have

CHRONIC URTICARIA

WHAT IT IS: Red, swollen, itchy hives on skin that linger for more than 6 weeks. Caused by exposure to heat, cold, and sunlight, as well as allergies to medication, pollen, insect bites, dust, and dander. Without treatment of underlying problem, recurrence likely. May be sign of other serious conditions such as lupus or hepatitis.

SPECIALIST TO SEE: Dermatologist

OTHER SYMPTOMS:

- Joint pain
- Fatigue
- Rash
- Fever
- General discomfort

PROGRESSION: Initially, rash appears. If accompanied by light-headedness and wheezing may indicate allergies or viral illness. Sudden allergic reactions present with throat tightening or loss of consciousness.

TREATMENT: Antihistamines, prednisone (steroid), and epinephrine shots. Palliative care for itching.

CONTAGION: **1** 2 3 4

PAIN: 1 **2** 3 4

SUFFERING: **1** 2 3 4

FATAL: Yes **No** Maybe

...or you might have

SJÖGREN'S SYNDROME

WHAT IT IS: Autoimmune disease targeting glands that produce tears and saliva. Can also affect joints, lungs, stomach, pancreas, and intestines. Results in dry eyes and mouth. Exact cause unknown; may appear in conjunction with

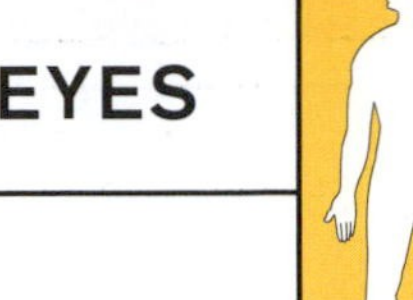

rheumatoid arthritis. Women are 9 times more susceptible than men.

SPECIALIST TO SEE: Rheumatologist, Ophthalmologist, Dentist

OTHER SYMPTOMS:

- Hoarse voice
- Rash
- Joint or muscle pain
- Dental cavities

PROGRESSION: Commonly starts with mild symptoms. Can take up to 6 years for symptoms to fully develop. Then, rapidly progresses to painful and life-threatening conditions such as pneumonia, scleroderma (hardening of skin and connective tissue), and lymphoma.

TREATMENT: No known cure. Artificial tears to treat dry eyes. Saliva stimulants to treat dry mouth. If lymphoma develops, chemotherapy and radiation.

CONTAGION: **1** 2 3 4

PAIN: 1 2 3 **4**

SUFFERING: 1 2 **3** 4

FATAL: Yes No **Maybe**

If you have watery eyes...

...you might have BLEPHARITIS

WHAT IT IS: Inflammation of eyelids. Tiny oil glands malfunction, causing bacterial overgrowth. Irritation and itchiness develop. Linked to seborrheic dermatitis (similar to dandruff) and *Staphylococcus* bacteria. Although recurring and uncomfortable, rarely results in permanent vision damage.

SPECIALIST TO SEE: Ophthalmologist, Dermatologist

OTHER SYMPTOMS:

- Swelling in eyes
- Burning sensation in skin
- Scaly, encrusted eyelashes
- Frothy tears

PROGRESSION: Begins as watery, itchy eyes. Painful styes develop near eyelash roots, and inner eyelids begin to swell. Inflammation can lead to recurrent bouts of conjunctivitis (pinkeye). Corneal ulcer or infection may develop.

TREATMENT: Antibiotic cream or ointment. Steroidal eyedrops.

CONTAGION: **1** 2 3 4

PAIN: **1** 2 3 4

SUFFERING: **1** 2 3 4

FATAL: Yes **No** Maybe

...or you might have CROCODILE TEARS SYNDROME

WHAT IT IS: Rare form of facial paralysis arising from conditions such as Bell's palsy. Nerve fibers controlling salivary glands become damaged and regrow into tear gland. Results in spontaneous eye tearing in conjunction with salivation. Can also be caused by lesion in seventh cranial nerve.

SPECIALIST TO SEE: Ophthalmologist, Neurologist

OTHER SYMPTOMS:

- Loss of taste
- Facial tics

PROGRESSION: Tearing may range from moderate to severe. Often followed by facial tics and loss of taste. Rarely progresses beyond primary symptoms.

TREATMENT: Anticholinergic (anti–nerve impulse) drugs.

CONTAGION: **1** 2 3 4

PAIN: 1 **2** 3 4

SUFFERING: 1 2 **3** 4

FATAL: Yes **No** Maybe

If your eye produces a discharge...

...you might have ECTROPION

WHAT IT IS: Relaxed muscles and tendons cause lower eyelids and eyelashes to sag and turn out. Eyelids are unable to close or function properly, leading to excessive dryness and inflammation. Common over age 60; may be congenital or result from burns, facial surgery, nerve paralysis, or lupus.

FACT | American workers out sick with the flu cost businesses $20 billion a year in lost productivity.

Let's Live in a Bubble

Disease Transmission

Infectious diseases lurk everywhere. But do we really know how they get from point A to point B? While germs exist in the obvious locales—toilet seats, shoe bottoms, used tissues—many more loiter in places we wouldn't expect. These germs have found numerous ways to hide, travel, and get into our systems, whether hitching a ride on an object like a pen or flying through the air in a droplet of mucus, whether entering through our noses or through a cut. Modes of disease transmission run the gamut from sneezing to sexual intercourse to needle sharing to eating food at restaurants—but by far the most common is our hands.

Reservoir

A reservoir is any source of a pathogen, and consists of 5 types: One, inanimate objects, called "fomites," are infected by contact—for example, a doorknob someone touches after sneezing. Two, contagious sick people transmit disease via both direct and indirect contact. Three, carriers that exhibit no symptoms are by far the most prevalent of reservoirs; they include "vectors," or organisms such as insects that transport disease pathogens. Four, other species can be reservoirs, though this is the least common transmission route. Communicable ailments transmitted from animals to humans are called "zoonotic." In some instances, as with Lyme disease, an ailment is both transmitted between species (with deer being the reservoir host) *and* by a vector (the reservoir of infection), the tick. Five, endogenous infections are a result of an infectious agent already in the body.

Portals of Entry

Pathogens have to get into the body to cause problems, with the exception of a few that are capable of breaching the skin barrier. The most typical routes are via mucous

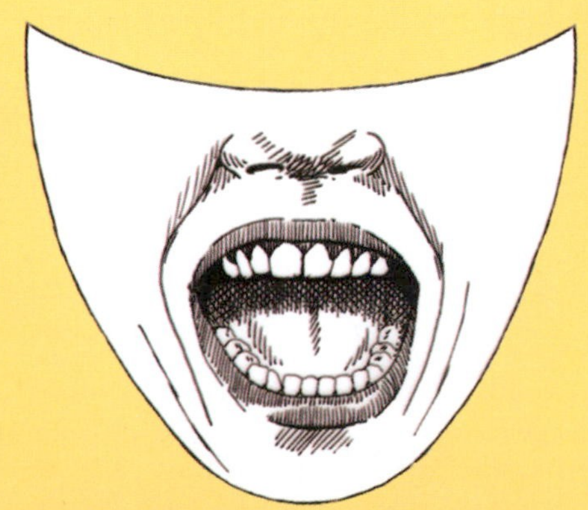

To avoid disease, all you have to do is wear gloves, face masks, and condoms, and refrain from eating, drinking, and breathing.

membranes (including the respiratory, gastrointestinal, and genitourinary tracts as well as the eyes) and through wounds.

Portals of Exit

What goes in must come out, and indeed portals of exit also play an important role in disease transmission, especially in respiratory infections (through the mouth and nose), gastrointestinal ailments (via the oral-fecal route), sexually transmitted diseases (via bodily fluids), and bloodborne infections (generally through insects or needles).

Transmission

Transmission is the process by which a pathogen moves between environments, from portal of exit to portal of entry. There are three types of transmission: contact (including direct, indirect, and droplet), vehicle, and vector.

Direct-Contact Transmission

Direct-contact transmission refers to germs spread from body part to body part without an intervening object, whether through handshaking, hugging, kissing, or sex.

Indirect-Contact Transmission

Indirect contact transmission occurs when an object with germs on it (called a "fomite") is touched. The germs generally travel from the hands to the eyes or nose through rubbing.

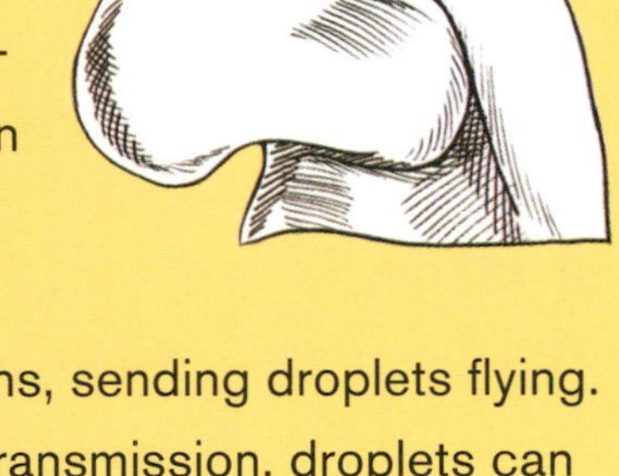

Droplet Transmission

Droplet transmission occurs when a person talks, sings, coughs, sneezes, or laughs, sending droplets flying. Unlike airborne transmission, droplets can only fly about 3 feet.

Vehicle Transmission

Vehicle transmission consists of food, air, and water, inanimate substances which, unlike fomites, are routinely taken into the body. With airborne transmission, germs are either aerosolized into very small droplets or they travel on dust particles. This is the least frequent mode of transmission, as it requires pathogens that are very durable.

Vector Transmission

As outlined in "Infectious Insects" (see pages 62–63), vectors are organisms such as insects that carry pathogens from one host to another without themselves becoming infected.

SPECIALIST TO SEE: Ophthalmologist

OTHER SYMPTOMS:

- Watery eyes
- Inadequate eye draining
- Redness in eyelids
- Sensitivity to wind or light

PROGRESSION: Untreated, leads to eye infection, cornea damage, and impaired vision. Rubbing eyes may cause further irritation. If not repaired, can result in thickened mucosal discharge, inflammation, and encrusted eyelids.

TREATMENT: Artificial tears, lubricating ointments, and sunglasses to prevent further drying. Surgery to repair muscles and tendons of eyelid.

CONTAGION: **1** 2 3 4

PAIN: **1** 2 3 4

SUFFERING: 1 **2** 3 4

FATAL: Yes **No** Maybe

...or you might have

TRACHOMA

WHAT IT IS: Chronic infectious eye disease caused by *Chlamydia trachomatis* bacteria. Transmitted by close contact with infected person or by flies that carry others' infected eye or nose discharge. Vision impairment frequently results; leading infectious cause of blindness worldwide.

SPECIALIST TO SEE: Ophthalmologist, Infectious Disease Specialist

OTHER SYMPTOMS:

- Inflammation in eyelids
- Swollen lymph nodes
- Cloudy or scratched cornea
- Turned-in eyelashes
- Vision loss

PROGRESSION: First, conjunctivitis appears. Then, repeated eye infections lead to more painful symptoms, including inflammation, eyelid scarring, ingrown eyelashes, and corneal clouding. Untreated, can lead to blindness.

TREATMENT: Antibiotics to prevent long-term complications. Eyelid surgery to reduce scarring.

CONTAGION: 1 2 3 **4**

PAIN: 1 2 **3** 4

SUFFERING: 1 **2** 3 4

FATAL: Yes **No** Maybe

If you have an earache...

...you might have

ACOUSTIC NEUROMA

WHAT IT IS: Slow-growing benign tumor on cranial nerve. Typically diagnosed between ages 30 and 60. Affects more women than men. Cause unknown, but may be hereditary. Untreated, tumor can fully occupy auditory canal, leading to permanent hearing loss. Ultimately, tumor may compress brain stem, resulting in death.

SPECIALIST TO SEE: Otolaryngologist

OTHER SYMPTOMS:

- Hearing loss
- Ringing in ears
- Dizziness
- Headache
- Confusion

PROGRESSION: First, few symptoms present. Then, as tumor grows, headaches and facial pain occur. If tumor encroaches on other brain tissue, nausea, vomiting, fever, vision distortions, and facial paralysis may develop.

TREATMENT: Surgery to remove tumor.

CONTAGION: **1** 2 3 4

PAIN: 1 **2** 3 4

SUFFERING: 1 **2** 3 4

FATAL: Yes No **Maybe**

...or you might have

CHOLESTEATOMA

WHAT IT IS: Epithelial cyst (composed of skin cells) located in middle ear behind eardrum. May be congenital; more commonly linked to complications from chronic ear infections, allergies, and colds. Can enlarge over time, destroying middle ear bones and causing persistent earache and hearing loss.

SPECIALIST TO SEE: Otolaryngologist

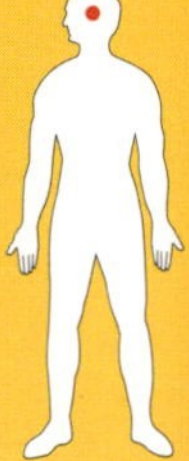

OTHER SYMPTOMS:

- Brown or yellow discharge from ear
- Foul odor
- Vertigo
- Hearing loss
- Facial paralysis

PROGRESSION: Begins with inner-ear pain. May lead to ear bone erosion, allowing bacteria to spread to brain. Untreated, permanent deafness, brain abscess, and meningitis can develop. In rare cases, fatal.

TREATMENT: Ear wash, oral antibiotics, and antibiotic drops to control infection. Surgery to remove large growths.

CONTAGION:	**1**	2	3	4
PAIN:	1	2	**3**	4
SUFFERING:	1	**2**	3	4
FATAL:	Yes	**No**	Maybe	

...or you might have
NASOPHARYNGEAL CANCER

WHAT IT IS: Starts in back of nose and throat and spreads through ear canal and lymph nodes. Mutated cells clump together, forming tumors that can metastasize to other areas. May be linked to Epstein-Barr virus and diet high in salted fish, eggs, and vegetables.

SPECIALIST TO SEE: Otolaryngologist, Oncologist

OTHER SYMPTOMS:

- Sore throat
- Headache
- Bloody nose
- Lump on nose or neck
- Hearing loss

PROGRESSION: Nose and ear blockage may result in hearing loss. Bloody pus, facial swelling, and paralysis can occur. Often diagnosed in late stage; death likely.

TREATMENT: Radiation and chemotherapy. Nasal surgery.

CONTAGION:	**1**	2	3	4
PAIN:	1	2	**3**	4
SUFFERING:	1	2	3	**4**
FATAL:	**Yes**	No	Maybe	

If your ear is bleeding...

...you might have
OTIC BAROTRAUMA

WHAT IT IS: Inflammation of middle ear. Caused by difference of pressure between middle ear and outside. May occur when descending from high altitudes or while scuba diving. Characterized by popping sound and intense pain in ear. May be accompanied by aching in face or teeth.

SPECIALIST TO SEE: Otolaryngologist

OTHER SYMPTOMS:

- Earache
- Dizziness
- Vomiting
- Hearing loss

PROGRESSION: Commonly starts as pain in ear, hearing disturbances, and bleeding. If paired with respiratory infection or blocked eustachian tube, tympanic membranes (eardrums) may rupture, causing nausea, vomiting, vertigo, and permanent hearing loss.

TREATMENT: Yawning or closed-nose swallowing for immediate relief. Penicillin. Surgery to repair ruptured membranes.

CONTAGION:	**1**	2	3	4
PAIN:	1	**2**	3	4
SUFFERING:	1	**2**	3	4
FATAL:	Yes	**No**	Maybe	

If you have hearing loss...

...you might have
PERFORATED EARDRUM

WHAT IT IS: Thin, oval layer of tympanic membrane (eardrum) bursts or tears, resulting in hearing loss. Blunt head trauma, loud noise, extreme pressure during airplane flights, or inserting cotton swabs too far into ear canal may cause puncture. Rarely fatal. Permanent hearing loss or brain infection may incur following recurrent ear infections.

SPECIALIST TO SEE: Otolaryngologist

FACT | After the age of 30, the human brain loses 50,000 neurons a day.

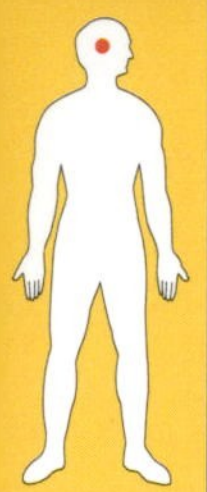

FACT | The small intestine is 22 feet long.

OTHER SYMPTOMS:

- Severe dizziness
- Vomiting
- Vertigo
- Tinnitus

PROGRESSION: Commonly starts with discomfort. Then, sharp pains and tinnitus (ringing in ears) develop. Pus-filled fluid or blood draining from ear warrants medical attention, as bacteria can reach middle ear.

TREATMENT: Generally self limiting. Surgery to treat holes that don't heal.

CONTAGION:	**1**	2	3	4
PAIN:	1	**2**	3	4
SUFFERING:	**1**	2	3	4
FATAL:	Yes	**No**	Maybe	

If your ears are ringing...

...you might have
LABYRINTHITIS

WHAT IT IS: Inflammation of inner-ear canals. Disconnect between information from eyes and labyrinth (inner-ear system that provides sense of balance) leads to hearing problems and vertigo. Caused by head injuries and bacteria from meningitis, cold, or flu. Sudden onset; symptoms may linger for days or weeks.

SPECIALIST TO SEE: Otolaryngologist, Neurologist

OTHER SYMPTOMS:

- Rushing sound
- Loss of balance
- Motion sickness
- Nausea or vomiting

PROGRESSION: Most cases resolve without treatment, though symptoms can recur. Commonly begins with

Cholesteatoma

[Fig. 103]

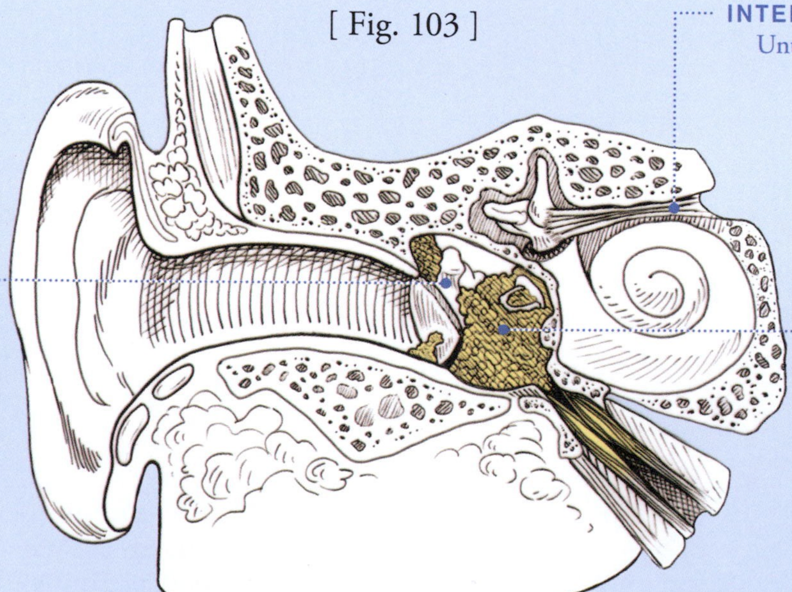

INTERCRANIAL CAVITY
Untreated, cyst can enter intracranial cavity, causing infection in or around brain.

OSSICLES
Middle ear bones: malleus, incus, and stapes. May be eroded by encroaching cyst, resulting in hearing loss.

CYST
Layers of cutaneous epithelial cells build up and cannot be expelled from ear, forming sac or cyst.

For disease description, see page 42.

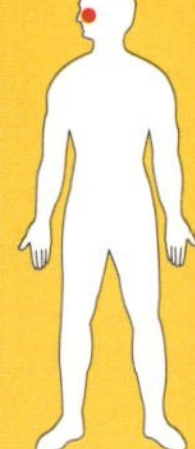

mild headaches, unsteady gait, and hearing deterioration. Hearing loss triggered by infection may be permanent.

TREATMENT: Antinausea medication to diminish vertigo. Antibiotics.

CONTAGION: **1** 2 3 4

PAIN: 1 **2** 3 4

SUFFERING: **1** 2 3 4

FATAL: Yes **No** Maybe

...or you might have

OTOSCLEROSIS

WHAT IT IS: Spongy, bonelike tissue grows and becomes fixed in middle ear. Prevents necessary vibrations in ear canal, leading to gradual distortion and eventual loss of hearing. Exact cause unknown; may be associated with viral infections or pregnancy-related hormonal changes. Often hereditary. Most common in white, middle-aged women.

SPECIALIST TO SEE: Otolaryngologist, Audiologist

OTHER SYMPTOMS:

- Loss of balance
- Inability to hear low-pitched sounds or whispers
- Dizziness
- Roaring, buzzing, or hissing sounds

PROGRESSION: First, hearing and balance are disrupted. Without medical attention, sensory cells and nerve fibers of inner ear may become damaged beyond repair.

TREATMENT: Hearing aids for mild hearing loss. Fluoride to harden spongy, diseased bone. Rarely, surgery.

CONTAGION: **1** 2 3 4

PAIN: 1 **2** 3 4

SUFFERING: **1** 2 3 4

FATAL: Yes **No** Maybe

If you have a bloody nose...

...you might have

LEUKEMIA

WHAT IT IS: Cancer of blood or bone marrow. Characterized by overproduction of abnormal leukocytes (white blood cells), which overcrowd other cells, leading to anemia, low blood clotting, and inability to fight infections. Exact cause unknown; exposure to high levels of radiation and chemotherapy increase risk.

SPECIALIST TO SEE: Oncologist, Hematologist

OTHER SYMPTOMS:

- Headache
- Fever or chills
- Night sweats
- Weakness and fatigue
- Reduced appetite

PROGRESSION: May go undiagnosed initially. Swollen lymph nodes (especially in neck or armpit), loss of muscle control, and seizures develop. Bone marrow damage can affect platelet production, necessary for blood clotting. Death possible.

TREATMENT: Chemotherapy, radiation, bone-marrow or stem-cell transplant.

CONTAGION: **1** 2 3 4

PAIN: 1 2 **3** 4

SUFFERING: 1 2 **3** 4

FATAL: Yes No **Maybe**

...or you might have

RHEUMATIC FEVER

WHAT IT IS: Rare inflammatory disease that results from complication of untreated strep throat or scarlet fever. Severe cases can lead to damage to joints, brain, and skin. Fifty percent chance of developing heart inflammation after first attack.

SPECIALIST TO SEE: Cardiologist, Infectious Disease Specialist

OTHER SYMPTOMS:

- Headache
- Muscle pain
- Fever
- Sore throat
- Swollen tonsils
- Rash

PROGRESSION: First symptoms generally appear after strep throat infection. In advanced cases, inflammation causes severe damage to muscles, brain, heart, and heart valves. Loss of coordination, chest pain, shortness of breath, and heart failure eventually develop.

QUOTE | "Doctors think a lot of patients are cured who have simply quit in disgust." —Herbert Hoover

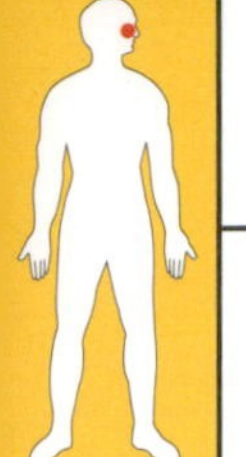

TREATMENT: No known cure. Antibiotics to treat strep infection. Surgery to repair heart damage.

CONTAGION: 1 2 3 4 (1)
PAIN: 1 2 3 4 (3)
SUFFERING: 1 2 3 4 (2)
FATAL: Yes No Maybe (Maybe)

If you have a stuffy nose...

...you might have
EMPHYSEMA

WHAT IT IS: Lung disease in which swollen, blocked lung tubes and damaged air sacs cause breathing difficulty. Cigarette smoking is most common cause, but may occur in nonsmokers who have rare genetic disorder called alpha-1-antitrypsin deficiency. Occurs most frequently in middle age. Often fatal.

SPECIALIST TO SEE: Pulmonologist

OTHER SYMPTOMS:
- Fatigue
- Runny nose
- Wheezing
- Unintended weight loss
- Pneumonia
- Flu

PROGRESSION: Causes recurring chest infections, which increase risk for abnormally high blood pressure and irregular heartbeat. Damage is permanent; respiratory failure and death likely.

TREATMENT: Bronchodilator medication to open lung air passages. Antibiotics, steroids, and supplemental oxygen to relieve symptoms.

CONTAGION: 1 2 3 4 (1)
PAIN: 1 2 3 4 (4)
SUFFERING: 1 2 3 4 (4)
FATAL: Yes No Maybe (Yes)

If you have a runny nose...

...you might have
HODGKIN'S DISEASE

WHAT IT IS: Cancer of lymphatic system (nodes, spleen, and bone marrow). Affects ability to fight infections. Exact cause unknown; may be linked to compromised immune system and previous Epstein-Barr infection. Typically occurs after age 55; more common in men.

SPECIALIST TO SEE: Oncologist

OTHER SYMPTOMS:
- Fever
- Fatigue
- Night sweats
- Unintended weight loss
- Itchy skin

PROGRESSION: Initial symptoms resemble flu. Often diagnosed after abnormalities are found on chest x-rays. Atypical cells in lymphatic system may spread to lungs, causing respiratory problems.

TREATMENT: Radiation and chemotherapy. Bone-marrow transplant if condition recurs.

CONTAGION: 1 2 3 4 (1)
PAIN: 1 2 3 4 (3)
SUFFERING: 1 2 3 4 (3)
FATAL: Yes No Maybe (Maybe)

...or you might have
RELAPSING POLYCHONDRITIS

WHAT IT IS: Immune system attacks cartilage, causing inflammation known as chondritis. Debilitating and often life-threatening. Can develop alone or in conjunction with other autoimmune disorders. Most often occurs between ages 30 and 60. Exact cause unknown, but may be inherited genetic component.

SPECIALIST TO SEE: Otolaryngologist, Rheumatologist

OTHER SYMPTOMS:
- Fever
- Unintended weight loss
- Vertigo
- Arthritis

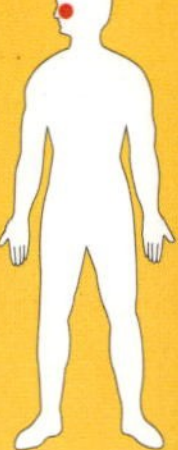

- Rash
- Floppy ears

PROGRESSION: Subtle early symptoms often delay diagnosis. Cartilage becomes irreversibly damaged. Respiratory failure due to collapse of tracheal cartilage or severe heart damage may result in death.

TREATMENT: Aspirin and nonsteroidal anti-inflammatory medication. Daily doses of corticosteroids for more severe cases.

CONTAGION:	**1**	2	3	4
PAIN:	1	2	**3**	4
SUFFERING:	1	2	**3**	4
FATAL:	Yes	No	**Maybe**	

If you have sinus pain...

...you might have

DRUG-RESISTANT STREPTOCOCCUS PNEUMONIAE

WHAT IT IS: Infection with bacteria that have developed resistance to drugs used for pneumococcal infections. Easily transmitted through coughing, sneezing, or direct contact. Excessive use of antimicrobial agents (e.g., among child-care workers, doctors, and nurses) increases risk of transmission. Major cause of illness and death worldwide.

SPECIALIST TO SEE: Infectious Disease Specialist

OTHER SYMPTOMS:

- Fever or chills
- Headache
- Stiff neck
- Rapid heartbeat
- Dark mucus
- Sneezing

PROGRESSION: May cause wide range of infection-related complications, including meningitis, pneumonia, bacteremia, sinusitis, and ear infection. Advanced bloodstream and upper respiratory tract infections may occur, which can lead to death.

TREATMENT: Moxifloxacin to kill some strains. Palliative care for symptoms.

CONTAGION:	1	2	3	**4**
PAIN:	1	**2**	3	4
SUFFERING:	1	2	**3**	4
FATAL:	Yes	No	**Maybe**	

...or you might have

WEGENER'S GRANULOMATOSIS

WHAT IT IS: Autoimmune disorder in which granulomas (inflamed masses) appear in kidneys and upper and lower respiratory tracts. Renal failure and necrosis (tissue death) may occur as inflammation disrupts blood flow to tissue. Cause unknown; not hereditary or contagious. Early diagnosis increases chance of effective treatment.

SPECIALIST TO SEE: Rheumatologist, Otolaryngologist

OTHER SYMPTOMS:

- Persistent runny nose
- Bloody noses
- Ear infection
- Hearing loss

PROGRESSION: Mild symptoms (e.g., coughing, ear infection) give way to eye or ear inflammation, skin sores, and kidney damage. Septum perforation may lead to saddle nose deformity. Permanent respiratory and neurological complications, as well as impaired sight or hearing, can occur. Potentially fatal if untreated.

TREATMENT: Corticosteroids and chemotherapy to suppress immune system and induce remission.

CONTAGION:	**1**	2	3	4
PAIN:	1	**2**	3	4
SUFFERING:	1	2	**3**	4
FATAL:	Yes	No	**Maybe**	

If you're sneezing excessively...

...you might have

RUBELLA

WHAT IT IS: Viral infection that primarily affects skin and lymph nodes, producing characteristic red rash. Highly contagious, though usually not fatal; commonly transmitted through respiratory

FACT | At least 1 in 2 Americans will contract an STD at some point in their lives.

Stressed Out by Stress
The Modern Malaise

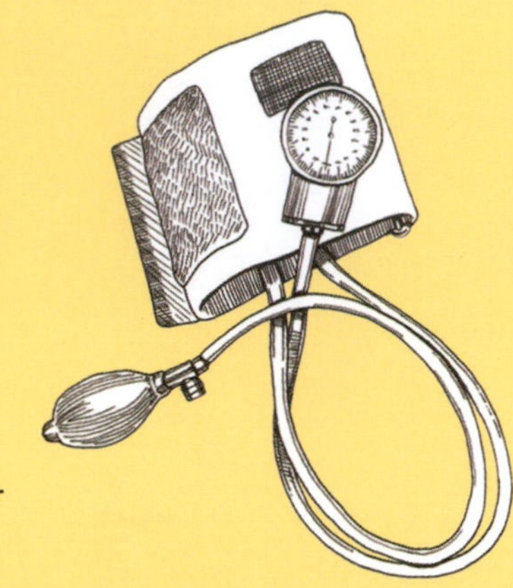

Stress has been called a "disease of civilization." Defined scientifically as a stimulus that interferes with normal physiologic equilibrium, stress comprises a broad spectrum of feelings, including fear, physical pain, being out of control, depression, anxiety, sadness, and loneliness. When stressed, our bodies put into play a cascade of physiological responses meant to help us when we're in harm's way—increased energy and strength to escape a prehistoric mastadon, for example—also known as our "fight or flight" mechanisms.

When we encounter a stressor, the hypothalamus, a gland at the base of the brain, prompts the adrenal glands, atop the kidneys, to release hormones, especially epinephrine (also known as adrenaline) and cortisol. Epinephrine increases heart rate, blood pressure, and reaction time. Cortisol pours glucose into the bloodstream to energize the brain and muscles, and curtails unnecessary physiological systems in order to conserve energy—particularly those for digestion, reproduction, and growth. While these biochemical responses are essential in a short-term crisis, when chronically triggered, they engender and intensify long-term health problems, likely decreasing lifespans by 15 to 20 years if untreated.

Obesity

Increased cortisol boosts appetite and causes weight gain, especially abdominal fat, which itself is a risk factor for diabetes and heart disease. Stress impairs sleep, and lack of sleep is associated with weight gain. Overeating is also used to soothe stress.

Depression

Some byproducts of cortisol act as a sedative, producing an overall feeling of lethargy and depression. Continued stress also decreases serotonin levels.

Weakened Immune System

Cortisol suppresses the immune system, leaving individuals especially susceptible to viral infections and possibly cancer.

Cardiovascular Disease

By raising heart rate, blood pressure, and cholesterol and triglyceride levels, chronic stress increases stroke and heart attack risk.

Drug, Alcohol, and Nicotine Use

Stress is the number-one cause of addiction relapse, with recent research linking the two biochemically.

droplets expelled during cough or sneeze. Can lead to fetal death or birth defects. Also known as German measles.

SPECIALIST TO SEE: Primary Care Physician

OTHER SYMPTOMS:
- Rash
- Mild fever
- Swollen or tender lymph nodes
- Reduced appetite

PROGRESSION: First, glands or lymph nodes swell. Rash appears on face, then spreads throughout body, eventually forming evenly colored patches. Later, headache, mild conjunctivitis, and pain and swelling in joints develop.

TREATMENT: Absent severe complications, condition will self-limit.

CONTAGION: 1 2 3 **4**

PAIN: 1 **2** 3 4

SUFFERING: **1** 2 3 4

FATAL: Yes **No** Maybe

...or you might have
WHOOPING COUGH

WHAT IT IS: Highly contagious airborne bacterial infection of respiratory system, spread from person to person through sneezing, coughing, or laughing. Severe coughing spells end in "whooping" sound when inhaling. More common in adults whose vaccination has lost potency over time.

SPECIALIST TO SEE: Primary Care Physician

OTHER SYMPTOMS:
- Runny or stuffy nose
- Red, watery eyes
- Mild fever
- Dehydration

PROGRESSION: First, sore throat, mild fatigue, and dry cough appear. Then, cough progresses to vomit-producing spasms. Tongue protrudes, eyes bulge and bleed, and face becomes discolored due to difficulty inhaling.

TREATMENT: Antibiotics.

CONTAGION: 1 2 3 **4**

PAIN: 1 2 **3** 4

SUFFERING: 1 **2** 3 4

FATAL: Yes **No** Maybe

If your gums are sore...

...you might have
ACATALASIA

WHAT IT IS: Genetic disorder characterized by lack of catalase enzyme, which breaks down hydrogen peroxide into oxygen and water. Excess hydrogen peroxide, produced by certain bacteria, destroys hemoglobin, depriving infected tissue of oxygen. Tissue dies, resulting in painful gangrenous mouth ulcers.

SPECIALIST TO SEE: Endocrinologist, Periodontist

OTHER SYMPTOMS:
- Mouth sores
- Gangrene
- Gum infection

PROGRESSION: Benign gum pain leads to open, oozing mouth sores. Untreated, mouth sores kill surrounding tissue, causing tissue to become gangrenous. Rarely progresses beyond mouth and oral tissue.

TREATMENT: Surgical removal of damaged tissue.

CONTAGION: **1** 2 3 4

PAIN: 1 **2** 3 4

SUFFERING: 1 **2** 3 4

FATAL: Yes **No** Maybe

...or you might have
GUM CANCER

WHAT IT IS: Cancer that invades tissue surrounding base of teeth. May result from chronic gum irritation, including smoking, chewing tobacco, excessive alcohol use, poor oral hygiene, and dentures. Eventual treatment can cause significant facial disfigurement. Sixth most commonly occurring cancer.

SPECIALIST TO SEE: Oncologist, Periodontist

OTHER SYMPTOMS:
- Discolored gums
- Lump on gums
- Loose teeth
- Persistent bloody sores in mouth

PROGRESSION: First, painful red or white patch or sore appears on gums and spreads quickly. At diagnosis, over one-half of cases have spread to throat or neck. Fifty percent fatality rate.

FACT | In its brief lifetime, a female housefly can lay up to 1,000 eggs.

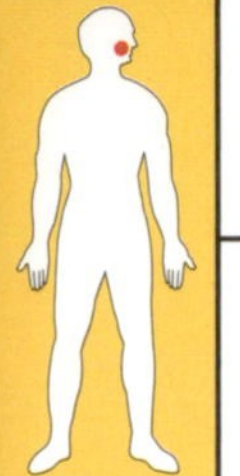

TREATMENT: Surgical removal of cancerous tumors from gums. Radiation or chemotherapy.

CONTAGION:	**1**	2	3	4
PAIN:	1	2	**3**	4
SUFFERING:	1	2	**3**	4
FATAL:	Yes	No	**Maybe**	

If your gums are bleeding...

...you might have
SCURVY

WHAT IT IS: Severe form of vitamin C deficiency. Caused by poor nutrition; specifically, not enough fresh fruits and vegetables. May appear alongside alcoholism or eating disorders. Develops slowly over long period of time. Historically, common among sailors at sea for longer than fruits or vegetables could be stored.

SPECIALIST TO SEE: Primary Care Physician, Dietitian

OTHER SYMPTOMS:

- Lethargy
- Spots on legs
- Easily bruised skin
- Slow wound healing
- Loose teeth
- Swollen, purple, or spongy gums
- Joint or muscle pain

PROGRESSION: Initially causes lethargy. Shortness of breath, weakness, joint abnormalities, and bone pain follow. In late stages, jaundice, fluid buildup, fever, and convulsions develop. Fatal if untreated.

TREATMENT: High doses of vitamin C daily.

CONTAGION:	**1**	2	3	4
PAIN:	1	**2**	3	4
SUFFERING:	1	**2**	3	4
FATAL:	Yes	No	**Maybe**	

...or you might have
TRENCH MOUTH

WHAT IT IS: Extreme form of gingivitis (infection of gums). Caused by overgrowth of bacteria in mouth, often due to poor oral hygiene, stress, diet, or smoking. Results in open, bleeding gum ulcers, foul taste in mouth, and halitosis (bad breath).

SPECIALIST TO SEE: Dentist, Periodontist

OTHER SYMPTOMS:

- Red or swollen gums
- Gray film on gums
- Swollen lymph nodes

PROGRESSION: Severe cases may result in tooth loss and trouble eating or swallowing. Untreated, can spread to surrounding tissue, such as cheeks, lips, and jawbone. May enter bloodstream, leading to potentially fatal systemic infection.

TREATMENT: Antibiotics. Removal of damaged gum tissue. Scaling and root planing to remove plaque and tartar from beneath gumline. Vigilant oral hygiene to prevent recurrence.

CONTAGION:	**1**	2	3	4
PAIN:	1	**2**	3	4
SUFFERING:	1	**2**	3	4
FATAL:	Yes	**No**	Maybe	

If your mouth is dry...

...you might have
BURNING MOUTH SYNDROME

WHAT IT IS: Mysterious condition resulting in burning sensation in mouth, dryness, and scalding pain. Cause unclear, but may be related to nutritional deficiencies, psychological problems, nerve damage, medication, and hormonal imbalances. Pain control and relaxation techniques often needed in absence of identifiable cause and treatment.

SPECIALIST TO SEE: Dermatologist, Dentist, Psychologist, Otolaryngologist

QUOTE | "Every human being is the author of his own health or disease." —Buddha

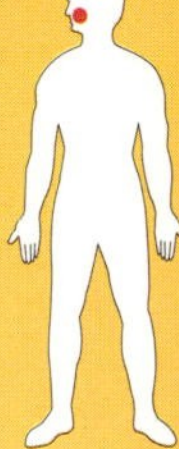

OTHER SYMPTOMS:
- Severe burning pain in mouth
- Tingling sensation in mouth or tongue
- Bitter or metallic taste

PROGRESSION: First onset is typically sudden, ranging from mildly irritating to unbearable symptoms. Pain and tingling often get worse throughout day but dissipate at night.

TREATMENT: Depends on underlying cause. Antidepressants, vitamin supplements, pain relievers, or antifungal medication may help.

CONTAGION:	**1**	2	3	4
PAIN:	1	2	3	**4**
SUFFERING:	1	**2**	3	4
FATAL:	Yes	**No**	Maybe	

...or you might have
TYPE 2 DIABETES

WHAT IT IS: Metabolic disorder marked by insulin resistance or deficiency. Cells, which require insulin to absorb glucose (blood sugar), become starved for energy. Over time, glucose buildup causes debilitating damage to nearly all body systems. Usually presents after age 35. Can be delayed or prevented by maintaining healthy lifestyle. Accounts for more than 90 percent of diabetes cases.

SPECIALIST TO SEE: Endocrinologist

OTHER SYMPTOMS:
- Persistent thirst
- Frequent urination
- Slow healing of wounds
- Extreme hunger
- Blurred vision

PROGRESSION: First, mild, short-term symptoms present. Long-term, debilitating damage, including heart disease, stroke, blindness, kidney failure, Alzheimer's disease, develops gradually. Excessively low or high blood sugar can abruptly cause coma or death.

TREATMENT: Lifelong, strict blood sugar control with medication. Insulin injections.

CONTAGION:	**1**	2	3	4
PAIN:	1	**2**	3	4
SUFFERING:	1	2	**3**	4
FATAL:	Yes	No	**Maybe**	

If you salivate excessively...

...you might have
GUILLAIN-BARRÉ SYNDROME

WHAT IT IS: Autoimmune condition. Body attacks its own peripheral nerves by producing antibody that damages myelin sheaths (fatty coverings that insulate nerve fibers). Cause unknown, though in rare instances may be precipitated by *Campylobacter* infection. Often occurs within days or weeks of respiratory or gastrointestinal infection. Risk increases with age.

SPECIALIST TO SEE: Neurologist, Immunologist, Rheumatologist

OTHER SYMPTOMS:
- Weakness throughout body
- Numbness or tingling in arms, legs, upper body, or face

PROGRESSION: Numbness or tingling in limbs appears first. Leads to complete limb paralysis within 24 hours. Symptoms resolve within months or years, or many persist indefinitely.

TREATMENT: No known cure. Intravenous immune globulin therapy to bolster immune system.

CONTAGION:	**1**	2	3	4
PAIN:	1	**2**	3	4
SUFFERING:	1	2	**3**	4
FATAL:	Yes	**No**	Maybe	

...or you might have
RABIES

WHAT IT IS: Viral disease that attacks brain cells and nervous system. Contracted through bites or scratches from infected animals. Causes extreme symptoms such as viciousness, rage, excitability, and paralysis before death. Infected bats have transmitted majority of recent cases in United States.

SPECIALIST TO SEE: Primary Care Physician

OTHER SYMPTOMS:
- Excessive thirst
- Fever

FACT | Health-destroying parasites inhabit 80 percent of the people in North America.

Managing Pain
The Evolution of Pain Relief

START

4000 BCE
Poppy documented as pain reliever in a Sumerian text.

2750 BCE
Egyptian carvings depict use of an electric fish to treat pain.

2000 BCE
In ancient India, first documented use of cannabis leaves (chewed) for pain.

1500 BCE
First documented use of acupuncture for pain relief in ancient Chinese medicine.

1500 BCE
First documented use of leeches, whose saliva is now known to contain anesthetic substances.

9th century BCE
Ice commonly used to dull pain in injured extremities.

1800
Mesmerism, commonly known as hypnosis, used to treat pain.

1800
Commonly "a blow to the jaw was used to induce a state of insensitivity," according to American Society of Anesthesiologists.

1800
Leech therapy experiences resurgence when American physicians recognize its anesthetic capabilities.

1803
Morphine, most potent part of opium, is isolated.

1804
Using herbal pain relievers, Japanese physician documents first use of general anesthesia during surgery.

1810
First known use of acupuncture in Western world, practiced by physician in Paris to treat abdominal pain.

1829
Early non-steroidal anti-inflammatory agent (NSAID) developed when salicylic acid—potent, pain-relieving ingredient in willow bark—is isolated.

1842
Ether first used as surgical anesthetic; prior to this, surgery was performed with minimal pain intervention.

1843
Morphine first dispensed intravenously.

1846
Oliver Wendell Holmes coins term "anæsthesia." Derived from Greek *anaisthésia* (insensibility), from *a-* (not) plus *aisthEsis* (perception).

1908
Intravenous regional anesthesia, known as the Bier block, invented. Consists of local anesthetic injected into limb below a high-pressure tourniquet, which traps the anesthetic.

1909
Acetaminophen isolated.

1919
Electreat pain-relief machine introduced: dispenses moderate electric shocks, thought to disrupt way in which brain receives pain signals.

1921
Epidural anesthesia first used during childbirth.

1937
Marijuana prescriptions illegalized in United States, despite testimony from American Medical Association asserting its beneficial uses.

1940
Anesthesiology is fully recognized as a medical specialty, with section in the American Medical Association, certification process, specialty board, and journal.

1940
Hyperventilation used to help alter pain perception during labor and childbirth, henceforth known as the Lamaze method.

1943
Local anesthetic lidocaine synthesized.

1955
First form of acetaminophen, marketed as Tylenol, available to consumers.

1960
Biofeedback, process of raising one's awareness of bodily functions to help control physiological reactions, introduced as pain-management technique.

"Given the choice between the experience of pain and nothing, I would choose pain."
—William Faulkner

6th century BCE
In *The Iliad*, Homer references poppy as source of pain relief.

5th century BCE
Greek physician Hippocrates writes about powder extracted from willow bark, precursor to aspirin, that eases pain and reduces fevers; this is also known by other cultures, including Native Americans.

46 CE
To relieve headache pain, Scribonius Largus, physician to Emperor Claudius, recommends standing on a live black torpedo fish for its electric shock.

1275 CE
Ether, a colorless, inhaled anesthetic, possibly discovered by Spanish philosopher Ramon Llull.

1540
Ether synthesized by Valerius Cordus.

1644
René Descartes proposes theory of pain that links mind and body together.

1680
Laudanum, mixture of opium and alcohol, introduced; becomes commonplace pain reliever.

1790
Henry Davy tests nitrous oxide (laughing gas) as pain-relief method.

19th century
Marijuana commonly prescribed by physicians to relieve pain, in form of tincture, liquid medication created by steeping marijuana leaves in alcohol.

1846
Revolutionary demonstration of surgical anesthesia at Massachusetts General Hospital: after using ether to anesthetize the patient, Dr. William Morton removes neck tumor.

1847
Introduction of chloroform, inhaled anesthetic with slightly sweet odor, offers first pain-relief option for childbirth.

1853
Hypodermic syringe invented.

1853
During childbirth, Queen Victoria uses choloroform, transforming it into respectable option for middle- and upper-class women.

1860
Cocaine isolated from leaves of coca plant.

1884
Cocaine first used as topical anesthetic.

1897
Dr. Felix Hoffman synthesizes salicylic acid and an acetyl group, creating acetylsalicylic acid, known today as aspirin. Acetylating addresses stomach upset caused by salicylic acid alone, and marks first synthesized, non-natural drug in history.

1899
First spinal anesthetic delivered in Germany: injection of cocaine effectively numbs lower half of patient's body.

1899
Bayer registers aspirin as trademark; marketed to physicians and hospitals in powder form.

1905
American Society of Anesthesiologists is formed.

1971
Acupuncture garners attention in United States following *New York Times* article about its pain-relieving effects.

1974
Patent issued for first transcutaneous electric nerve stimulator (TENS), modern-day machine that delivers electric shocks for pain reduction.

1988
Patient-controlled epidurals introduced, reducing amount of pain medication used during childbirth by 30 percent.

1996
National Institutes of Health and Food and Drug Administration give acupuncture long-awaited recognition as a viable medical treatment.

2004
They're back. Food and Drug Administration approves leeches as modern-day medical devices.

END

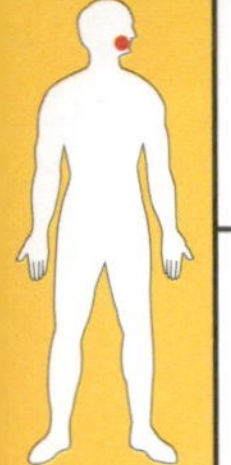

FACT | Each year, Americans come down with 1 billion colds.

- Headache
- Pain throughout body
- Hallucinations

PROGRESSION: Symptoms appear 30 days after transmission. Virus travels to brain and causes encephalitis (brain inflammation). Followed by death in 3 to 10 days if untreated.

TREATMENT: Preventable by vaccination. Postexposure prophylaxis within 2 weeks of infection.

CONTAGION: 1 **2** 3 4

PAIN: 1 2 **3** 4

SUFFERING: 1 2 **3** 4

FATAL: Yes No **Maybe**

If you have sores in your mouth...

...you might have

LEUKOPENIA

WHAT IT IS: Low white blood cell count leads to complications throughout body. Risk of serious and life-threatening infection rises. Cause often unknown, though commonly linked to viral infections, leukemia, chemotherapy, and vitamin and nutrient deficiencies.

SPECIALIST TO SEE: Primary Care Physician, Hematologist

OTHER SYMPTOMS:
- Fever or chills
- Frequent infections
- Dark urine
- Painful urination
- Redness, swelling, or pain around wounds

PROGRESSION: Depends on underlying cause. May be asymptomatic. Serious cases lead to mouth sores, liver problems, and pneumonia.

TREATMENT: Steroid injections. High doses of vitamins.

CONTAGION: **1** 2 3 4

PAIN: 1 **2** 3 4

SUFFERING: 1 **2** 3 4

FATAL: Yes **No** Maybe

If you have white spots in your mouth...

...you might have

ORAL THRUSH

WHAT IT IS: Painful mouth infection. Characterized by white lesions on tongue and cheeks. Caused by unrestrained growth of fungus *Candida albicans*. Commonly occurs in infants and in adults with compromised immune systems. Benign and harmless for most, but can cause more severe complications when paired with weakened immune system.

SPECIALIST TO SEE: Primary Care Physician

OTHER SYMPTOMS:
- Difficulty swallowing
- Mouth pain
- Bleeding from mouth

PROGRESSION: Swift onset. Begins as white lesions that resemble cottage cheese. Starts on tongue and cheeks; can spread to gums and tonsils. Rarely, may reach esophagus. In compromised immune system, can lead to widespread infection and resistance to treatment.

TREATMENT: Unsweetened yogurt to kill bacteria. Antifungal medication for more serious cases.

CONTAGION: **1** 2 3 4

PAIN: 1 **2** 3 4

SUFFERING: **1** 2 3 4

FATAL: Yes **No** Maybe

If your mouth has a metallic taste...

...you might have

LEAD POISONING

WHAT IT IS: Poisoning caused by ingestion or inhalation of tiny particles of disintegrating lead. Often found in paint and plumbing of structures built before 1978, stained glass, batteries, and jewelry. Resulting buildup of lead in hair, nails, teeth, and organs leads to interference with body's ability to carry oxygen.

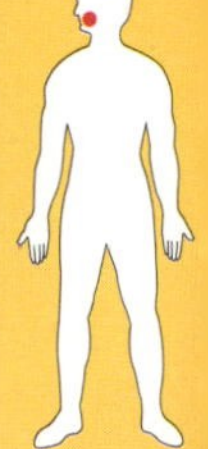

SPECIALIST TO SEE: Primary Care Physician, Hematologist

OTHER SYMPTOMS:

- High blood pressure
- Gastrointestinal disorders
- Joint or muscle pain
- Loss of memory
- Inability to concentrate
- Miscarriage

PROGRESSION: Lead accumulates slowly, seeping into kidney, liver, brain, and nervous system. Fatigue, lethargy, stomach pain, and cramping occur. Oxygen deficit results, altering brain function and causing swelling in skull, seizures, coma, and, possibly, death.

TREATMENT: Chelate (metal ion) therapy to allow excretion of lead.

CONTAGION: **1** 2 3 4

PAIN: 1 2 **3** 4

SUFFERING: 1 2 **3** 4

FATAL: Yes No **Maybe**

...or you might have

ZOLLINGER-ELLISON SYNDROME

WHAT IT IS: Engenders multiple tumors of pancreas, stomach, or duodenum (small intestine). Gastrinomas (tumors) secrete excessive amounts of digestive acid or gastrin, creating ulcers in stomach and duodenum. Cause unknown; may be genetic. Usually manifests after age 40. Ulcers resist treatment and often recur.

SPECIALIST TO SEE: Gastroenterologist, Endocrinologist

OTHER SYMPTOMS:

- Heartburn
- Nausea
- Vomiting or diarrhea
- Unintended weight loss
- Weakness throughout body
- Bloody vomit or stool

PROGRESSION: Starts as mild pain and heartburn. Multiple peptic ulcers develop, causing vomiting, bloody diarrhea, and weight loss. Ulcers may erode lining of affected organs, leading to perforation and, possibly, death. Tumors sometimes malignant and often metastasize to liver, another cause of death.

TREATMENT: Medication to reduce secretion of gastrin, decrease pain, and heal ulcers. Surgery to repair severe ulcers and remove tumors.

CONTAGION: **1** 2 3 4

PAIN: **1** 2 3 4

SUFFERING: 1 2 **3** 4

FATAL: Yes No **Maybe**

If you lose your sense of taste...

...you might have

BELL'S PALSY

WHAT IT IS: Facial muscles on one side become weak or paralyzed due to temporary paralysis of seventh cranial nerve. Rarely occurs on both sides of face. Often confused with having stroke. Cause unknown, but linked to viral infections such as herpes, immune disorders, or Lyme disease.

SPECIALIST TO SEE: Neurologist

OTHER SYMPTOMS:

- Drooping of one eye and corner of mouth
- Drooling
- Facial tics

PROGRESSION: Sudden onset of paralysis. Symptoms remain for 2 days, then subside. Majority of cases resolve within 6 months, though some never recover.

TREATMENT: No known cure. Prednisone (steroid) to decrease nerve inflammation and ease paralysis.

CONTAGION: **1** 2 3 4

PAIN: **1** 2 3 4

SUFFERING: 1 **2** 3 4

FATAL: Yes **No** Maybe

...or you might have

WALLENBERG'S SYNDROME

WHAT IT IS: Neurological disorder caused by occlusion of blood flow to certain parts of brain. May also result from serious, penetrating head wounds or stroke. Usually affects brain stem and areas related to sensation, motor skills, and

FACT | A typical mattress may contain up to 2 million dust mites.

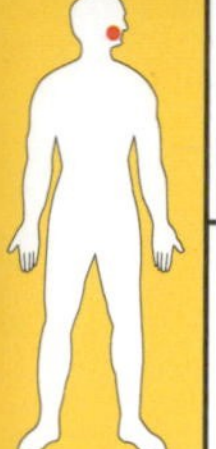

ambulation. Symptoms range from numbness to severe pain.

SPECIALIST TO SEE: Neurologist

OTHER SYMPTOMS:

- Hiccups
- Hoarse voice
- Rapid involuntary eye movement
- Clumsiness

PROGRESSION: Facial pain and numbness develop. Progressive loss of muscle control leads to inability to talk and eat. Walking also becomes difficult. May cause permanent damage.

TREATMENT: No known cure. Feeding tube if swallowing is impaired. Long-term care for permanent disabilities.

CONTAGION: **1** 2 3 4

PAIN: 1 2 **3** 4

SUFFERING: 1 2 **3** 4

FATAL: Yes **No** Maybe

If your tongue is sore...

...you might have

NOMA

WHAT IT IS: Centuries-old oral bacterial disease, also called gangrenous stomatitis. Causes destruction of tongue, mouth, and face. Starts as small painless blister, but bacteria ultimately eat away at oral and facial tissue. May be triggered by oral herpes; often associated with suppressed immune system.

SPECIALIST TO SEE: Dermatologist, Infectious Disease Specialist

OTHER SYMPTOMS:

- Bleeding from mouth
- Excessive salivation
- Gray or white patches on face or mouth
- Difficulty speaking

PROGRESSION: Blisters, followed by disintegration of oral and facial tissue, and accompanied by severe pain and impaired ability to eat, drink, and speak. Tube feeding eventually needed. Death likely, often due to starvation.

TREATMENT: Antibiotics to kill bacteria. Surgery to remove dead skin and tissue.

CONTAGION: **1** 2 3 4

PAIN: 1 2 3 **4**

SUFFERING: 1 2 3 **4**

FATAL: **Yes** No Maybe

...or you might have

TONGUE CANCER

WHAT IT IS: Cancerous tumors of tongue, occurring most often after age 45. Typically presents in postmenopausal women, smokers, and excessive drinkers. Difficult to diagnose, especially if tumor is located at base of tongue. May remain undetected until swallowing and speech are compromised.

SPECIALIST TO SEE: Oncologist, Otolaryngologist

OTHER SYMPTOMS:

- Numbness in tongue
- Bleeding from mouth
- Difficulty speaking, swallowing, or chewing
- Stiff neck

PROGRESSION: Reddish or gray-pink patches develop. Sores bleed easily and harden. Pain increases as tumor eats away nerve endings. Without rapid treatment, death likely.

TREATMENT: Surgery, radiation, and chemotherapy. Removal of affected tissue, teeth, and lymph nodes. Speech therapy.

CONTAGION: **1** 2 3 4

PAIN: 1 2 **3** 4

SUFFERING: 1 2 **3** 4

FATAL: Yes No **Maybe**

If your tongue is swollen...

...you might have

ACROMEGALY

WHAT IT IS: Noncancerous tumor on pituitary gland causes abundant production of growth hormone, spurring excessive growth in various parts of body. Rarely, tumors may be located in pancreas or lungs. Also called giantism. Can cause height to reach 99th percentile of growth charts (between 7 and 8 feet tall).

QUOTE | "Common sense is in medicine the master workman." —Peter Latham

Tongue Cancer

[Fig. 104]

EARLY STAGE

Tumors on oral tongue (visible, front two-thirds of tongue) usually appear as white, red, or gray lesions. May bleed when touched.

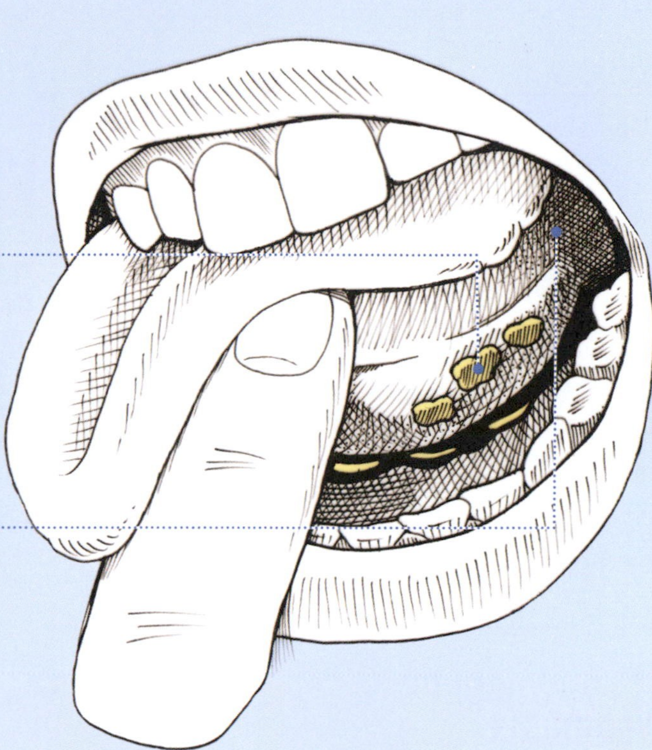

TONGUE BASE

On tongue base (posterior third of tongue, near throat), tumor may not be visible or symptomatic, increasing potential for metastasis before diagnosis.

LATE STAGE

Initially a few spots appear. Then, without treatment, tumors quickly spread, consuming large area of tongue.

RISK FACTORS

Heavy alcohol and tobacco usage strongly correlated with incidence of mouth cancer.

TREATMENT

Surgery to remove tumor from oral tongue; radiation therapy for base of tongue.

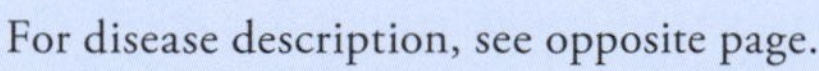

For disease description, see opposite page.

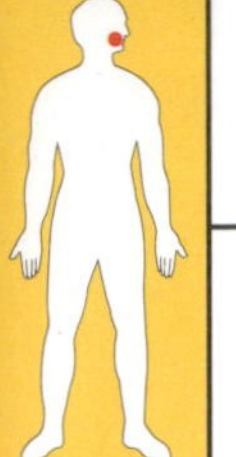

SPECIALIST TO SEE: Endocrinologist, Neurologist

OTHER SYMPTOMS:
- Thickened or oily skin
- Coarse hair
- Deepened voice
- Excessive sweating
- Body odor
- Erectile dysfunction

PROGRESSION: Slow, insidious progress spanning years. Arthritis-like symptoms occur, often causing misdiagnosis. Facial features and internal organs become enlarged, followed by diabetes, high blood pressure, and organ failure. Compression of nerves in brain may lead to blindness.

TREATMENT: Surgery. Medication to lower growth hormone. Radiation to treat pituitary gland.

CONTAGION: **1** 2 3 4
PAIN: 1 2 **3** 4
SUFFERING: 1 2 **3** 4
FATAL: Yes No **Maybe**

...or you might have
AMYLOIDOSIS

WHAT IT IS: Large amounts of amyloid protein produced by plasma cells and deposited within body interfere with organ function. Cause unknown, but may be triggered by tuberculosis, autoimmune disorders, or rheumatoid arthritis. Attacks men more often than women; may lead to cancer.

SPECIALIST TO SEE: Immunologist, Hematologist

OTHER SYMPTOMS:
- Joint pain or numbness
- Swelling in arms or legs
- Shortness of breath
- Irregular heartbeat
- Difficulty swallowing

PROGRESSION: As excessive amyloid spreads throughout body, organs harden, then malfunction. Hormone disorders develop, urine output drops, and heart function decreases. Following cardiac, respiratory, and kidney failure, death within 5 years.

TREATMENT: No known cure. Chemotherapy to reduce inflammation and protein production. Stem-cell transplant to replace abnormal cells.

CONTAGION: **1** 2 3 4
PAIN: 1 2 **3** 4
SUFFERING: 1 2 3 **4**
FATAL: **Yes** No Maybe

If your jaw is sore...

...you might have
RHEUMATOID ARTHRITIS

WHAT IT IS: Immune-system disorder in which body's own defense system attacks tissue surrounding joints. Characterized by inflammation of joint lining. Typically, affects joints symmetrically, i.e., both wrists or both knees. Results in difficulty completing simple day-to-day tasks. Affects more women than men. Long-term smoking increases risk. Chronic condition.

SPECIALIST TO SEE: Orthopedist, Rheumatologist

OTHER SYMPTOMS:
- Swollen, red, or painful joints
- Deformed joints
- Fever

PROGRESSION: Commonly starts with pain in hands, wrists, knees, and feet. Followed by sore jaw, shoulders, and hip joints. Then, joints swell, making movement difficult. Finally, joints become deformed and inflexible.

TREATMENT: No known cure. Steroids, pain relievers, and medication to limit joint damage or suppress immune system.

CONTAGION: **1** 2 3 4
PAIN: 1 2 **3** 4
SUFFERING: 1 **2** 3 4
FATAL: Yes **No** Maybe

...or you might have
TETANUS

WHAT IT IS: Serious condition caused when bacteria contaminate wound. *Clostridium tetani* bacterium produces toxin that poisons muscles and nervous system, leading to uncontrollable muscle spasms. May lead to permanent organ damage.

FACT | As many as 1.2 million illnesses per year are caused by *Salmonella* infections.

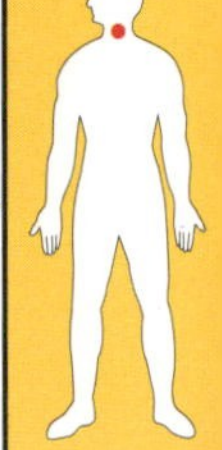

Can be fatal, even with treatment. Also known as lockjaw.

SPECIALIST TO SEE: Primary Care Physician, Infectious Disease Specialist

OTHER SYMPTOMS:

- Fever
- Excessive sweating
- Stiff neck
- Muscle spasms
- Difficulty swallowing
- Rapid heartbeat

PROGRESSION: First symptoms may appear within days to weeks following wound contamination. Then, muscle spasms spread from jaw to chest, abdomen, and back. Finally, severe spasms affect respiratory muscles, making breathing difficult or impossible.

TREATMENT: Intensive care. Antitoxin medication or antibiotics. Ventilator support. Sedation to control muscle spasms.

CONTAGION: **1** 2 3 4

PAIN: 1 2 3 **4**

SUFFERING: 1 2 **3** 4

FATAL: Yes No **Maybe**

If you have a dry cough...

...you might have
ASBESTOSIS

WHAT IT IS: Life-threatening breathing disorder caused by asbestos exposure. Asbestos particles embed in lungs, leading to inflammation and scarring. Lung walls become rigid. Minimal exposure required to trigger symptoms; may take years to materialize. Results in severely restricted breathing and increases risk for lung cancer.

SPECIALIST TO SEE: Pulmonologist, Oncologist

OTHER SYMPTOMS:

- Chest pain
- Lethargy
- Shortness of breath
- Bloody cough
- Deformed fingernails
- Clubbed fingers

PROGRESSION: Commonly starts with increasingly restricted breathing, especially on exertion. In advanced cases, may lead to total respiratory failure and potentially death.

TREATMENT: Flu vaccine as preventative step. Blood-thinning medication, analgesics, bronchodilators. Oxygen therapy. Lung-fluid drainage.

CONTAGION: **1** 2 3 4

PAIN: 1 2 **3** 4

SUFFERING: 1 2 **3** 4

FATAL: Yes No **Maybe**

...or you might have
ASTHMA

WHAT IT IS: Chronic condition in which airways become inflamed and fill with mucus, restricting breathing. Severe attacks can be life-threatening. Usually inherited, but environmental factors (allergens, obesity, urban living, and, in some cases, exercise) can contribute to onset and severity. Can surface at any age in response to allergens.

SPECIALIST TO SEE: Pulmonologist

OTHER SYMPTOMS:

- Wheezing
- Shortness of breath
- Chest pain
- Difficulty sleeping
- Poor stamina

PROGRESSION: Progress varies greatly. Chronic coughing and wheezing. Frequency of severe asthma attacks may increase. May also spark sleep apnea and chronic acid reflux. In extreme cases, loss of consciousness occurs, increasing risk of respiratory arrest and death.

TREATMENT: Inhaled and oral corticosteroids. Leukotriene modifiers. Long-acting beta-2 agonists (bronchodilators). Immunotherapy.

CONTAGION: **1** 2 3 4

PAIN: 1 **2** 3 4

SUFFERING: 1 **2** 3 4

FATAL: Yes No **Maybe**

FACT | Of the 76 million Americans who contract foodborne illnesses each year, 300,000 are hospitalized and 5,000 die.

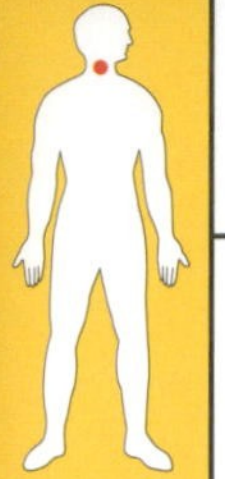

FACT | Humans are color-blind at birth.

...or you might have

AVIAN FLU

WHAT IT IS: Potentially deadly viral infection spread from birds to humans directly, or through another animal (e.g., pigs). Transmitter often exhibits no symptoms, and virus can live in host without consequence. Can mutate into more debilitating and deadly strain and transfer from person to person. Also known as bird flu.

SPECIALIST TO SEE: Infectious Disease Specialist

OTHER SYMPTOMS:

- Fever
- Headache
- Sore throat
- Muscle pain
- Eye infection

PROGRESSION: Mild, flu-like symptoms appear within days of exposure. Pronounced respiratory distress may trigger viral pneumonia. Fifty percent fatality rate.

TREATMENT: Antiviral medication.

CONTAGION:	1	2	**3**	4
PAIN:	1	**2**	3	4
SUFFERING:	1	2	**3**	4
FATAL:	Yes	No	**Maybe**	

...or you might have

LUNG CANCER

WHAT IT IS: Most common cancer killer. Smokers account for 90 percent of cases. Also caused by exposure to asbestos, radon gas, secondhand smoke, or genetics. May indicate spread of cancer elsewhere in body. Usually not detected until advanced stage, with 85 percent fatality rate after 5 years.

SPECIALIST TO SEE: Pulmonologist, Oncologist

Scurvy

[Fig. 105]

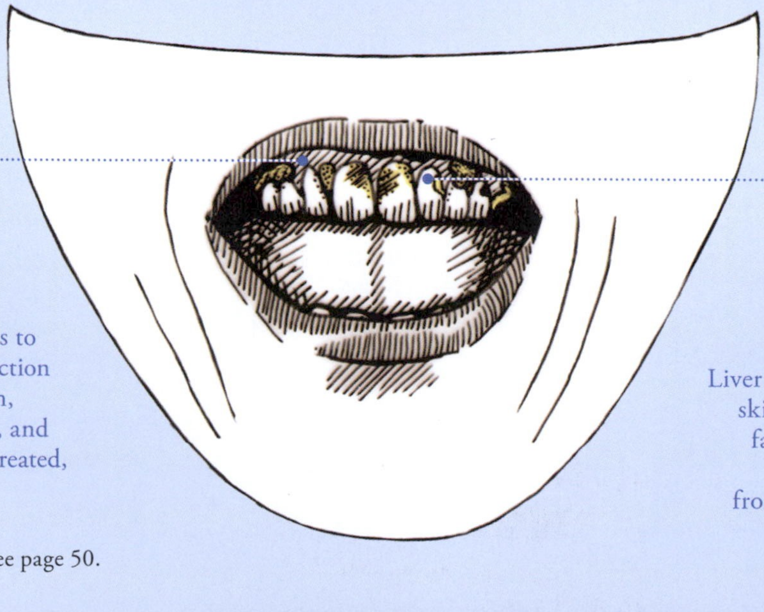

GUMS
Spongy, swollen, and bleeding gums.

TEETH
Loose teeth, leading to tooth loss.

WHAT IT IS
Lack of vitamin C leads to reduced collagen production and destruction of skin, cartilage, mouth, bone, and blood-vessel tissue. Untreated, nearly always fatal.

SYMPTOMS
Liver spots (bleeding under skin) on thighs and legs; fatigue; fever; diarrhea, or vomiting; bleeding from any and all orifices.

For disease description, see page 50.

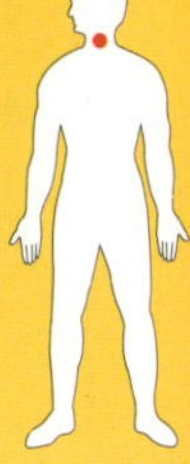

OTHER SYMPTOMS:
- Chest pains
- Chronic coughing
- Recurring bronchitis
- Hoarse voice
- Swelling in neck
- Weight loss

PROGRESSION: Starts as nagging cough. If caught early, tumor can be removed surgically and treated effectively. Typically diagnosed in later stages when successful treatment is unlikely and death is imminent.

TREATMENT: Surgery to remove tumors. Chemotherapy and radiation.

CONTAGION: **1** 2 3 4
PAIN: 1 2 **3** 4
SUFFERING: 1 2 3 **4**
FATAL: **Yes** No Maybe

If you have a wet cough...

...you might have
CYSTIC FIBROSIS

WHAT IT IS: Inherited chronic and often fatal disorder that attacks respiratory and digestive systems. Thick, sticky mucus buildup in lungs causes difficulty breathing and respiratory infections. Pancreas similarly affected by mucus production, which lowers enzyme production and prevents body from absorbing nutrients.

SPECIALIST TO SEE: Gastroenterologist, Pulmonologist

OTHER SYMPTOMS:
- Thick, sticky mucus
- Respiratory and digestive complications
- Diarrhea

PROGRESSION: First, lungs host bacterial infections alongside bouts of bronchitis and sinusitis. Then, combination of respiratory and nutritional problems weakens body, resulting in death from many possible causes, including pneumonia, emphysema, and cirrhosis.

TREATMENT: No known cure. Mucus-thinning medication, bronchodilators, bronchial drainage, and antibiotics to manage lung and digestive complications.

CONTAGION: **1** 2 3 4
PAIN: 1 2 **3** 4
SUFFERING: 1 2 3 **4**
FATAL: **Yes** No Maybe

...or you might have
PNEUMONIA

WHAT IT IS: Acute illness of respiratory system in which alveoli (air-filled sacs in lungs) become inflamed and filled with fluids. Caused by bacterial, viral, fungal, or parasitic infection. More than 50 types exist, each with different symptoms. Often mimics cold or flu, masking seriousness of actual condition. Severity may range from mildly debilitating to fatal. Infections like flu or chronic emphysema increase risk of repeated bouts.

SPECIALIST TO SEE: Primary Care Physician, Pulmonologist

OTHER SYMPTOMS:
- Chest or abdominal pain
- Fever or chills
- Difficulty breathing
- Headache
- Diarrhea

PROGRESSION: Commonly begins with chest and breathing pain, fever, chills, and fatigue. Then, lungs may fill with fluid, damaging respiratory cells. Death can result if not treated promptly, especially in elderly and immunocompromised persons.

TREATMENT: Antibiotics, antivirals, corticosteroids. Supplemental oxygen. Pain relievers.

CONTAGION: 1 2 **3** 4
PAIN: 1 2 **3** 4
SUFFERING: 1 **2** 3 4
FATAL: Yes No **Maybe**

FACT | Breast augmentation has tripled since 1997 and is now the leading cosmetic-surgery procedure.

Infectious Insects
Terror in Tiny Packages

Insects come in more species than all other animal groups combined. They're annoying, but they can also be deadly. The plague, spread by fleas, has killed tens of millions of people in single pandemics—the 14th-century Black Death killed one-third of the population of Europe in under 5 years. Today, mosquito-borne malaria is responsible for as many as 2.7 million deaths per year worldwide. When organisms carry pathogens (viruses, bacteria, fungi, protozoa, and parasites) from one host to another without themselves causing the infection, they're called "vectors." "Mechanical" vectors (like cockroaches and houseflies) are merely transporters, while "biological" vectors have longstanding ecological relationships with pathogens and support their replication (as with fleas and mosquitoes). Whatever the vector, there's plenty of infection to go around.

Cockroach

The German cockroach is the domestic culprit in the United States, preferring indoor locations and reproducing the fastest of all pest cockroaches. Descendents of a single female can number 30,000 in one year. Roaches love human food, and hide out in cracks as small as 1.6 millimeters wide when we try to hunt them down. Cockroaches crawl through and eat decaying matter and sewage, picking up germs on their legs then depositing them on food and food surfaces. They pass pathogens through their digestive tracts then defecate on or near the food they eat, leaving their droppings behind and walking through them to transport them elsewhere. In 2005, it was confirmed that cockroaches contribute significantly to childhood asthma. Allergens in cockroach secretions, droppings, cast skins, and dead bodies trigger the attacks; 1 in 5 children is susceptible. Beyond asthma, cockroaches spread at least fifty pathogens and diseases, including *Salmonella*, *Staphylococcus*, *Streptococcus*, hepatitis, and dysentery.

Housefly

Flies are toxic from day-one: they reproduce in manure, garbage, and rotting flesh because they're excellent sources of food for hatching fly maggots. Like cockroaches, houseflies deposit pathogens in a few different ways. With no mouths, flies can only eat food in

The diseases insects transmit have killed more people throughout history than all wars combined.

liquid form. They secrete saliva onto solid food to dissolve it, then suck it back in. They also vomit partially digested food for reconsumption. Both these activities, along with defecation, leave pathogens behind. Flies have sticky pads on their feet—it's how they're able to land on ceilings and walls, but it's also an effective way to transport pathogens after dining on dung, rotting carcasses, or decaying plant matter. A single housefly can carry over 30 million bacteria internally and another half billion outside its body. Housefly-transmitted diseases include typhoid fever, tuberculosis, anthrax, dysentery, chlamydia, and polio.

Flea

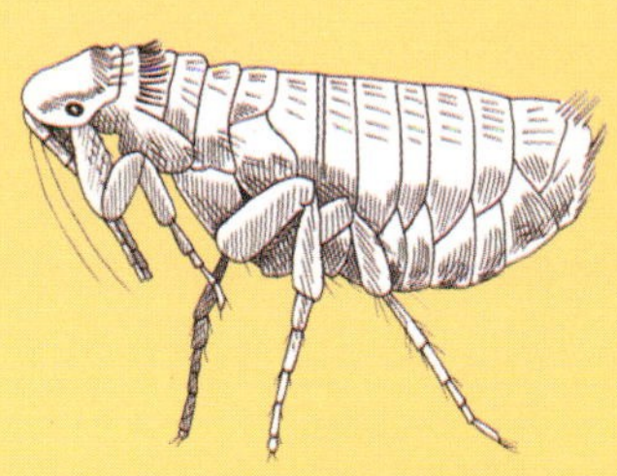

Fleas are most infamous for transmitting plague, whether bubonic, pneumonic, or septicemic, but they can also transmit typhoid and tapeworm. While there hasn't been an epidemic of plague in a hundred years or so, the disease hasn't disappeared—in 2006, 13 American cases were diagnosed. Infection generally occurs when a person is bitten by a flea that previously fed on an infected rodent. The bacteria multiply inside the flea and form a stomach-blocking plug. The starving flea feeds vigorously, but because it can't pass the blood past the bacteria, it vomits bacteria-tainted blood in the bite wound, causing infection. In contemporary times, plague has been confined to wild rodents, but public health officials fear that it could pass to city rats and cause another epidemic.

Mosquito

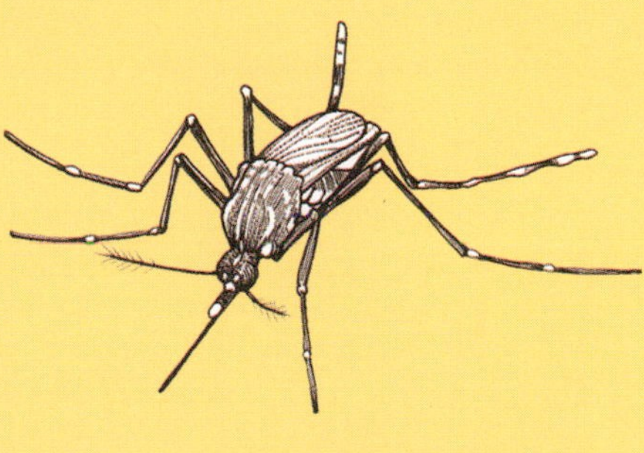

While fleas have been the cause of devastating epidemics in past centuries, the mosquito is currently a bigger public health problem, transmitting diseases to almost 70 million people every year. Only the females feast on blood, as they need the protein for egg development; males feed on nectar. When a mosquito bites, it injects saliva containing anti-coagulants to keep the blood from clotting. Also in mosquito saliva are pathogens for diseases, which the mosquito first ingests by feeding on an infected human carrier. Diseases transmitted by the mosquito include malaria, Dengue and yellow fevers, West Nile virus, encephalitis, and elephantiasis.

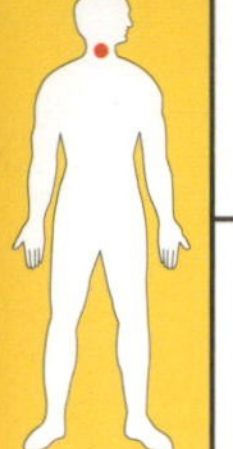

FACT | Each year, 90,000 patients die of infections acquired *after* being admitted to a hospital.

If you're coughing blood...

...you might have
ARTERIOVENOUS MALFORMATION

WHAT IT IS: Defect of circulatory system resulting in strangling entanglement of veins and arteries in brain, spleen, lung, spine, and kidneys. Causes lesions that may rupture. Usually present at birth but remains largely undetected until symptoms appear later. May occur in conjunction with another disease (e.g., Von Hippel-Lindau disease).

SPECIALIST TO SEE: Neurologist

OTHER SYMPTOMS:

- Seizures
- Muscle weakness or paralysis
- Vision loss
- Loss of comprehension
- Numbness or tingling sensation throughout body
- Hallucinations

PROGRESSION: Symptoms often arise suddenly and without warning. Immediate debilitation occurs. Hemorrhaging leads to serious long-term neurological defects. May cause paralyzing and potentially fatal stroke or cerebral aneurysm. Thirty percent mortality rate.

TREATMENT: Surgery to correct defect.

CONTAGION: **1** 2 3 4

PAIN: 1 2 **3** 4

SUFFERING: 1 2 **3** 4

FATAL: Yes No **Maybe**

...or you might have
GOODPASTURE'S SYNDROME

WHAT IT IS: Autoimmune disease that quickly destroys kidneys and causes lung hemorrhaging. Usually undetected until rapid deterioration has already taken hold. Only 10 percent fatality rate from actual condition; related kidney disease presents more dangerous threat.

SPECIALIST TO SEE: Nephrologist, Pulmonologist

OTHER SYMPTOMS:

- Mild coughing
- Shortness of breath
- Fatigue
- Nausea
- Painful urination
- Bloody or frothy urine

PROGRESSION: Initial symptoms may last several weeks or up to 2 years. If detected early, lung hemorrhage can be stemmed. Irreversible kidney damage, if present, may be fatal.

TREATMENT: Corticosteroids, immunosuppressants, plasmapheresis (plasma transfusion), antibiotics (for lungs). Dialysis. Kidney transplant.

CONTAGION: **1** 2 3 4

PAIN: 1 2 **3** 4

SUFFERING: 1 2 **3** 4

FATAL: Yes No **Maybe**

If you gag repeatedly...

...you might have
CYCLIC VOMITING SYNDROME

WHAT IT IS: Bouts of pronounced nausea and vomiting of unknown origin last several hours or days and may disappear and resume without warning. Triggered by stress, heat, menstruation, food (e.g., chocolate, cheese), motion sickness, and even excitement. Personal or family history of migraines, depression, irritable bowel syndrome, and hypothyroidism increase risk.

SPECIALIST TO SEE: Gastroenterologist

OTHER SYMPTOMS:

- Drowsiness
- Sensitivity to light or sound
- Excessive thirst
- Diarrhea or abdominal pain
- Dizziness
- Headache or fever

PROGRESSION: Commonly starts with vomiting several times per hour for several hours. May last up to 10 days. Debilitating effects may cause semi-comatose state.

TREATMENT: Anti-migraine and anti-emetic medication, antidepressants, triptans, and analgesics.

CONTAGION: **1** 2 3 4

PAIN: 1 2 **3** 4

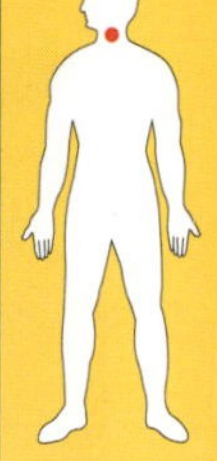

SUFFERING: 1 2 **3** 4

FATAL: Yes **No** Maybe

...or you might have
MYASTHENIA GRAVIS

WHAT IT IS: Chronic neuromuscular disease caused by defective gene in which antibodies mistakenly attack motor-function nerve cells. Produces fluctuating weakness and fatigue in voluntary muscles. May take up to 2 years to correctly diagnose through blood and neurological tests. Ranges in severity. May affect one or all muscles, including pulmonary muscles.

SPECIALIST TO SEE: Neurologist

OTHER SYMPTOMS:
- Double vision
- Slurred speech
- Facial paralysis
- Difficulty chewing

PROGRESSION: Sudden onset of weakness in eye or throat muscles, difficulty swallowing, and speech problems. In severe cases, general paralysis develops. May affect respiratory functions, requiring assisted ventilation.

TREATMENT: Immunosuppressants, neurotransmitter stimulants. Surgery. Physical therapy.

CONTAGION: **1** 2 3 4

PAIN: **1** 2 3 4

SUFFERING: 1 2 **3** 4

FATAL: Yes No **Maybe**

If you have a sore throat...

...you might have
DIPHTHERIA

WHAT IT IS: Affliction of upper respiratory tract. Highly contagious; usually spread from person to person directly or through objects worn or touched by carriers. Symptoms may remain dormant for up to 6 weeks following exposure. Though inoculation exists, effects weaken over time. Lack of widespread vaccination leads to resurgence in outbreaks.

SPECIALIST TO SEE: Infectious Disease Specialist

OTHER SYMPTOMS:
- Mild fever and chills
- Fatigue
- Difficulty swallowing
- Nausea or vomiting

PROGRESSION: First, flu-like symptoms appear. Then, toxins attack mucous membranes, making respiration difficult. Recovery slow. Side effects include heart, kidney, or motor-system damage. Fatality rate between 10 and 20 percent.

TREATMENT: Intensive care. Erythromycin, penicillin, and intravenous hydration. In severe cases, tracheotomy and treatment with diphtheria antitoxin.

CONTAGION: 1 2 3 **4**

PAIN: 1 2 **3** 4

SUFFERING: 1 **2** 3 4

FATAL: Yes No **Maybe**

...or you might have
EPSTEIN-BARR VIRUS

WHAT IT IS: Infectious virus of herpes family that can cause mononucleosis. Virus housed in throat. Very common; high likelihood of infection, though symptoms usually remain dormant. Transmission requires contact with saliva of infected person. Contraction through air or blood uncommon.

SPECIALIST TO SEE: Primary Care Physician

OTHER SYMPTOMS:
- Fever
- Swollen lymph nodes
- Enlarged liver or spleen
- Fatigue

PROGRESSION: First, swelling of throat glands accompanied by fever, muscle aches, fatigue, and jaundice. In some cases, swollen liver or spleen appear. May also progress into rare cancers, Burkitt's lymphoma and nasopharyngeal carcinoma.

TREATMENT: Bed rest. Steroids.

CONTAGION: 1 2 3 **4**

PAIN: 1 **2** 3 4

SUFFERING: 1 2 **3** 4

FATAL: Yes No **Maybe**

QUOTE | "If I had my way I'd make health catching instead of disease." —Robert Ingersoll

Hashimoto's Thyroiditis

[Fig. 106]

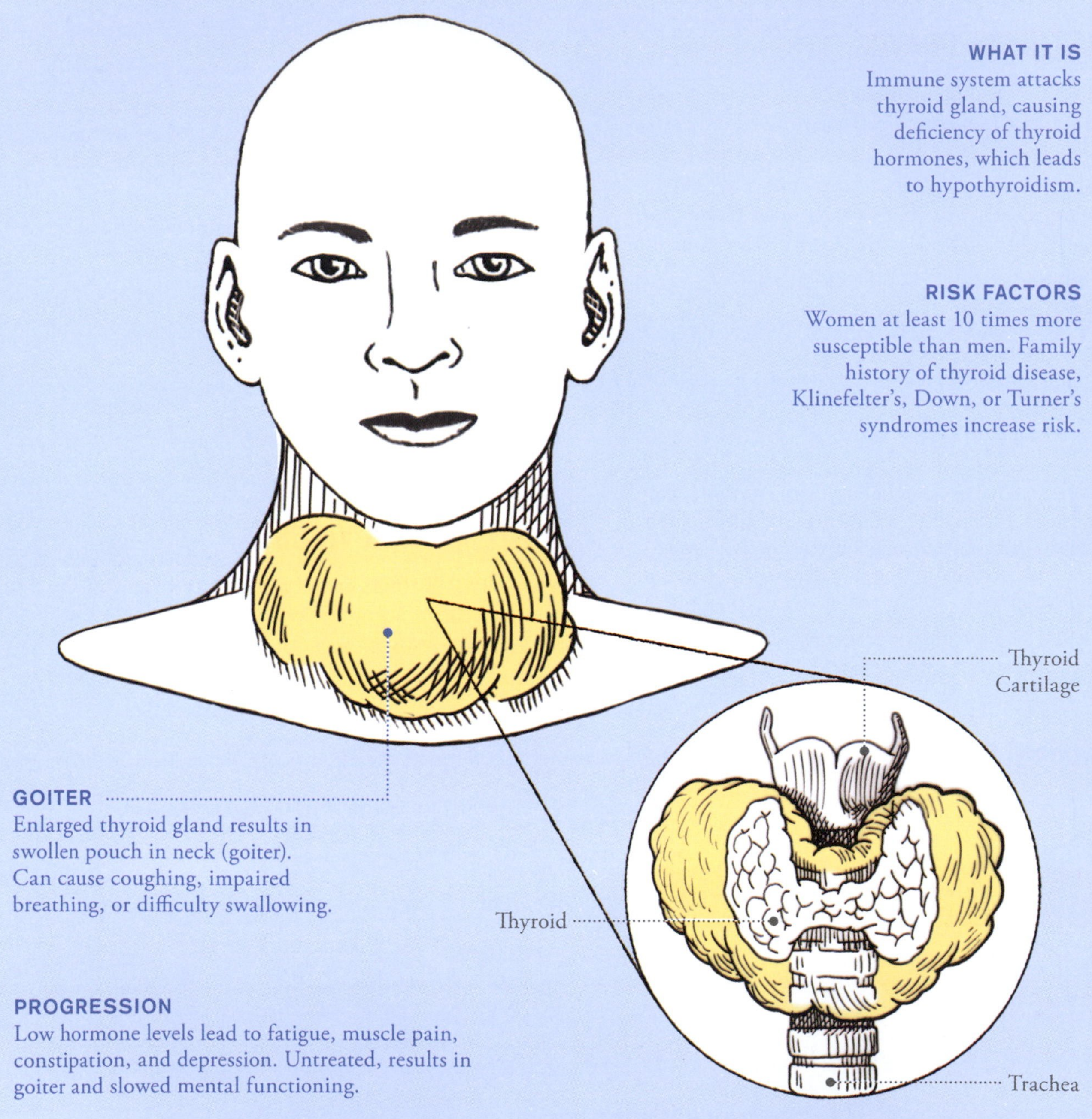

WHAT IT IS
Immune system attacks thyroid gland, causing deficiency of thyroid hormones, which leads to hypothyroidism.

RISK FACTORS
Women at least 10 times more susceptible than men. Family history of thyroid disease, Klinefelter's, Down, or Turner's syndromes increase risk.

GOITER
Enlarged thyroid gland results in swollen pouch in neck (goiter). Can cause coughing, impaired breathing, or difficulty swallowing.

PROGRESSION
Low hormone levels lead to fatigue, muscle pain, constipation, and depression. Untreated, results in goiter and slowed mental functioning.

For disease description, see opposite page.

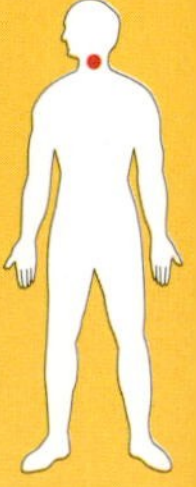

...or you might have
SCARLET FEVER

WHAT IT IS: Highly contagious streptococcal infection. Acute manifestation of strep throat that causes high fever, sore throat, and red impetigo-like rash (oozing, crusting sores) on chest. Rashes eventually spread to entire body.

SPECIALIST TO SEE: Primary Care Physician, Infectious Disease Specialist

OTHER SYMPTOMS:
- Headache
- Chills
- Rapid heartbeat
- Swollen tonsils
- Redness or blistering on tongue

PROGRESSION: First, starts with common signs of strep throat. Then, red rash appears on face and body. Rash fades and begins to peel after several days. May progress to rheumatic fever if untreated.

TREATMENT: Penicillin, antibiotics, and erythromycin.

CONTAGION: 1 2 3 **4**

PAIN: 1 2 **3** 4

SUFFERING: 1 2 **3** 4

FATAL: Yes No **Maybe**

If your voice is hoarse...

...you might have
ESOPHAGEAL CANCER

WHAT IT IS: Malignant tumors in esophagus. Especially prevalent among heavy drinkers and smokers. Other risk factors include chronic heartburn, acid reflux, and exposure to silica dust. Three times more prevalent in men than women. Ninety percent mortality after 5 years.

SPECIALIST TO SEE: Oncologist, Otolaryngologist

OTHER SYMPTOMS:
- Sensation of food sticking in throat or chest
- Chronic coughing
- Weight loss
- Muscle atrophy
- Vomiting
- Bloody cough

PROGRESSION: Commonly asymptomatic at first. Then, tumor causes chronic coughing and gagging, leading to vomiting and weight loss. By time of diagnosis, cancer likely has spread to other organs, resulting in high likelihood of death.

TREATMENT: Surgical removal of affected areas of esophagus. Chemotherapy, radiation, and photodynamic and laser therapy.

CONTAGION: **1** 2 3 4

PAIN: 1 2 **3** 4

SUFFERING: 1 2 3 **4**

FATAL: **Yes** No Maybe

...or you might have
HASHIMOTO'S THYROIDITIS

WHAT IT IS: Most common form of hypothyroidism in United States. Inherited autoimmune disorder causes immune system to attack thyroid gland. Results in underproduction of thyroid hormones; may be accompanied by occasional adrenaline-like excess, followed by periods of depression, fatigue, and constipation. Affects more women than men.

SPECIALIST TO SEE: Endocrinologist

OTHER SYMPTOMS:
- Lethargy
- Swelling in mouth or lips
- Brittle fingernails
- Decreased libido
- Cognitive impairment
- Goiter

PROGRESSION: Slowly leads to chronic obesity, heart disease, pain in joints, and noticeable goiter (neck growth) that can complicate breathing and swallowing. Untreated, can be fatal.

TREATMENT: Synthetic hormone replacement.

CONTAGION: **1** 2 3 4

PAIN: 1 2 **3** 4

SUFFERING: 1 2 **3** 4

FATAL: Yes No **Maybe**

VOCAB | Superinfector: An infected person with an above-average ability to pass a contagious disease on to others.

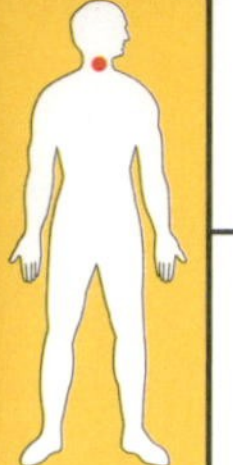

FACT | Heart disease is the number-one cause of death in the United States.

...or you might have
SILICOSIS

WHAT IT IS: Progressive respiratory disease characterized by inflammation and scarring of lung tissue due to long-term exposure to silica dust. Silica, world's most common mineral, can be found in glass, paint, and concrete. Dust becomes trapped in lungs, causing tissue to swell. Symptoms may not appear for up to 20 years after exposure. Also called "potter's rot."

SPECIALIST TO SEE: Pulmonologist

OTHER SYMPTOMS:
- Chronic coughing
- Difficulty breathing
- Weight loss
- Blue skin
- Fever
- Fatigue

PROGRESSION: Starts as shallow breathing, nagging cough, fatigue, weight loss, and sickly blue skin. Then, life-threatening diseases, such as tuberculosis, emphysema, and pulmonary hypertension follow. Symptoms may be irreversible.

TREATMENT: Damage is irreparable. Antibiotics, bronchodilators, cough suppressants, and oxygen supplementation to treat symptoms. Lung transplant in severe cases.

CONTAGION: **1** 2 3 4

PAIN: 1 2 **3** 4

SUFFERING: 1 2 **3** 4

FATAL: Yes No **Maybe**

If you have difficulty swallowing...

...you might have
HERPETIC STOMATITIS

WHAT IT IS: Highly contagious viral mouth infection sparked by herpes simplex. Characterized by blisters on tongue, gums, and lips, as well as oral inflammation. Passed from person to person, sometimes through indirect contact. Can lead to secondary herpes eye infection. First outbreak is usually most severe, after which body develops antibodies.

SPECIALIST TO SEE: Primary Care Physician, Periodontist

OTHER SYMPTOMS:
- Reduced appetite
- High fever
- Fatigue

PROGRESSION: Inside of cheeks and tongue develop painful ulcers, causing drooling, difficulty swallowing, and inability to ingest food. Clears in about 10 days. If immune system compromised, may lead to brain damage or meningitis.

TREATMENT: Acetaminophen. Antiviral medication. Pain and fever relievers.

CONTAGION: 1 2 3 **4**

PAIN: 1 **2** 3 4

SUFFERING: 1 **2** 3 4

FATAL: Yes **No** Maybe

If you have swollen glands...

...you might have
AFRICAN SLEEPING SICKNESS

WHAT IT IS: Parasitic disease spread by bites of tsetse fly. Has symptom-free incubation period of up to 1 month. Can cause paralysis of eye muscles and severe muscular weakness throughout body. Untreated, overcomes body's immune system, causing gland and organ failure and death within weeks.

SPECIALIST TO SEE: Infectious Disease Specialist

OTHER SYMPTOMS:
- Headache
- Tremors
- Convulsions
- Anemia

PROGRESSION: Commonly starts with mild symptoms, followed shortly by mental confusion and alternating periods of mania and insomnia. Then, heart and nervous systems affected. Extreme sleepiness and coma occur before death.

Deadly Handshake

Etiquette Can Be Fatal

Manners are one thing, but the handshake is another—most germs are transmitted via the hands.

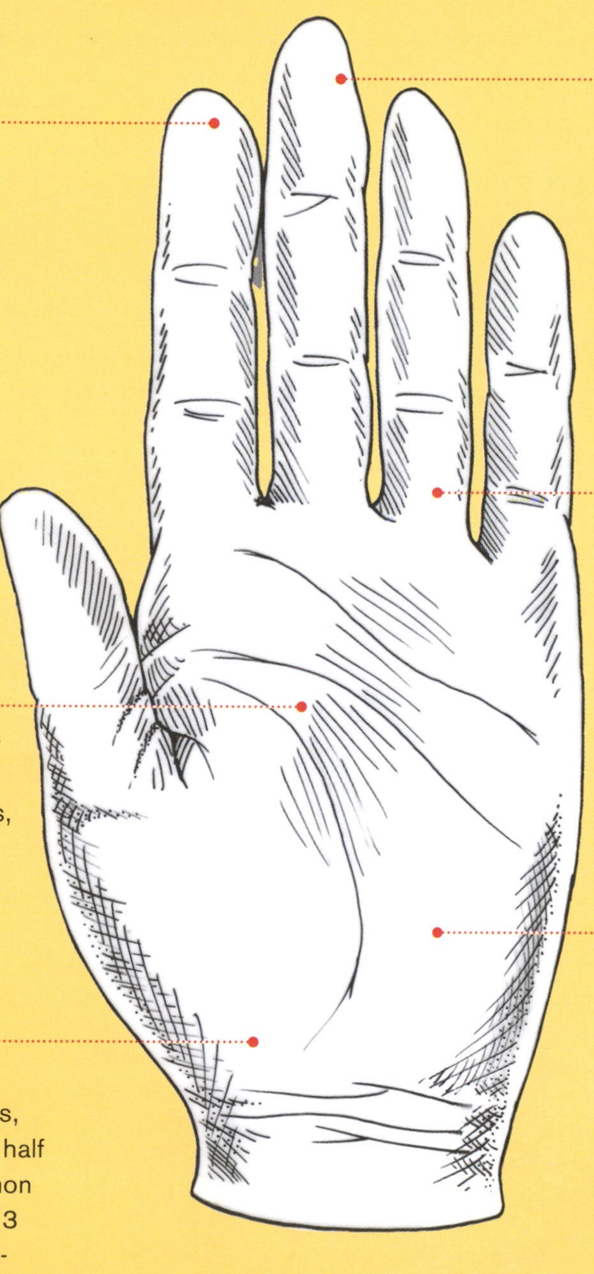

Adenovirus
This contagious, diarrhea-causing virus accounts for about 10 percent of acute upper-respiratory infections. It can also cause bronchiolitis, croup, pneumonia, pinkeye, middle-ear infections, swollen lymph nodes, gastroenteritis, and urinary-tract infections.

Pseudomonas aeruginosa
This opportunistic pathogen can lead to ear, eye, and respiratory infections, acne vulgaris, sepsis, pharyngitis, dermatitis, bacteremia, meningitis, and brain abscesses.

Rhinovirus
The most prevailing viral agent in the United States, rhinovirus causes almost half of the cases of the common cold. Its lifespan of up to 3 hours on the skin or inanimate objects allows colds to spread easily.

Staphylococcus aureus
Causing a variety of pus-forming infections and skin lesions like pimples, boils, and sties, this bacterium can deteriorate into more serious infections such as mastitis, phlebitis, folliculitis, and toxic shock syndrome.

Shigella
This microscopic germ causes the intestinal ailments shigellosis and dysentery. About 18,000 cases are reported in the United States each year, with joint pain, chronic arthritis, eye irritation, and painful urination appearing in untreated cases.

Haemophilus influenzae
A bacterium estimated to be responsible for millions of serious illnesses and thousands of deaths per year, chiefly from meningitis and pneumonia, *H. influenzae* can also lead to obstructive laryngitis, ear and joint diseases, and blood poisoning. Despite its name, it does not cause the flu.

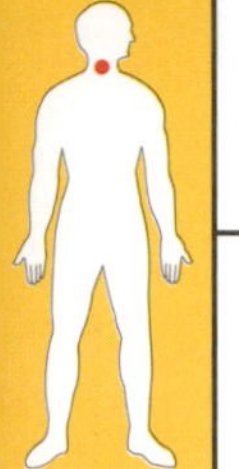

TREATMENT: Variety of medication. Hospitalization and follow-up exams that include spinal tap.

CONTAGION:	**1**	2	3	4
PAIN:	1	**2**	3	4
SUFFERING:	1	2	**3**	4
FATAL:	Yes	No	**Maybe**	

...or you might have
MONONUCLEOSIS

WHAT IT IS: Viral infection, often spread through contact with saliva (popularly called "kissing disease"). Can be contracted by coughing, sneezing, or sharing utensils. Caused by Epstein-Barr virus and, to lesser degree, Cytomegalovirus. Known for lengthy incubation period and long-lasting symptoms.

SPECIALIST TO SEE: Primary Care Physician, Endocrinologist

OTHER SYMPTOMS:
- Headache
- Fever
- Weakness in muscles or joints
- Disorientation
- Night sweats
- Sore throat
- Reduced appetite

PROGRESSION: Commonly starts a month after infection, with fever and sore throat. Then, fatigue; weakness; swelling in lymph nodes, spleen, and liver; and skin rash appear. Symptoms take several months to subside.

TREATMENT: Bed rest. Painkillers, aspirin, and antibiotics to treat symptoms.

CONTAGION:	1	2	3	**4**
PAIN:	1	**2**	3	4
SUFFERING:	**1**	2	3	4
FATAL:	Yes	**No**	Maybe	

...or you might have
MUMPS

WHAT IT IS: Highly contagious virus spread through saliva. Long-term effects include infertility and damage to other body parts, such as breasts and prostate. Additional complications may include brain inflammation and deafness. Largely eradicated through vaccine.

SPECIALIST TO SEE: Primary Care Physician, Endocrinologist

OTHER SYMPTOMS:
- Fever
- Fatigue
- Swelling in testicles or ovaries
- Rash
- Difficulty swallowing

PROGRESSION: Following 1-month incubation period, fever, headache, and sore throat occur, followed by swelling in glands. Finally, subsides without treatment in 2 weeks. Can cause painful swelling of testicles or ovaries, compromising fertility.

TREATMENT: Pain relievers. Warm baths to soothe swelling.

CONTAGION:	1	2	3	**4**
PAIN:	1	**2**	3	4
SUFFERING:	1	**2**	3	4
FATAL:	Yes	**No**	Maybe	

If your neck is sore...

...you might have
ANKYLOSING SPONDYLITIS

WHAT IT IS: Systemic rheumatic disorder similar to rheumatoid arthritis. Characterized by chronic inflammation of spine and sacroiliac joints, located on either side of buttocks. Prolonged inflammation can lead to fusion of vertebrae.

SPECIALIST TO SEE: Rheumatologist, Orthopedist

OTHER SYMPTOMS:
- Fatigue
- Fever
- Weight loss

PROGRESSION: Degree of lower back pain and stiffness varies. If vertebrae fuse together, decreased mobility will result. Can also affect area where ribs attach to spine, which can obstruct breathing.

TREATMENT: Physical therapy and exercise. Joint-replacement surgery for severe cases.

FACT | Shopping-cart handles contain more bacteria than public bathrooms.

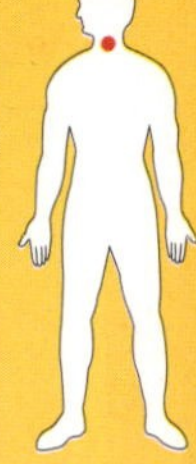

CONTAGION: 1 2 3 4
PAIN: 1 2 3 4
SUFFERING: 1 2 3 4
FATAL: Yes No Maybe

...or you might have
TORTICOLLIS

WHAT IT IS: Condition caused by brain nerve palsy in which head is tilted forward, back, or to one side, and chin is elevated and turned to other side. Can be genetic or acquired. Acquired version results from neck trauma, undetected tumor, or awkward sleeping position. More common in women. Also known as "wry neck."

SPECIALIST TO SEE: Neurologist

OTHER SYMPTOMS:
- Twisted neck
- Tremors
- Repetitive, jerking head movement
- Limited range of motion in neck

PROGRESSION: Twisting of neck begins gradually. Neck remains contorted and may spasm involuntarily. Contortion is painful and can damage neck nerves, leading to permanent physical deformity.

TREATMENT: No known cure. Physical therapy, anti-inflammatory medication, and plastic surgery to alleviate symptoms.

CONTAGION: 1 2 3 4
PAIN: 1 2 3 4
SUFFERING: 1 2 3 4
FATAL: Yes No Maybe

If your neck is stiff...

...you might have
LISTERIOSIS

WHAT IT IS: Bacterial infection primarily caused by eating food contaminated by *Listeria monocytogenes.* Can also be contracted through contact with infected calves and fowl. Once bacteria reach intestines, may be absorbed into bloodstream and transported to central nervous system and other body systems.

SPECIALIST TO SEE: Gastroenterologist, Infectious Disease Specialist

OTHER SYMPTOMS:
- Skin lesions
- Pink eye
- Fever
- Lethargy
- Muscle pain
- Nausea, vomiting, and diarrhea
- Headache

PROGRESSION: Symptoms may take weeks to appear. Can lead to confusion, loss of balance, convulsions, meningitis, pneumonia, and hepatitis. Reinfection is possible.

TREATMENT: Antibiotics.

CONTAGION: 1 2 3 4
PAIN: 1 2 3 4
SUFFERING: 1 2 3 4
FATAL: Yes No Maybe

...or you might have
POLIO

WHAT IT IS: Contagious viral disease resulting in paralysis, compromised breathing, and death; can lead to multi-organ failure. Commonly recognized by deformation in hips, ankles, and feet. Spread through fecal contamination of water or food. Most carriers asymptomatic. No known cure; mass immunization began in mid-1950s.

SPECIALIST TO SEE: Infectious Disease Specialist, Orthopedist

OTHER SYMPTOMS:
- Headache
- Constipation
- Vomiting
- Extreme sensitivity to touch
- Stiff joints
- Impaired reflexes

PROGRESSION: After exposure, virus multiplies in throat and intestinal tract. Travels to brain, destroying neurotransmitters and causing muscular damage and temporary or permanent paralysis. Compromises other organs, leading to chronic and often fatal diseases.

QUOTE | "Health is merely the slowest possible rate at which one can die." —Unknown

10 Most Deadly Cancers
Which One Will You Get?

After heart disease, cancer is the second leading cause of death in the United States, responsible for over half a million deaths per year. It's pretty hard to avoid: for men, the overall likelihood of lifetime diagnosis is 1 in 2.17; women fare a little better at 1 in 2.63.

Men	
1	**Lung and Bronchus** Lifetime probability you'll get it: 1 in 12
2	**Prostate** Lifetime probability you'll get it: 1 in 6
3	**Colon and Rectum** Lifetime probability you'll get it: 1 in 17
4	**Pancreas** Lifetime probability you'll get it: 1 in 79
5	**Leukemia (all types)** Lifetime probability you'll get it: 1 in 67
6	**Liver and Intrahepatic Bile Duct** Lifetime probability you'll get it: 1 in 114
7	**Esophagus** Lifetime probability you'll get it: 1 in 131
8	**Urinary Bladder** Lifetime probability you'll get it: 1 in 28
9	**Non-Hodgkin's Lymphoma** Lifetime probability you'll get it: 1 in 47
10	**Kidney and Renal Pelvis** Lifetime probability you'll get it: 1 in 61

Women	
1	**Lung and Bronchus** Lifetime probability you'll get it: 1 in 16
2	**Breast** Lifetime probability you'll get it: 1 in 8
3	**Colon and Rectum** Lifetime probability you'll get it: 1 in 19
4	**Pancreas** Lifetime probability you'll get it: 1 in 79
5	**Ovary** Lifetime probability you'll get it: 1 in 69
6	**Leukemia (all types)** Lifetime probability you'll get it: 1 in 95
7	**Non-Hodgkin's Lymphoma** Lifetime probability you'll get it: 1 in 55
8	**Uterus** Lifetime probability you'll get it: 1 in 40
9	**Brain and Nervous System** Lifetime probability you'll get it: 1 in 192
10	**Liver and Intrahepatic Bile Duct** Lifetime probability you'll get it: 1 in 249

*Most statistics drawn from the American Cancer Society for 2007.

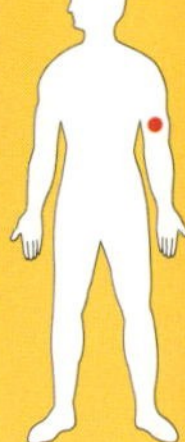

TREATMENT: No known cure. Antibiotics, analgesics, portable ventilators, and surgery to correct deformities.

CONTAGION: 1 2 3 **4**

PAIN: 1 2 3 **4**

SUFFERING: 1 2 **3** 4

FATAL: Yes No **Maybe**

...or you might have

TYPHUS

WHAT IT IS: Group of potentially life-threatening diseases caused by *Rickettsia* bacteria. Spread from rodents to humans through mites, fleas, and lice. Can be endemic (restricted to certain region or population, e.g., Texas and southern California) or epidemic (spreading into regions or among people not normally affected). Epidemic form considered potential bioterrorism agent.

SPECIALIST TO SEE: Infectious Disease Specialist

OTHER SYMPTOMS:

- Headache
- Fever or chills
- Exhaustion
- Rash
- Muscle pain
- Dry cough

PROGRESSION: Symptoms appear within 3 weeks following exposure. Fever, chills, headaches, convulsions, and rashes develop. Leads to life-threatening complications, such as pneumonia, uremia (toxic levels of waste), encephalitis (brain inflammation), and pulmonary edema (fluid-filled lungs). Untreated, over 60 percent mortality rate.

TREATMENT: Antibiotics, intensive care, intravenous fluids, and oxygen.

CONTAGION: 1 2 3 **4**

PAIN: 1 2 **3** 4

SUFFERING: 1 2 3 **4**

FATAL: Yes No **Maybe**

If you have shoulder pain...

...you might have

MYELOPATHY

WHAT IT IS: Disorder of or injury to nerves in spinal cord that may result from degenerative disease, such as polio, or severe trauma, such as automobile accident or fall. Destruction of nerves in spinal cord can cause loss of sensation or mobility, or paralysis.

SPECIALIST TO SEE: Orthopedist, Neurologist

OTHER SYMPTOMS:

- Prickling or itching sensation
- Difficulty walking
- Bladder incontinence
- Numbness
- Paralysis

PROGRESSION: Lower spinal cord injuries affect legs, hips, and bowels. Injury to nerves in upper spinal cord near neck results in loss of function in upper body. Mid-spine nerve injuries affect trunk or hands.

TREATMENT: Immunosuppressants, steroids, anti-inflammatory medication, painkillers, and antidepressants.

CONTAGION: **1** 2 3 4

PAIN: 1 2 **3** 4

SUFFERING: 1 2 **3** 4

FATAL: Yes **No** Maybe

...or you might have

PYOGENIC LIVER ABSCESS

WHAT IT IS: Occurs when bacteria invade liver. Bacteria and liquefied liver cells form pocket of pus, which becomes walled off from healthy liver tissue by dead tissue. Abscesses may be singular or appear in groups. May result from prior liver trauma or after complications such as pneumonia, peritonitis, appendicitis, or endocarditis.

SPECIALIST TO SEE: Hepatologist, Gastroenterologist

OTHER SYMPTOMS:

- Pain on right side
- Weight loss
- Fever or chills

FACT | Flying on an airplane with an ear infection can result in imploded eardrums.

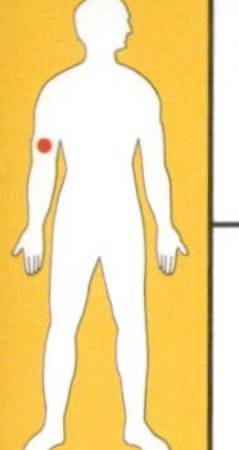

FACT | According to one survey, 42 percent of patients believe they have experienced a medical mistake.

PROGRESSION: Fever and chills evolve into more complications. Abscess may rupture into peritoneum. Can result in potentially fatal sepsis (bloodstream infection).

TREATMENT: Antibiotics to stem infection. Surgery in extreme cases.

CONTAGION:	**1**	2	3	4
PAIN:	1	2	**3**	4
SUFFERING:	1	**2**	3	4
FATAL:	Yes	No	**Maybe**	

If you have pain in your armpit...

...you might have
CASTLEMAN'S DISEASE

WHAT IT IS: Large, noncancerous growths, typically located in stomach, chest, or neck. Rare variety affecting plasma may deplete red blood cell count. Origin unknown. Mimics other diseases, often misdiagnosed. Also known as giant lymph node hyperplasia.

SPECIALIST TO SEE: Otolaryngologist

OTHER SYMPTOMS:

- Difficulty breathing
- Vomiting
- Abdominal pain
- Night sweats

PROGRESSION: Hyaline-vascular form may present as dry cough or respiratory difficulties if tumor grows in chest. Plasma-cell form may cause fever, weight loss, fatigue, or rash. Generalized form affects entire body and may cause liver and spleen complications.

TREATMENT: Antiviral medication. Surgical removal of growths. Radiation and chemotherapy.

CONTAGION:	**1**	2	3	4
PAIN:	1	**2**	3	4
SUFFERING:	1	2	**3**	4
FATAL:	Yes	No	**Maybe**	

...or you might have
ERYTHRASMA

WHAT IT IS: Chronic bacterial infection of top layers of skin. Occurs in moist skin folds, such as between toes and in groin. Tends to be persistent. Often diagnosed using Wood's lamp to shine ultraviolet light on skin; under lamplight, affected skin glows vivid coral-red color. Can recur, necessitating additional treatment.

SPECIALIST TO SEE: Dermatologist

OTHER SYMPTOMS:

- Pink, irregularly shaped rash
- Red or brown scales on skin
- Itching skin

PROGRESSION: Affected skin slowly turns from pink to red. Appearance of slightly raised patches with central clearing follow. Can spread to torso.

TREATMENT: Antibacterial soap. Antibiotic gel. Oral antibiotics, such as tetracycline, for more extensive lesions.

CONTAGION:	**1**	2	3	4
PAIN:	1	**2**	3	4
SUFFERING:	**1**	2	3	4
FATAL:	Yes	**No**	Maybe	

If your arm is stiff...

...you might have
ALEXANDER DISEASE

WHAT IT IS: Rare disorder of central nervous system. Characterized by growth of fatty sheath surrounding nerve fibers in brain. Hereditary, degenerative disease most common in children, although cases have been observed in adults with symptoms akin to multiple sclerosis. Causes wide variety of neurological complications and eventual death.

SPECIALIST TO SEE: Neurologist

OTHER SYMPTOMS:

- Loss of coordination
- Difficulty speaking
- Stiffness in arms or legs
- Seizures
- Swelling in head

PROGRESSION: Commonly starts with worsening neurological defects. Late-onset symptoms include ataxia (lack of muscle coordination) and bulbar palsy (weakness of lower cranial nerves), leading to difficulty swallowing, chewing, breathing, and talking. Juvenile

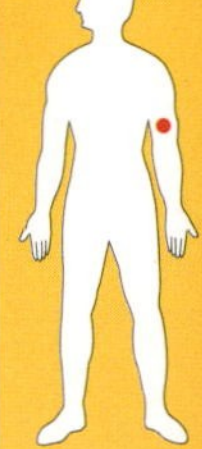

form usually causes death within 10 years after emergence of symptoms.

TREATMENT: No known cure. Anticonvulsants to control seizures.

CONTAGION: **1** 2 3 4

PAIN: 1 2 **3** 4

SUFFERING: 1 2 3 **4**

FATAL: **Yes** No Maybe

...or you might have

FIBRODYSPLASIA OSSIFICANS PROGRESSIVA

WHAT IT IS: Severe disorder that causes connective tissue and muscles to ossify (turn into bone). Malfunction of body's repair mechanism ultimately turns skeleton into solid shell. Difficult to predict where and how bone will grow. Life expectancy never exceeds 40 years.

SPECIALIST TO SEE: Orthopedist

OTHER SYMPTOMS:

- Rapidly spreading, tumorlike bumps
- Deformed toes

PROGRESSION: Small lumps appear almost overnight on neck or spine. Most connective tissue and skeletal muscles turn to bone with age. Eventually, body completely ossifies. Often death results from respiratory failure due to chest constriction.

TREATMENT: No known cure. Lifestyle changes to prevent further complications.

CONTAGION: **1** 2 3 4

PAIN: 1 2 3 **4**

SUFFERING: 1 2 3 **4**

FATAL: **Yes** No Maybe

If you feel tingling in your hands...

...you might have

ALIEN HAND SYNDROME

WHAT IT IS: Also known as Dr. Strangelove syndrome. Neurological disorder characterized by feeling of disconnection from hand and inability to control hand movements. Often occurs following brain surgery, strokes, or infections. Although regular muscle function exists, hand operates independent of will.

SPECIALIST TO SEE: Neurologist

OTHER SYMPTOMS:

- Memory loss
- Emotional changes
- Involuntary clenching of hand

PROGRESSION: Swift loss of hand control.

TREATMENT: No known cure. May be controlled by keeping hand occupied. Oven mitt or cloak to restrict sensory feedback in hand.

CONTAGION: **1** 2 3 4

PAIN: 1 **2** 3 4

SUFFERING: 1 2 **3** 4

FATAL: Yes **No** Maybe

...or you might have

CARPAL TUNNEL SYNDROME

WHAT IT IS: Results from swelling of tendons that pass through canal in wrist called carpal tunnel, causing pain and weakness in arm. Symptoms increase over time, making early diagnosis difficult. Gained notoriety in 1990s with increased computer usage. Especially common in assembly-line workers; more likely in women.

SPECIALIST TO SEE: Physical Therapist

OTHER SYMPTOMS:

- Loss of sensation in hand
- Pain or weakness in arm

PROGRESSION: Symptoms present slowly in palm and finger. Discomfort and pain from swelling may lead to difficulty clenching fist. Untreated, can cause deterioration of thumb muscles. High blood pressure, diabetes, and tuberculosis increase risk.

TREATMENT: Physical therapy. Splint to restrict wrist movement. Surgery in some cases.

CONTAGION: **1** 2 3 4

PAIN: 1 **2** 3 4

SUFFERING: **1** 2 3 4

FATAL: Yes **No** Maybe

QUOTE | "The first wealth is health." —Ralph Waldo Emerson

I've Got the Flu
Mundane but Deadly

Short for "influenza," the flu is a common but dangerous disease that can strike entire populations and, in worst-case scenarios, trigger pandemics (global epidemics) killing millions. New vaccines are constantly developed and manufactured to combat new influenza strains. The Centers for Disease Control's National Strategic Stockpile has large supplies of medicine, as do the Department of Health and Human Services and county health departments. Every year, however, strains of the disease shift, and these groups must again build their supplies with new vaccines. Most health officials agree that the chance of another pandemic is high. Because the influenza virus constantly mutates, prophylactic vaccination is difficult and our immune systems are unprepared for the flu's deadly assault. Booming merchant economies and global travel have made it possible for local viruses to spread quickly throughout the world. And as vaccination increases, flu strains become stronger and more easily transmitted from one person to another.

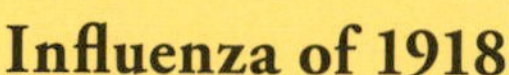

Influenza of 1918

Often called the Spanish flu, the pandemic of 1918 was swift and destructive, with a global death toll ranging from 50 million to 100 million—2 to 5 percent of the world's population. Considered one of the worst pandemics in history, this flu stood out for ravaging the strong rather than the weak. It sparked a healthy, vigorous immune response that assaulted the respiratory system, filling the lungs with fluid and causing the sufferer to drown. Spreading just as World War I was ending, the virus was first seen in a soldier at a Kansas military hospital. Sharing close quarters, soldiers passed the virus to one another as well as everywhere they traveled. Highly contagious, the Spanish flu killed entire families in just a few days; in some cases, whole towns were decimated.

Around the world, influenza kills between 500,000 and 1 million people each year.

Asian Flu

In 1957, a new influenza appeared in China and soon spread globally as carriers traveled along merchant routes. Considered one of the world's first bird influenzas, the Asian flu killed 1 to 4 million people in 1 year. Because it came from birds, the virus encountered no defenses in the human immune system. Health officials believe the strain later shifted and caused another pandemic, the Hong Kong flu. In October 2004, this virus was accidentally released from an American research lab to 3,700 other facilities via flu-testing kits; it was a year before all the deadly kits were retrieved.

Hong Kong Flu

In 1968, 11 years after the deadly Asian flu, the Hong Kong flu infected more than 40 percent of the global population, killing hundreds of thousands. Because people's immune systems were better equipped to handle this derivative of the Asian flu, the Hong Kong flu wasn't as devastating as other pandemics, but its effects were far-flung. In the United States, over 30,000 people died.

SARS

In 2002 and 2003, SARS (severe acute respiratory syndrome) caused a small epidemic in China, with approximately 8,100 cases reported. After an American businessman traveling from Hong Kong died from pneumonia-like symptoms in Hanoi, the disease drew international media attention. Within days, SARS coverage sent Asian travelers into a panic and forced health officials to implement restrictive travel policies. Towns throughout Asia were quarantined to contain the virus. While the death toll is estimated at only 800, this figure is most likely grossly underreported.

Avian Flu

Also called the bird flu, avian flu is a strand of influenza found in birds. It first appeared in Italy in the early 20th century and has since spread worldwide, sparking speculation about a pandemic. Each fall, potential outbreaks are monitored, especially in parts of Europe, Australia, the Near East, Asia, and Africa where casual contact with poultry, either at open markets or through farming practices, is commonplace. The avian flu is one of the most prevalent global health concerns, as its rapid transmission and ability to overtake healthy immune systems mean an avian flu pandemic could be as lethal as the Asian and Hong Kong flu pandemics.

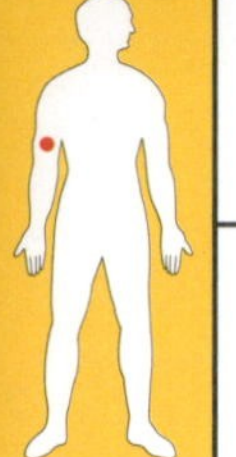

FACT | 2.5 million people die in the United States each year.

...or you might have

NEUROTOXIC SHELLFISH POISONING

WHAT IT IS: Form of food poisoning acquired from contaminated shellfish. Occurs when dinoflagellates (single-cell algae) combine with toxin that collects in shellfish. Commonly results in gastroenteritis (inflammation of intestinal tract), ataxia (lack of muscle coordination), and vertigo. Excessive toxin consumption leads to severe neurological reactions.

SPECIALIST TO SEE: Neurologist, Poison Control Specialist

OTHER SYMPTOMS:

- Numbness in mouth
- Tingling sensation in mouth or legs
- Burning pain in rectum
- Excessive sweating
- Muscle cramping

PROGRESSION: Symptoms appear within hours of eating contaminated shellfish. Alternating feelings of hot and cold body temperature, as well as tremors and nausea, may occur. Typically resolves within 48 hours without treatment.

TREATMENT: Symptom-driven treatment. Gastrointestinal decontamination within 4 hours of ingestion.

CONTAGION: **1** 2 3 4

PAIN: 1 **2** 3 4

SUFFERING: **1** 2 3 4

FATAL: Yes **No** Maybe

If your hands feel cold...

...you might have

LUPUS

WHAT IT IS: Disorder in which immune system attacks healthy tissue; nearly all organ systems susceptible. Most common form causes rash, swelling and pain in joints, persistent fever, and generalized pain and fatigue. More common in women; thought to result from combination of inherited and environmental risk factors. Individual cases vary significantly in presentation.

SPECIALIST TO SEE: Rheumatologist

OTHER SYMPTOMS:

- Sensitivity to light
- Mouth ulcers
- Arthritis
- Chest pain during inhalation
- Fatigue
- Seizures

PROGRESSION: Unpredictable. Flaring of symptoms alternates with extended periods of remission. Kidney failure is common fatal complication.

TREATMENT: No known cure. Anti-inflammatory or corticosteroid medication. Anti-rheumatic medication to reduce flares.

CONTAGION: **1** 2 3 4

PAIN: 1 2 **3** 4

SUFFERING: 1 2 **3** 4

FATAL: Yes No **Maybe**

...or you might have

RAYNAUD'S PHENOMENON

WHAT IT IS: Disorder of blood vessels in which fingers, toes, ears, and nose become abnormally cold and numb. During "attack," blood vessels constrict, limiting blood flow to affected areas. Often triggered by cold temperatures or stress. More common in women.

SPECIALIST TO SEE: Rheumatologist, Hematologist

OTHER SYMPTOMS:

- Discolored hands or feet
- Tingling sensation in nose, fingers, toes, or ears
- Deformed fingernail or toenail
- Stinging pain upon warming of skin

PROGRESSION: Areas of restricted blood flow may first turn pinkish-white, then blue, then red. Swelling frequently occurs. Throbbing and tingling follow improved circulation. Ulceration or gangrene may develop.

TREATMENT: Calcium-channel blockers to dilate blood vessels. Biofeedback (alternative medicine technique). In severe cases, nerves signaling blood vessels in fingertips are surgically cut.

CONTAGION: **1** 2 3 4

PAIN: 1 **2** 3 4

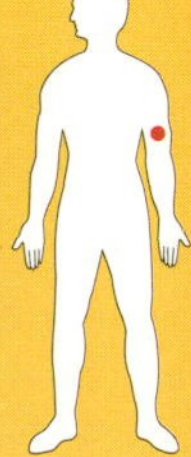

SUFFERING: 1 **2** 3 4

FATAL: Yes **No** Maybe

If your fingers are numb or weak...

...you might have

GERSTMANN'S SYNDROME

WHAT IT IS: Neurological disorder generally associated with lesions near intersection of parietal (controls shape and word recognition, calculations, and writing) and temporal (controls auditory perception, language, memory, and emotion) lobes of brain. Leads to disability and other developmental complications. Causes may include tumors and exposure to toxins.

SPECIALIST TO SEE: Neurologist

OTHER SYMPTOMS:

- Difficulty speaking or listening
- Impaired reading or writing
- Inability to distinguish right from left

PROGRESSION: Swift onset, with noticeable deficits in mathematical ability. Commonly results in inability to differentiate between individual fingers. Symptoms may diminish over time.

TREATMENT: No known cure. Occupational therapy.

CONTAGION: **1** 2 3 4

PAIN: **1** 2 3 4

SUFFERING: 1 **2** 3 4

FATAL: Yes **No** Maybe

...or you might have

INCLUSION BODY MYOSITIS

WHAT IT IS: "Wasting disease" that causes arms or legs to deteriorate via fat or protein cells replacing muscle. Results in visibly deformed muscles and weak or frail appearance. Progresses slowly, sometimes over 30 or more years.

SPECIALIST TO SEE: Neurologist

OTHER SYMPTOMS:

- Loss of balance
- Muscle atrophy
- Weakness in legs or arms
- Difficulty swallowing

PROGRESSION: First, weakness in hands and difficulty grasping objects. Then, gait becomes increasingly unstable. Holes and clumps of protein or fat develop within muscle fiber. Often causes immobility, requiring wheelchair usage.

TREATMENT: Physical therapy. Body-building supplements.

CONTAGION: **1** 2 3 4

PAIN: 1 **2** 3 4

SUFFERING: 1 2 3 **4**

FATAL: Yes **No** Maybe

If your fingernails are discolored...

...you might have

METHEMOGLOBINEMIA

WHAT IT IS: Blood disorder in which oxygen-carrying capacity of hemoglobin is impaired. Congenital form is relatively harmless. In acquired form, prolonged exposure to chemicals can result in harmful side effects. Toxin-induced cases are particularly prevalent in infants.

SPECIALIST TO SEE: Hematologist

OTHER SYMPTOMS:

- Blue skin
- Nausea
- Headache
- Fatigue
- Loss of consciousness

PROGRESSION: Lack of oxygen causes blood to turn from vibrant red to dark brown. Skin takes on blue tint. Severe chemically acquired cases may cause seizures, coma, and death.

TREATMENT: Supplemental oxygen and fluids to restore hemoglobin level.

CONTAGION: **1** 2 3 4

PAIN: 1 2 **3** 4

SUFFERING: 1 2 **3** 4

FATAL: Yes No **Maybe**

FACT | Each year, nearly 1,500 patients in the United States have objects left inside them following surgery.

Fibrodysplasia Ossificans Progressiva

[Fig. 107]

WHAT IT IS
Severe disorder in which mutation of body's repair mechanism causes muscles and connective tissue to become bone.

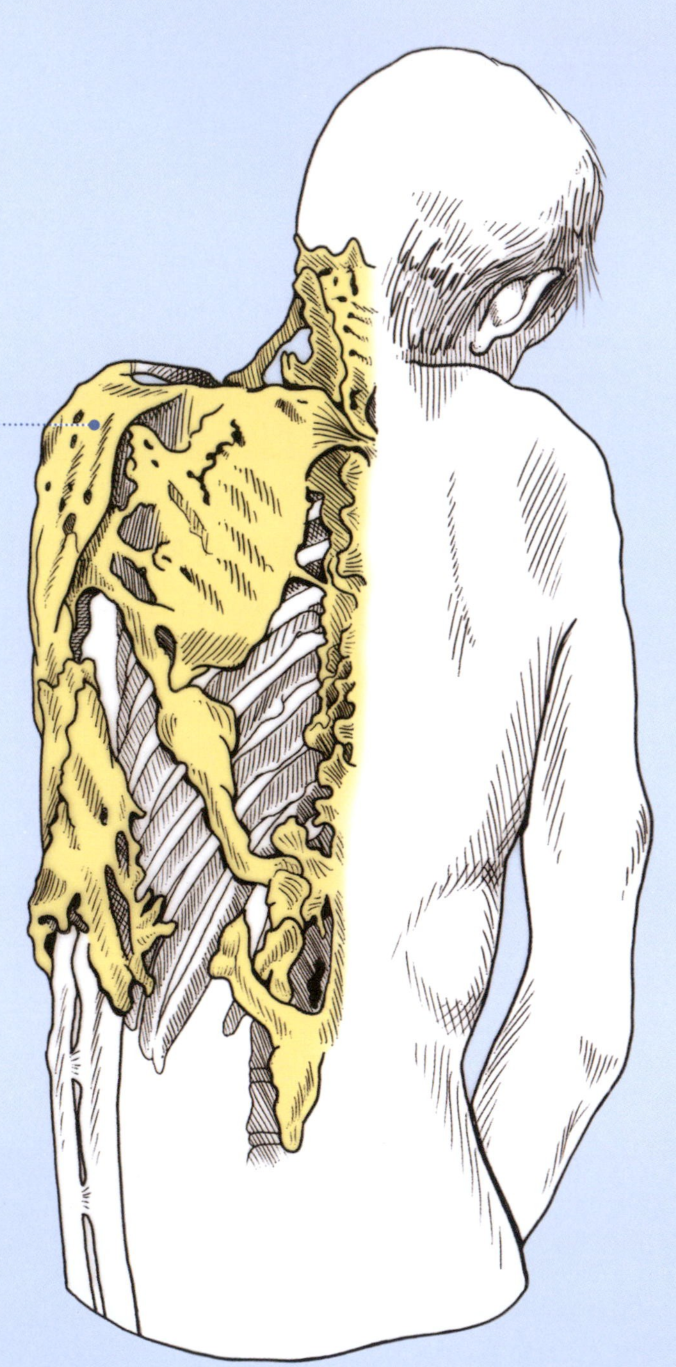

OSSIFICATION
As damaged soft tissue (e.g., muscles, tendons, and ligaments) transforms into bone, body stiffens.

PROGRESSION
Movement in affected areas is restricted and sometimes impossible. Ossified tissue cannot be removed due to likelihood of further ossification in trauma area. Because of inevitable paralysis of diaphragm, ultimately fatal.

TREATMENT
No known cure. Avoidance of injury, stretching, or physical exertion crucial for stemming bone growth.

For disease description, see page 75.

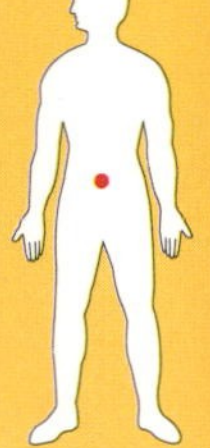

...or you might have
NAIL-PATELLA SYNDROME

WHAT IT IS: Rare genetic disorder that affects nail and skeletal development. Often results in abnormal or missing fingernails or patellae (kneecaps) and other skeletal malformations. May lead to scoliosis, glaucoma, or kidney disease.

SPECIALIST TO SEE: Orthopedist, Ophthalmologist

OTHER SYMPTOMS:
- Underdeveloped kneecaps or fingernails
- Deformed elbow
- Clubfoot

PROGRESSION: Abnormalities may be subtle, such as triangular-shaped cuticles or square-shaped kneecaps. Joints can become unstable, causing decreased mobility and susceptibility to dislocation. Kidney damage may occur.

TREATMENT: Medication to treat symptoms. Dialysis or kidney transplant in severe cases.

CONTAGION:	**1**	2	3	4
PAIN:	1	**2**	3	4
SUFFERING:	1	**2**	3	4
FATAL:	Yes	No	**Maybe**	

If you have back pain...

...you might have
SCOLIOSIS

WHAT IT IS: Side-to-side curvature of spine. Often congenital; usually develops in childhood. May also present in adults, typically as secondary symptom of another disorder, such as cerebral palsy or spinal muscular atrophy. More prevalent in females. Exact cause unknown. In severe cases (i.e., curvature greater than 100 degrees), can lead to lung and heart damage.

SPECIALIST TO SEE: Orthopedist

OTHER SYMPTOMS:
- Arthritis
- Difficulty breathing
- Uneven waist
- Leaning to one side

PROGRESSION: Presents as abnormal curvature of spine from side to side. May lead to prominent shoulder blade or rib "humps," asymmetric breast size in women, and uneven hips.

TREATMENT: Back brace. Metal rods surgically inserted in spine in severe cases.

CONTAGION:	**1**	2	3	4
PAIN:	1	2	**3**	4
SUFFERING:	1	**2**	3	4
FATAL:	Yes	**No**	Maybe	

...or you might have
SYRINGOMYELIA

WHAT IT IS: Syrinx (fluid-filled, tubular cavity) or cyst forms in center of spinal cord. Usually occurs in upper portion, but may expand to consume spine's full length. Results in pain and weakness in back, arms, or legs. Severity of symptoms depends on size and location of cavity. May arise as complication of trauma, meningitis, tumor, or hemorrhage.

SPECIALIST TO SEE: Neurologist

OTHER SYMPTOMS:
- Shoulder or arm pain
- Difficulty walking
- Weakness throughout body
- Loss of sensation in hands
- Headache
- Incontinence

PROGRESSION: In primary form, brain abnormality causes development of cavity; in second form, catalyst is trauma, hemorrhage, or tumor. Cavity elongates and destroys center of spinal cord. Leads to pain, weakness, and sensory impairment.

TREATMENT: Surgery to drain syrinx.

CONTAGION:	**1**	2	3	4
PAIN:	1	2	**3**	4
SUFFERING:	1	**2**	3	4
FATAL:	Yes	**No**	Maybe	

FACT | Prescription-drug deaths in the United States have risen 68 percent since 1999.

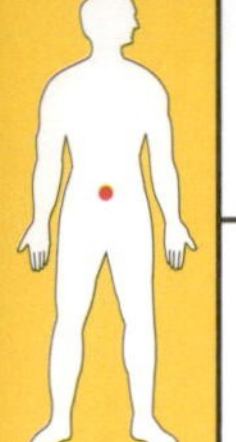

If your back is stiff...

...you might have
STIFF-PERSON SYNDROME

WHAT IT IS: Progressive neurological disorder. Causes pain, muscle spasms, and stiffness in trunk, back, and limbs (especially upper legs). Heightened sensitivity to touch, noise, and stress can induce more severe spasms. Exact cause unknown; may be linked to autoimmune disorder. Often misdiagnosed as Parkinson's disease, fibromyalgia, or multiple sclerosis.

SPECIALIST TO SEE: Neurologist

OTHER SYMPTOMS:
- Difficulty walking
- Hunched posture
- Contracted muscles

PROGRESSION: Irregular muscle spasms slowly become unremitting. Anxiety or sudden motion exacerbates symptoms. Sudden movements become difficult and unsteady gait develops. In severe cases, constant falls may cause bone fractures, and breathing may be impaired.

TREATMENT: No known cure. Anticonvulsants and muscle relaxants. Intravenous immunoglobulin to reduce stiffness and lower sensitivity.

CONTAGION: **1** 2 3 4

PAIN: 1 2 3 **4**

SUFFERING: 1 2 **3** 4

FATAL: Yes **No** Maybe

If you have muscle spasms...

...you might have
HYPOCALCEMIA

WHAT IT IS: Caused by low calcium levels in blood. Results in many symptoms, including tetany (spasms in hands, feet, and larynx caused by overactive reflexes). Often triggered by vitamin D deficiency or hypoparathyroidism, which impairs calcium regulation. Chronic form may lead to poor bone development, osteoporosis, and, in severe cases, cardiovascular collapse and death.

SPECIALIST TO SEE: Endocrinologist

OTHER SYMPTOMS:
- Abdominal cramping
- Dry skin, coarse hair, or brittle fingernails
- Muscle pain
- Shortness of breath

PROGRESSION: First, muscle cramping, tetany, breathing problems, and tingling sensations present. Skin, hair, and nails may become dry and brittle. Untreated, neurological complications can follow.

TREATMENT: Vitamin D and calcium supplements. Calcium salts administered intravenously in severe cases.

CONTAGION: **1** 2 3 4

PAIN: 1 **2** 3 4

SUFFERING: 1 **2** 3 4

FATAL: Yes No **Maybe**

...or you might have
SCIATICA

WHAT IT IS: Nerve compression causes pain in leg, buttock, lower back, or foot. Symptoms typically occur only on one side of body. Can result from trauma, spinal-disc herniation, unhealthy posture, insufficient exercise, or pregnancy.

SPECIALIST TO SEE: Primary Care Physician, Orthopedist

OTHER SYMPTOMS:
- Numbness
- Tingling sensation in legs
- Weakness in legs

PROGRESSION: Pain radiates from lower back or hips through buttock, back of thigh, and down leg. May lead to numbness and difficulty controlling movement.

TREATMENT: Anti-inflammatory or pain medication. Massage therapy. Surgery in severe cases.

CONTAGION: **1** 2 3 4

PAIN: 1 **2** 3 4

SUFFERING: 1 2 **3** 4

FATAL: Yes **No** Maybe

Misdiagnosed

Suffering from the Wrong Disease

The only thing worse than being diagnosed with a life-threatening disease, is being diagnosed with the *wrong* disease. Incorrect or delayed diagnoses comprise 40 percent of all medical errors, as reported by the National Patient Safety Foundation, which could result in as many as 40,000 deaths per year. According to a Kaiser Family Foundation study, 34 percent of all patients claim they've been the victim of medical error or misdiagnosis.

Some diagnosis mistakes derive from the doctor's or insurance carrier's reticence to incur the costs of specialized medical tests or expensive treatments, as documented in a "Patient Safety in Hospitals" study. Before their brain tumors are identified, many patients with headaches suffer frequent and repeated misdiagnosis, as reported to the Brain Tumor Society. The society notes, however, that the rarity of brain tumors and the prevalence of headaches puts doctors in a difficult position: headaches account for almost 20 million visits to American health-care providers annually, but only 200,000 people are ultimately diagnosed with a brain tumor; of those, primary (non-metastatic) tumors constitute only 40,000.

Among the most commonly misdiagnosed and potentially fatal conditions are heart attacks, strokes, tuberculosis, diabetes, meningitis, and appendicitis, as well as prostate, lung, breast, cervical, ovarian, and testicular cancers. The journal *Cancer* maintains that 12 percent of all cancer patients are initially diagnosed with the wrong ailment. Other reports conclude that as many as 40 percent of biopsies are wrong, producing a false negative or positive, which can delay the start of life-saving treatment—or send healthy patients into a panic.

Patients and their families have struck back with a rash of lawsuits that have made malpractice insurance for both doctors and hospitals one of the fastest-rising costs in health care. Most of these suits cite misdiagnosis or delayed diagnosis. When these conditions lead to the death of a patient, the monetary awards to families of the deceased can climb into the millions. Lobbyists for doctors and insurance companies attempt to persuade Congress to enact legislation to curb or cap "frivolous" lawsuits, while those representing lawyers and victims contend that limiting lawsuits and damages will do nothing to reduce the spiraling costs of insurance premiums nor make misdiagnosis any rarer.

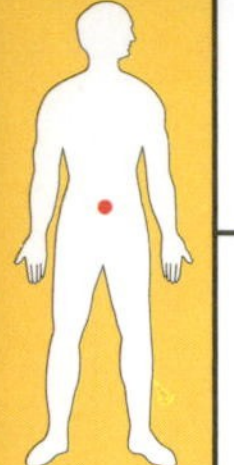

FACT | Cold and flu viruses can live on dry surfaces for 3 days.

If you have pain on your side...

...you might have
ACUTE PYELONEPHRITIS

WHAT IT IS: Potentially life-threatening infection, typically originating in urinary tract. Characterized by sudden kidney inflammation. Results in scarring of and possibly significant damage to kidneys. Can lead to chronic kidney disease, sepsis (bloodstream infection), and shock. Especially severe in elderly.

SPECIALIST TO SEE: Urologist, Nephrologist

OTHER SYMPTOMS:
- Painful urination
- Bloody or cloudy urine
- Severe abdominal pain
- Fever

PROGRESSION: Bacteria ascend from urinary tract to kidney, causing extreme side pain and urinary complications. Damp skin, chills, and fatigue may occur. With treatment, symptoms usually subside within 3 days. Untreated, permanent kidney damage may result. If sepsis occurs, can be fatal.

TREATMENT: Intravenous antibiotics.

CONTAGION: **1** 2 3 4

PAIN: 1 2 **3** 4

SUFFERING: 1 **2** 3 4

FATAL: Yes No **Maybe**

...or you might have
SHINGLES

WHAT IT IS: Also known as herpes zoster. Painful skin blisters caused by chicken-pox virus. Nerves foster dormant virus and can reactivate infection. Causes more pain and less itching than chicken pox. Although not usually serious, may lead to prolonged tenderness of skin. Typically presents after age 50.

SPECIALIST TO SEE: Dermatologist

OTHER SYMPTOMS:
- Rash or blisters around waistline
- Swelling in eyelids
- Fever
- Lethargy

PROGRESSION: Commonly begins as burning pain. Bumps and blisters on skin develop within days. Usually subsides in 3 to 5 weeks. Potential serious effects include partial facial paralysis (usually temporary), ear damage, or encephalitis (inflammation of brain). If eyes are affected, can lead to glaucoma years later.

TREATMENT: Antiviral medication, steroids, or anticonvulsants. Topical agents to treat skin blisters.

CONTAGION: **1** 2 3 4

PAIN: 1 **2** 3 4

SUFFERING: 1 **2** 3 4

FATAL: Yes **No** Maybe

If you have chest pain...

...you might have
ACUTE PORPHYRIA

WHAT IT IS: Four similar inherited forms of disorder, all affecting production of heme (iron-containing pigment in the blood). Characterized by acute, painful attacks throughout body. Often misdiagnosed as Guillain-Barré syndrome or lupus due to rarity. Can lead to liver cancer. More common in women.

SPECIALIST TO SEE: Hematologist

OTHER SYMPTOMS:
- Abdominal pain
- Depression, anxiety, or paranoia
- Convulsions or paralysis

PROGRESSION: Attacks may result from drug or alcohol intake or hormonal changes. Begins with severe pain in abdomen, back, or thighs, and may be accompanied by nausea, vomiting, and constipation. Hallucinations or confusion—and in extreme cases, respiratory paralysis or coma—can occur. Usually last up to 2 weeks.

TREATMENT: Heme arginate or glucose. Painkillers and anti-nausea medication.

CONTAGION: **1** 2 3 4

PAIN: 1 2 **3** 4

SUFFERING: 1 2 **3** 4

FATAL: Yes No **Maybe**

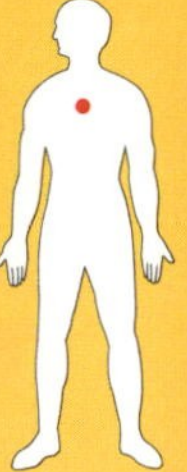

...or you might have
COSTOCHONDRITIS

WHAT IT IS: Painful inflammation of cartilage in ribs and breastbone. May result from physical strain, injury, or vigorous laughter. Pain may be sharp or dull. One of most common causes of chest pain. Occurs more frequently after age 40 and in women.

SPECIALIST TO SEE: Primary Care Physician, Emergency Physician

OTHER SYMPTOMS:

- Shoulder or arm pain
- Painful coughing
- Difficulty breathing

PROGRESSION: Closely mimics heart-attack symptoms. Can cause debilitating tenderness and soreness in sternum. Pain generally lasts up to 2 weeks.

TREATMENT: Usually self-limiting. Muscle relaxants and anti-inflammatory medication. Rest and heating pads.

CONTAGION:	**1**	2	3	4
PAIN:	1	**2**	3	4
SUFFERING:	1	**2**	3	4
FATAL:	Yes	**No**	Maybe	

...or you might have
LEGIONNAIRES' DISEASE

WHAT IT IS: Severe pulmonary infection caused by *Legionella pneumophila* bacteria. First identified after outbreak at American Legion convention in 1976. Usually occurs in summer and early fall, though can present anytime. *L. pneumophila* often found in hot tubs, cooling towers, plumbing, and air conditioning systems of large buildings.

SPECIALIST TO SEE: Pulmonologist

FACT | 15,000 people die from falls each year.

Shingles
[Fig. 108]

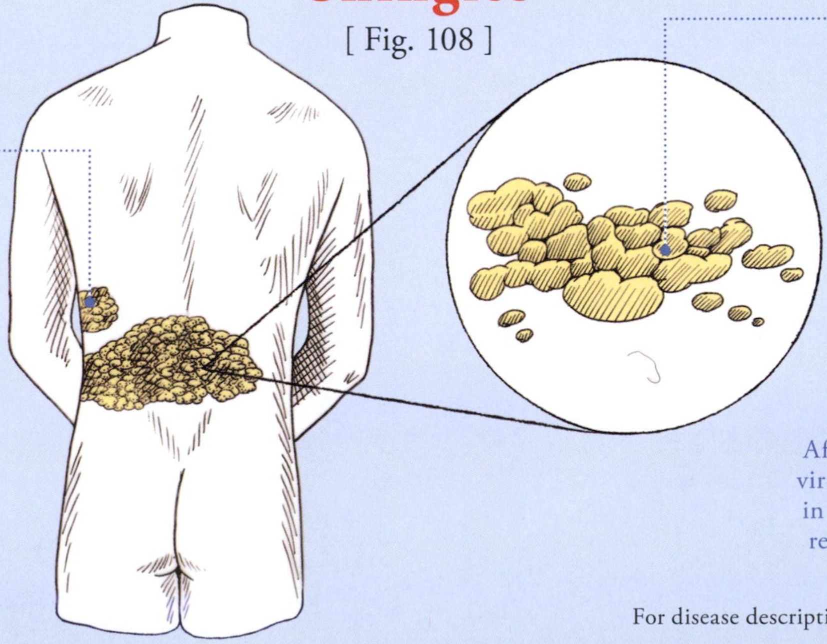

BLISTERS
Painful, itchy, fluid-filled blisters appear on back, side, or chest. On face, may result in facial paralysis or permanent vision or hearing loss.

VARICELLA-ZOSTER VIRUS
Responsible for chicken pox, cold sores, and genital herpes.

RECURRENCE
After initial infection, virus remains dormant in nervous system and reactivates years later.

For disease description, see opposite page.

QUOTE | "Medicine sometimes snatches away health, sometimes gives it." —Ovid

OTHER SYMPTOMS:
- Coughing
- Headache
- Fatigue
- Reduced appetite

PROGRESSION: Symptoms similar to pneumonia. Muscle aches, lethargy, and cough may lead to more severe symptoms, such as kidney damage. Delayed treatment may result in death.

TREATMENT: Antibiotics for respiratory tract infection. Fluid replacement and supplemental oxygen.

CONTAGION: 1 2 3 **4**

PAIN: 1 **2** 3 4

SUFFERING: 1 2 **3** 4

FATAL: Yes No **Maybe**

...or you might have
MARBURG HEMORRHAGIC FEVER

WHAT IT IS: Severely infectious fever caused by Filoviridae virus (closely related to Ebola virus). Resembles malaria and typhoid fever, making diagnosis difficult. Transmitted from person to person through body fluids. Indigenous to Africa; often spread by travelers. First cases passed from monkeys to humans.

SPECIALIST TO SEE: Infectious Disease Specialist

OTHER SYMPTOMS:
- Fever or chills
- Headache
- Muscle pain
- Rash

PROGRESSION: Starts as fever and headache, followed by nausea, chest and abdominal pain, and diarrhea. Oral or nasal hemorrhaging may result. Death often occurs within one week.

TREATMENT: Maintenance of blood pressure. Blood transfusions and fluid replacement.

CONTAGION: 1 2 **3** 4

PAIN: 1 2 **3** 4

SUFFERING: 1 2 **3** 4

FATAL: Yes No **Maybe**

If you have chest pressure...

...you might have
GASTROESOPHAGEAL REFLUX DISEASE

WHAT IT IS: Chronic condition caused by abnormal reflux of stomach contents into esophagus. Results in burning and sharp chest pain, sore throat, heartburn, and difficulty swallowing. May damage esophageal lining. Symptoms increase when lying down or after eating.

SPECIALIST TO SEE: Gastroenterologist

OTHER SYMPTOMS:
- Coughing
- Hoarse voice
- Voice changes
- Nausea
- Ulcers in esophagus
- Hiatal hernia

PROGRESSION: Commonly presents as persistent heartburn (more than twice a week) or chest pain. Chronic form may increase risk for esophageal cancer.

TREATMENT: Lifestyle modifications, including weight loss and avoidance of spicy and acidic foods. Proton pump inhibitors and antacids. Surgery in extreme cases.

CONTAGION: **1** 2 3 4

PAIN: 1 **2** 3 4

SUFFERING: 1 **2** 3 4

FATAL: Yes **No** Maybe

...or you might have
MYOCARDIAL INFARCTION

WHAT IT IS: Heart attack. Caused by blockage of heart's blood vessels. Usually presents as chest discomfort, fullness, and pain, as well as pain radiating down left arm. Cardiovascular tissue death results from lack of oxygen; often fatal. Stress, diabetes, obesity, and high blood pressure and cholesterol increase risk.

SPECIALIST TO SEE: Cardiologist

OTHER SYMPTOMS:
- Fainting
- Shortness of breath

A Fungus Among Us
So Much More than Mushrooms

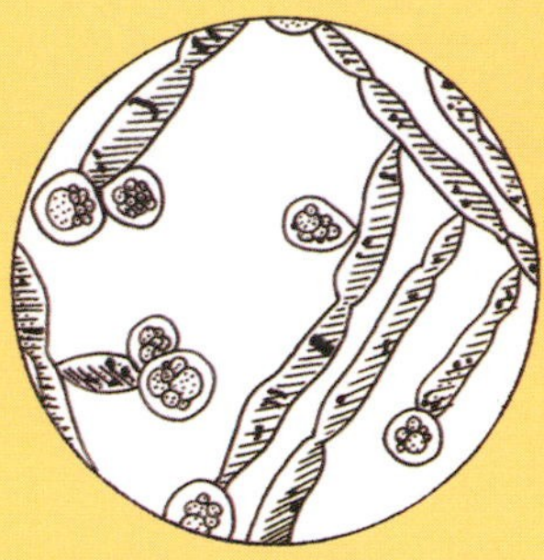

Microsporum canis
(Tinea, AKA Ringworm)

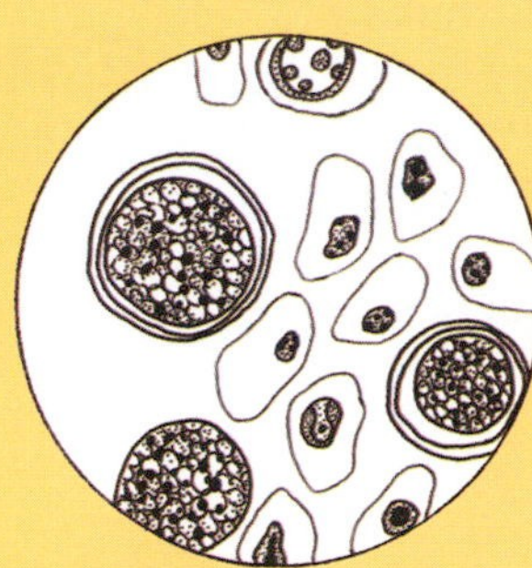

Blastomyces dermatitidis
(Blastomycosis)

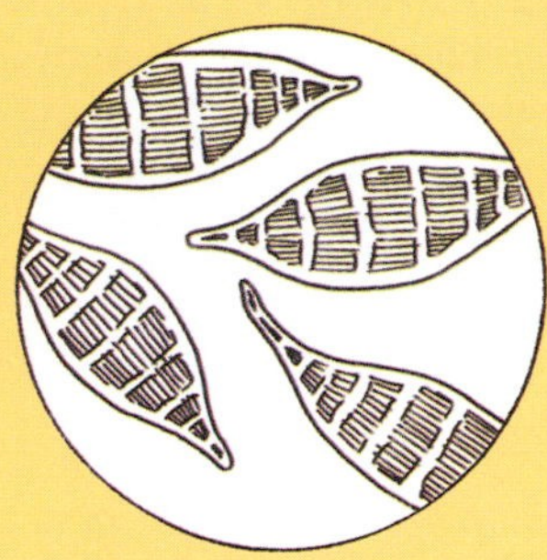

Candida sp.
(Yeast Infection)

While fungi provide such life-saving medications as penicillin, help to decompose our garbage, and grace our pizzas with delicious edibles, some 400 out of more than one million species cause harm. Neither plant nor animal, fungus is classified within its own kingdom, and individual species fall into one of two groups: mold or yeast. Rather than deriving nutrition through photosynthesis, as plants do, fungi draw nutrition from decaying organic matter. Problems arise when fungi feed on organic matter that hasn't yet started decaying—live plants, animals, or humans—causing mycosis, an infection caused by a fungus.

Tineas

The vast majority of mycotic infections are the tineas, an umbrella term for common fungal skin ailments. Caused by fungi called dermatophytes, the tineas range from jock itch (tinea cruris) to athlete's foot and onchycomychosis (tinea pedis and tinea unguium) to scalp inflammation (tinea capitis). The round lesions are called ringworm, but there are no worms involved.

Candidiasis

Candida are more than 150 species of small yeasts, around ten of which cause disease in humans. Candidiasis of skin and mucosal surfaces is most common, including diaper rash, oral thrush, and *Candida* vulvovaginitis (vaginal yeast infections). Invasive candidiasis intrudes beyond the skin, life-threatening ailments that are almost exclusively associated with specific surgeries and medical treatments and with compromised immune systems.

Respiratory Infections

When inhaled, certain fungi infect the lungs. While these infections can afflict the healthy, they are most frequent as opportunistic infections in the immunocompromised, and include cryptococcosis and histoplasmosis.

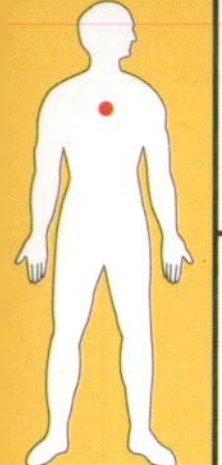

- Nausea
- Excessive sweating
- Pale skin

PROGRESSION: Clots form in arteries, interrupting flow of blood and oxygen to heart. Attack can occur anytime, at rest or during activity, and is often sudden. Causes acute pain in chest. Loss of consciousness, collapse, and death may follow.

TREATMENT: CPR or defibrillation. Blood-thinning medication to dissolve clots. Angioplasty to clear artery.

CONTAGION: 1 2 3 4

PAIN: 1 2 3 4

SUFFERING: 1 2 3 4

FATAL: Yes No Maybe

...or you might have

SARCOIDOSIS

WHAT IT IS: Immune disease that usually affects lungs or lymph nodes. Can also occur in eyes, skin, liver, bones, heart, and brain. Causes microscopic granulomas (masses of immune-system cells) to form. Typically affects multiple organs at once. Often results in permanent lung damage.

SPECIALIST TO SEE: Rheumatologist

OTHER SYMPTOMS:

- Joint pain
- Shortness of breath
- Red bumps on face, arms, and shins
- Fatigue
- Night sweats

PROGRESSION: Starts with fatigue, joint pain, weight loss, or trouble breathing. Rash forms on skin and eyes may become irritated. May result in organ failure. Individual cases vary widely.

TREATMENT: Corticosteroids and immunosuppressants. Transplantation if organ failure occurs.

CONTAGION: 1 2 3 4

PAIN: 1 2 3 4

SUFFERING: 1 2 3 4

FATAL: Yes No Maybe

If you have heartburn...

...you might have

ACHALASIA

WHAT IT IS: Disorder of esophagus in which muscles lose ability to move food into stomach. Lower esophagus does not relax properly when swallowing. Cause unknown; may be complication of esophageal cancer or Chagas' disease (parasitic illness transmitted by insects).

SPECIALIST TO SEE: Gastroenterologist

OTHER SYMPTOMS:

- Vomiting
- Weight loss
- Pain in chest, back, jaw, neck, or arm

PROGRESSION: Frequent hiccups and difficulty swallowing or belching. Often misdiagnosed. Eventually, malnutrition can result.

TREATMENT: Botox injections into esophagus to mitigate spasms. Balloon inserted into esophagus to stretch muscle fibers.

CONTAGION: 1 2 3 4

PAIN: 1 2 3 4

SUFFERING: 1 2 3 4

FATAL: Yes No Maybe

...or you might have

CHOLECYSTITIS

WHAT IT IS: Inflammation of gallbladder, usually caused by gallstones. Can also be result of infection of bile duct, tumor on pancreas or liver, or bile "sludge" that cannot exit gallbladder. May occur suddenly or over many years.

SPECIALIST TO SEE: Gastroenterologist

OTHER SYMPTOMS:

- Fever or chills
- Abdominal bloating
- Jaundice

PROGRESSION: Extreme upper-right back pain and nausea. Severe pain may last for several hours, usually after eating fatty meals. In extreme cases, gallbladder may rupture.

FACT | 1 of every 5 deaths in the United States is tobacco-related.

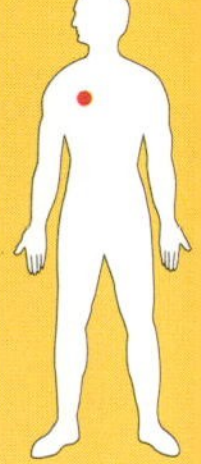

TREATMENT: Dietary supplements or medication to dissolve gallstones. Cholecystectomy (surgical removal of gallbladder).

CONTAGION: 1 2 3 4 (1)

PAIN: 1 2 3 4 (4)

SUFFERING: 1 2 3 4 (2)

FATAL: Yes No Maybe (No)

If your ribs are sore...

...you might have
MULTIPLE MYELOMA

WHAT IT IS: Cancer of plasma cells in bone marrow. Group of abnormal cells multiply, resulting in bone erosion. Can occur in several areas of body. Increases likelihood of developing recurrent infections, such as pneumonia. Exact cause unknown. Commonly presents after age 50 and in African Americans.

SPECIALIST TO SEE: Oncologist

OTHER SYMPTOMS:
- Excessive thirst
- Frequent urination
- Constipation
- Weight loss
- Bone pain
- Confusion

PROGRESSION: As excessive plasma cells interfere with red and white cell production, bone pain develops. Anemia and poor kidney function may result. If spreads to spine, paralysis can occur.

TREATMENT: No known cure. Chemotherapy, radiation, and stem-cell transplants.

CONTAGION: 1 2 3 4 (1)

PAIN: 1 2 3 4 (4)

SUFFERING: 1 2 3 4 (3)

FATAL: Yes No Maybe (Maybe)

...or you might have
TUBERCULOSIS

WHAT IT IS: Infection that commonly affects lungs. Generally characterized by lingering, severe cough. Spread by droplets expelled through sneezing, coughing, or spitting. HIV/AIDS, diabetes, and other immunosuppressive illnesses increase risk. Approximately one-third of population is infected. Often misdiagnosed; may recur or develop into drug-resistant strain.

SPECIALIST TO SEE: Pulmonologist, Infections Disease Specialist

OTHER SYMPTOMS:
- Chronic coughing
- Bloody cough
- Fever, chills, and night sweats
- Reduced appetite
- Fatigue

PROGRESSION: Bacteria can remain dormant in body for years. Usually infects lungs, causing shortness of breath. May also affect kidneys, spine, brain, and even skin. Spreads quickly through weakened immune system and can be life-threatening.

TREATMENT: Antibiotics to destroy bacteria. Usually cures within 12 months.

CONTAGION: 1 2 3 4 (4)

PAIN: 1 2 3 4 (2)

SUFFERING: 1 2 3 4 (3)

FATAL: Yes No Maybe (Maybe)

If you have an irregular heartbeat...

...you might have
MARFAN SYNDROME

WHAT IT IS: Hereditary condition. Affects connective tissue throughout body. Effects range from minor (e.g., loose joints) to severe (e.g., ruptured aorta). Body unable to produce fibrillin, protein that strengthens connective tissue. Causes weak and abnormally elastic tissue.

SPECIALIST TO SEE: Rheumatologist

OTHER SYMPTOMS:
- Overly flexible joints
- Spinal curvature
- Vision loss
- Shortness of breath

VOCAB | Nocebo: Opposite of placebo; an inert substance that causes harmful effects because negative results are expected.

Myocardial Infarction

[Fig. 109]

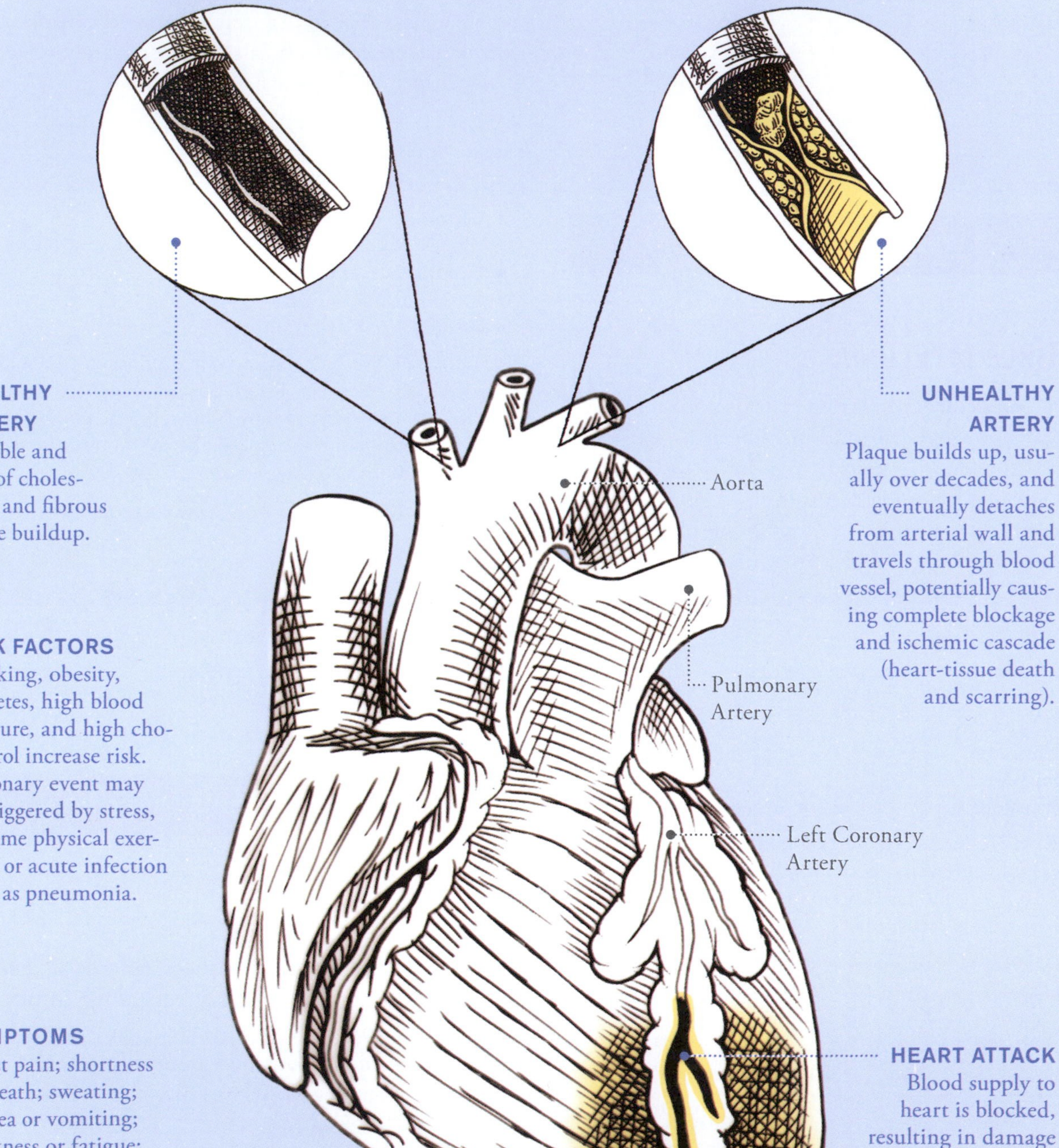

HEALTHY ARTERY
Flexible and free of cholesterol and fibrous tissue buildup.

UNHEALTHY ARTERY
Plaque builds up, usually over decades, and eventually detaches from arterial wall and travels through blood vessel, potentially causing complete blockage and ischemic cascade (heart-tissue death and scarring).

RISK FACTORS
Smoking, obesity, diabetes, high blood pressure, and high cholesterol increase risk. Coronary event may be triggered by stress, extreme physical exertion, or acute infection such as pneumonia.

SYMPTOMS
Chest pain; shortness of breath; sweating; nausea or vomiting; weakness or fatigue; dizziness; anxiety; loss of consciousness.

HEART ATTACK
Blood supply to heart is blocked, resulting in damage to heart tissue due to oxygen shortage.

For disease description, see page 86.

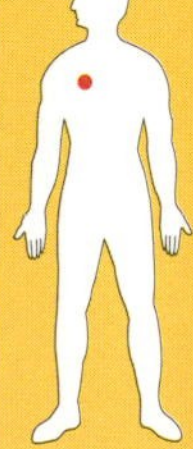

PROGRESSION: Can cause wide range of complications affecting musculoskeletal, pulmonary, and cardiac systems. Visual disturbances may increase, including retinal detachment. Severe cases can result in fatal aortic rupture.

TREATMENT: Medication to prevent aortic rupture. Surgery to repair damaged heart valves.

CONTAGION: **1** 2 3 4

PAIN: 1 **2** 3 4

SUFFERING: 1 2 **3** 4

FATAL: Yes No **Maybe**

...or you might have

MITRAL VALVE PROLAPSE

WHAT IT IS: Often undetected birth defect. Mitral valve in heart unable to open and close properly, allowing slight leakage of blood into heart. Often hereditary. Family history of Marfan syndrome or connective tissue disorders increases risk. Not fatal, and rarely requires treatment.

SPECIALIST TO SEE: Cardiologist

OTHER SYMPTOMS:

- Dizziness
- Chest pain
- Fatigue

PROGRESSION: Severe cases may lead to heart palpitations or mitral insufficiency, characterized by significant leakage in heart valves.

TREATMENT: No known cure. Beta-blockers to regulate heartbeat. Surgery.

CONTAGION: **1** 2 3 4

PAIN: **1** 2 3 4

SUFFERING: **1** 2 3 4

FATAL: Yes **No** Maybe

...or you might have

TETRALOGY OF FALLOT

WHAT IT IS: Severe birth defect characterized by 4 specific abnormalities within heart. Reduces blood flow to lungs, resulting in lower oxygen levels in blood. Especially problematic for pregnant women; condition poses potentially fatal strain on heart.

SPECIALIST TO SEE: Cardiologist

OTHER SYMPTOMS:

- Blue skin
- Rapid breathing
- Shortness of breath
- Fainting

PROGRESSION: First, cyanosis (blue skin) appears due to lack of oxygen in blood. Detection of heart murmur also leads to diagnosis. Death common if untreated.

TREATMENT: Heart surgery to repair defects.

CONTAGION: **1** 2 3 4

PAIN: 1 **2** 3 4

SUFFERING: 1 2 **3** 4

FATAL: Yes No **Maybe**

...or you might have

TOXIC MULTINODULAR GOITER

WHAT IT IS: Form of hypothyroidism in which autonomously functioning nodules grow in thyroid, each secreting thyroid hormone, resulting in overload of hormone. Causes goiter (lump in neck from enlarged thyroid). Often occurs after age 55. Also known as Plummer's disease.

SPECIALIST TO SEE: Endocrinologist

OTHER SYMPTOMS:

- Swelling in neck
- Weight loss
- Restlessness
- Fatigue
- Hand tremors
- Excessive sweating

PROGRESSION: Small nodules may grow quickly. Symptom onset is sudden, often beginning with rapid or irregular heartbeat. In rare cases, may lead to debilitating or potentially fatal conditions, such as atrial fibrillation and congestive heart failure.

TREATMENT: Radioactive iodine to control thyroid hormone production. Surgery in rare cases.

CONTAGION: **1** 2 3 4

PAIN: 1 **2** 3 4

SUFFERING: 1 **2** 3 4

FATAL: Yes **No** Maybe

FACT | The biggest tapeworm ever recorded was over 60 feet long.

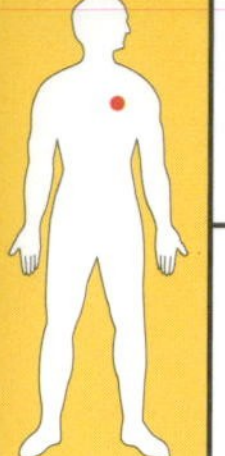

If you have a rapid heartbeat...

...you might have
BERIBERI

WHAT IT IS: Nervous system disorder caused by lack of vitamin B1 (thiamine); may be side effect of gastric bypass surgery. Alcoholism and excessive consumption of milled rice increase risk. May be passed from mother to child through breast milk. Can also affect cardiovascular, muscular, and gastrointestinal systems.

SPECIALIST TO SEE: Neurologist

OTHER SYMPTOMS:

- Weight loss
- Muscle weakness
- Pain in arm or leg

PROGRESSION: Starts with muscle pain and weakness, followed by weight loss and edema (swelling of bodily tissue). Dry form damages peripheral nerves and may lead to partial or full paralysis. Wet form can result in heart failure and, ultimately, death.

TREATMENT: Thiamine hydrochloride injections or pills.

CONTAGION:	1	**2**	3	4
PAIN:	1	2	**3**	4
SUFFERING:	1	2	**3**	4
FATAL:	Yes	No	**Maybe**	

...or you might have
PAROXYSMAL SUPRAVENTRICULAR TACHYCARDIA

WHAT IT IS: Episodic presence of rapid heartbeat that starts in upper ventricles of heart. Generally not fatal, but may appear in conjunction with other, more serious heart conditions. Smoking, excessive caffeine and alcohol intake, and drug use increase risk.

SPECIALIST TO SEE: Cardiologist

OTHER SYMPTOMS:

- Anxiety
- Chest pressure
- Shortness of breath
- Fainting

PROGRESSION: May start and stop suddenly. Regular recurrence is typical. Symptoms generally do not worsen over time.

TREATMENT: Breathing exercises and carotid-artery massage to help end episode. Intravenous medication, such as verapamil (to relax blood vessels). Electrical cardioversion (shock).

CONTAGION:	**1**	2	3	4
PAIN:	1	**2**	3	4
SUFFERING:	**1**	2	3	4
FATAL:	Yes	**No**	Maybe	

...or you might have
WOLFF-PARKINSON-WHITE SYNDROME

WHAT IT IS: Cardiac defect resulting from extra electrical connection between upper and lower heart chambers. Belongs to category of "pre-excitation syndromes," in which electrical signal reaches ventricles too early. Usually asymptomatic, but can be detected by electrocardiogram. May lead to extremely rapid heart rate. In rare cases, causes sudden death.

SPECIALIST TO SEE: Cardiologist

OTHER SYMPTOMS:

- Chest pain
- Irregular heartbeat
- Dizziness
- Loss of consciousness
- Crackling sensation in lungs

PROGRESSION: Heart palpitations are most common symptom. May also cause chest pain and dizziness.

TREATMENT: Breathing exercises. Medication to treat arrhythmia. Surgery to destroy extra connection.

CONTAGION:	**1**	2	3	4
PAIN:	1	**2**	3	4
SUFFERING:	1	**2**	3	4
FATAL:	Yes	No	**Maybe**	

QUOTE | "A good laugh and a long sleep are the best cures in the doctor's book." —Irish proverb

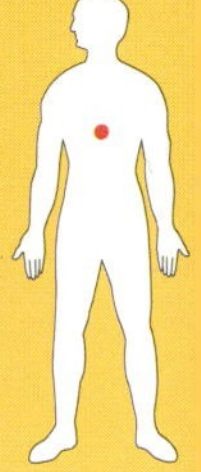

If you have difficulty breathing...

...you might have
ASCARIASIS

WHAT IT IS: Common infection of *Ascaris lumbricoides* worm. Worms grow in small intestine and migrate throughout body, feeding on semidigested food. May reach up to 1 foot in length and live for up to 1 year. Female worms can lay up to 200,000 eggs per day. Untreated, can cause fatal nutritional deficiency or intestinal perforation.

SPECIALIST TO SEE: Infectious Disease Specialist

OTHER SYMPTOMS:

- Wheezing
- Fever
- Bloody stool
- Abdominal pain
- Weight loss
- Worms in mouth, nose, or stools

PROGRESSION: Inside stomach, *Ascaris* eggs move to small intestine and hatch. Worms then burrow into bloodstream, liver, and lungs, eventually migrating into throat to be swallowed again. Squirming clumps of worms are passed during defecation.

TREATMENT: Antiparasitic medication. In extreme cases, surgery to eliminate worm clusters. Worms may also exit through mouth.

CONTAGION:	**1**	2	3	4
PAIN:	1	**2**	3	4
SUFFERING:	1	2	**3**	4
FATAL:	Yes	No	**Maybe**	

...or you might have
BRONCHITIS

WHAT IT IS: Bronchi (primary air passages of lungs) become inflamed, often from bacteria or virus. Typically, acute form appears after viral infection has reached nose, sinuses, and throat. Also may be caused

FACT | Human ears and noses never stop growing.

Shots Gone Wrong

Trypanophobia, or fear of injections, is one of the most common phobias—an estimated 1 out of 10 individuals suffers from it.

There are 4 types of trypanophobia, one of which may arise from an "inherited vasovagal reflex that causes shock with needle puncture," according to Dr. James G. Hamilton in the *Journal of Family Practice.* Unlike other phobias, this fear produces a slowed rather than rapid heart rate, among other symptoms—and can actually result in death. The other 3 forms of trypanophobia are more typical: associative, caused by a traumatic event; resistive, having to do with fear of being controlled; and hyperalgesic, due to a physiologically low tolerance for pain.

While a phobia is defined as an *un*substantiated fear, there are still potential injection mishaps, especially nerve injuries, either from puncturing the nerve, severing it, or creating a neuroma (an enlarging in the nerve). Some nerve injuries require surgery to remedy resulting chronic pain or to address "claw hand," a condition in which the fingers curl inward.

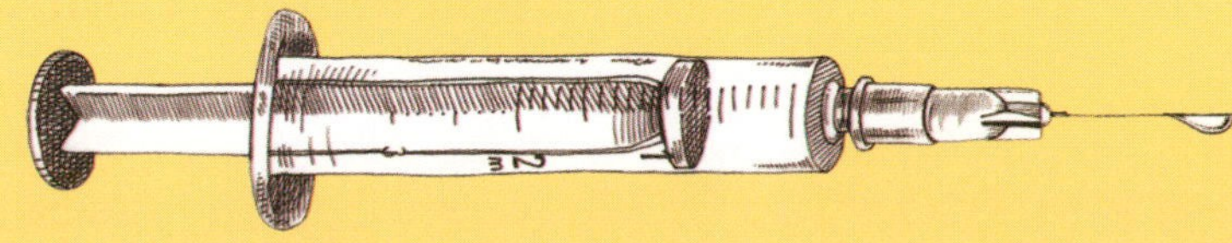

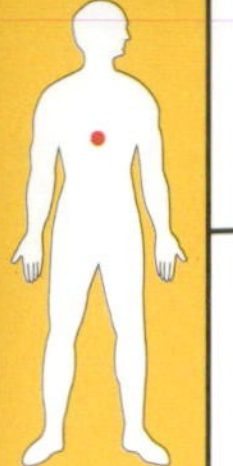

by cigarette smoke or pollutants. Chronic form may result in coughing with mucus for at least 3 months.

SPECIALIST TO SEE: Primary Care Physician

OTHER SYMPTOMS:
- Yellow, green, or gray mucus
- Sore throat
- Wheezing
- Fatigue
- Swelling in legs, ankles, or feet
- Blue lips

PROGRESSION: For acute form, often accompanies or follows cold or flu. Generally resolves within 7 to 10 days. May lead to secondary infection, and cough can continue for months. Chronic form may result in asthmatic conditions and increase risk of possibly fatal lung cancer.

TREATMENT: For acute form, aspirin, acetaminophen, fluids, and humidifier. For chronic form, bronchodilators to open airways and clear mucus. Smoking cessation.

CONTAGION: 1 2 **3** 4

PAIN: 1 **2** 3 4

SUFFERING: 1 **2** 3 4

FATAL: Yes **No** Maybe

...or you might have
HISTOPLASMOSIS

WHAT IT IS: Fungal infection contracted through inhalation of contaminated soil or dust. *Histoplasma capsulatum* fungus grows in soil enriched with bat or bird guano (defecation). Mainly affects lungs; may spread to other organs, evolving into life-threatening disseminated form. Fungus found mostly in areas bordering lower Mississippi Valley and Ohio River Valley.

SPECIALIST TO SEE: Pulmonologist, Infectious Disease Specialist

OTHER SYMPTOMS:
- Coughing
- Chest pain
- Fever
- Weight loss
- Arthritis

PROGRESSION: Symptoms usually appear 10 days following exposure and vary from mild to severe. When many spores are inhaled, acute pulmonary syndrome may develop.

TREATMENT: Antifungal medication.

CONTAGION: **1** 2 3 4

PAIN: 1 **2** 3 4

SUFFERING: 1 **2** 3 4

FATAL: Yes **No** Maybe

...or you might have
THALASSEMIA

WHAT IT IS: Inherited disorder resulting in destruction of red blood cells and interference with production of hemoglobin, thereby causing anemia. One of 2 forms, alpha and beta, may be diagnosed depending upon which component of hemoglobin is affected. May require frequent transfusions.

SPECIALIST TO SEE: Hematologist

OTHER SYMPTOMS:
- Weakness throughout body
- Fatigue
- Facial deformity
- Abdominal swelling
- Dark urine

PROGRESSION: Severity varies by number of affected genes. Presents risk of iron overload, which may damage heart, liver, and hormone production. Increases risk for blood infections. Untreated, death may occur.

TREATMENT: Blood transfusion. Bone-marrow or stem-cell transplant.

CONTAGION: **1** 2 3 4

PAIN: 1 **2** 3 4

SUFFERING: 1 2 **3** 4

FATAL: Yes No **Maybe**

If you have the hiccups...

...you might have
DIAPHRAGM TUMOR

WHAT IT IS: Soft-tissue masses that protrude into lungs and resemble hernia or pleural lesion. Often caused by mesothelioma (often fatal disease due to asbestos exposure). Once in diaphragm, mesothelioma has become stage III cancer and has likely

FACT | Malaria has been responsible for over half of all human deaths since the Stone Age.

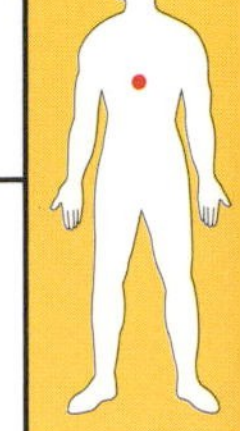

metastasized from other organs such as lungs, lymph nodes, testicles, or ovaries.

SPECIALIST TO SEE: Pulmonologist

OTHER SYMPTOMS:

- Abdominal swelling
- Anemia
- Gastrointestinal obstruction
- Change in bowel habits
- Weight loss

PROGRESSION: Except for unexplained symptoms like anemia and weight loss, symptoms largely go unnoticed. Associated cancers, such as mesothelioma and round-cell tumor, often result in death.

TREATMENT: Surgery, chemotherapy, radiation.

CONTAGION: **1** 2 3 4

PAIN: 1 2 **3** 4

SUFFERING: 1 2 **3** 4

FATAL: Yes No **Maybe**

...or you might have

EBOLA

WHAT IT IS: Gruesome virus of unknown origin, first identified in 1976. Highly contagious through person-to-person contact or contaminated needles. Virus rapidly replicates, infecting and destroying cells, with 90 percent fatality rate. Considered Category A bioterrorism agent.

SPECIALIST TO SEE: Infectious Disease Specialist

OTHER SYMPTOMS:

- Vomiting
- Diarrhea
- Discolored skin
- Bleeding from all orifices

PROGRESSION: High fever, weakness, nausea, and vomiting appear suddenly. Then, progresses quickly to severe internal and external bleeding. Finally, seizures, coma, and organ failure follow within weeks, with death shortly thereafter.

TREATMENT: No known vaccine or cure. Supportive measures to treat complications.

CONTAGION: 1 2 3 **4**

PAIN: 1 2 3 **4**

SUFFERING: 1 2 3 **4**

FATAL: **Yes** No Maybe

...or you might have

PLEURISY

WHAT IT IS: Sudden and painful inflammation of double membrane that lines chest cavity and encircles lungs. Commonly occurs as complication of other afflictions, such as pneumonia, pancreatitis, rheumatoid arthritis, cancer, chest injury, and flu. Can make breathing extremely painful. Effects may persist after condition resolves.

SPECIALIST TO SEE: Pulmonologist

OTHER SYMPTOMS:

- Fever or chills
- Coughing
- Reduced appetite
- Yellow, green, gray, or bloody saliva

PROGRESSION: First, sudden stabbing pain when breathing, sneezing, moving, or coughing. Then, pain can spread to neck, shoulder, or abdomen. May cause permanent lung damage.

TREATMENT: Treatment of underlying affliction. Anti-inflammatory medication, analgesics, codeine, and nerve blockers. Tube insertion to drain fluid from chest.

CONTAGION: **1** 2 3 4

PAIN: 1 2 **3** 4

SUFFERING: 1 2 **3** 4

FATAL: Yes **No** Maybe

If you're hyperventilating...

...you might have

ACUTE MOUNTAIN SICKNESS

WHAT IT IS: Also known as altitude sickness. Series of medical complications linked to high altitude. Caused by reduced level of air pressure coupled with lower concentration of oxygen. Can be life-threatening if edema (fluid accumulation) occurs in certain organs. May affect lungs, heart, or brain.

SPECIALIST TO SEE: Emergency Physician

FACT | One-third of people using public restrooms don't wash their hands, though 95 percent claim to.

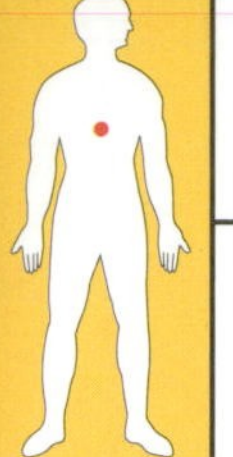

FACT | Health care accounts for 15.5 percent of the gross national product in the United States.

OTHER SYMPTOMS:

- Headache
- Vomiting
- Difficulty sleeping
- Bloody cough
- Congestion in chest
- Blue, gray, or pale skin
- Confusion

PROGRESSION: HAPE (high-altitude pulmonary edema) may occur quickly. Fluid builds up in lungs, making breathing difficult. With HACE (high-altitude cerebral edema), brain swelling occurs, causing psychotic behavior, hallucinations, and loss of eyesight. Without quick treatment, both lead to coma and death.

TREATMENT: Supplemental oxygen. Emergency medical care.

CONTAGION: **1** 2 3 4

PAIN: 1 2 **3** 4

SUFFERING: 1 2 **3** 4

FATAL: Yes No **Maybe**

...or you might have

LACTIC ACIDOSIS

WHAT IT IS: Cells lose ability to convert food into usable energy. Results in lactic-acid buildup that may damage vital organs, such as liver and pancreas. Possibly associated with underlying illnesses, including AIDS, cancer, and kidney failure. Rigorous exercise is most frequent cause.

SPECIALIST TO SEE: Emergency Physician

OTHER SYMPTOMS:

- Nausea
- Abdominal pain
- Weakness in legs or arms
- Blue or cold hands
- Irregular heartbeat

PROGRESSION: Immediate dehydration and lethargy. Severe cases induce hyperventilation, vomiting, or even shock. Without early diagnosis, may be life-threatening.

TREATMENT: Treatment of underlying cause. Removal of carbohydrates from diet. Intravenous fluids.

CONTAGION: **1** 2 3 4

PAIN: 1 **2** 3 4

SUFFERING: 1 **2** 3 4

FATAL: Yes No **Maybe**

If you have lung pain...

...you might have

DA COSTA'S SYNDROME

WHAT IT IS: Anxiety disorder characterized by poor concentration, irritability, excessive worry, and hypochondria. May cause numbness or painful sensations throughout body. Initially identified as war-related malady during American Civil War; often referred to as "soldier's heart." Some similarities to post-traumatic stress disorder (PTSD).

SPECIALIST TO SEE: Psychiatrist

OTHER SYMPTOMS:

- Shortness of breath
- Chest pain
- Smothering sensations throughout body
- Dizziness
- Cold or clammy hands or feet
- Fidgeting
- Excessive sweating
- Insomnia

PROGRESSION: No physical symptoms, despite similarity to heart disease. Fatigue, shaking, and fainting may occur. Without intervention, can continue indefinitely.

TREATMENT: Therapy for psychiatric complications. Often, anti-anxiety and antidepressant medication.

CONTAGION: **1** 2 3 4

PAIN: 1 2 **3** 4

SUFFERING: 1 2 **3** 4

FATAL: Yes **No** Maybe

...or you might have

XIPHOIDALGIA

WHAT IT IS: Inflammation of xiphoid process, cartilaginous protrusion located at base of sternum that fills gaps between ribs. Characterized by significant sensitivity and discomfort in chest region, which can be aggravated by movement (e.g., coughing, deep breathing). Cause unknown.

Bronchitis

[Fig. 110]

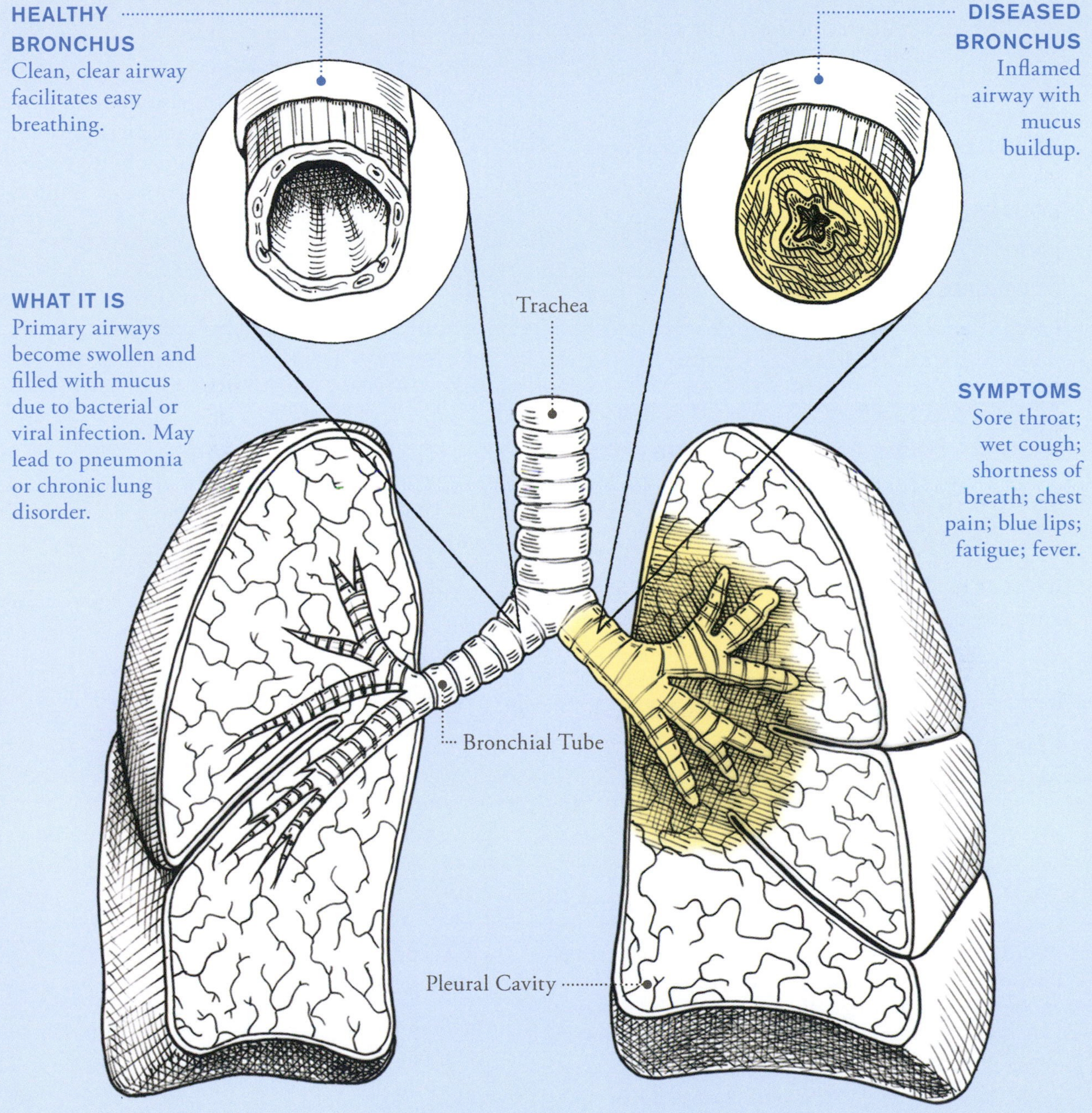

For disease description, see page 93.

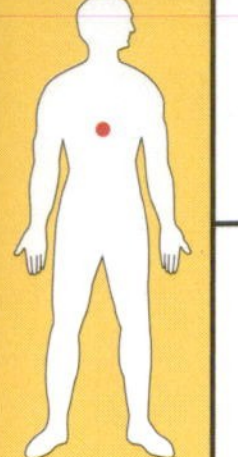

SPECIALIST TO SEE: Primary Care Physician, Orthopedist

OTHER SYMPTOMS:
- Pain or tenderness in chest
- Nausea
- Vomiting

PROGRESSION: Tenderness and pain which often worsen with activity. Sleep may be disturbed, and irritation of stomach can occur, causing vomiting.

TREATMENT: Anti-inflammatory medication and muscle relaxants. Anesthetic injections and steroids may completely or partially eliminate pain.

CONTAGION: **1** 2 3 4

PAIN: 1 **2** 3 4

SUFFERING: **1** 2 3 4

FATAL: Yes **No** Maybe

If you have abdominal pain...

...you might have
AMOEBIASIS

WHAT IT IS: Infection of large intestine caused by amoebic parasite *Entamoeba histolytica.* Transmitted largely through fecal matter of infected person and passed on through contaminated food or water. Often found in developing countries.

SPECIALIST TO SEE: Infectious Disease Specialist

OTHER SYMPTOMS:
- Bloody diarrhea
- Abdominal cramping
- Rectal pain
- Dehydration
- Nausea

PROGRESSION: After ingestion, amoebae attack intestinal walls, traveling through blood and occasionally entering liver and surrounding organs, and even brain. May cause formation of large cysts, leading to kidney failure and blood poisoning.

TREATMENT: Antibiotics to kill amoebae and microorganisms in intestine.

CONTAGION: 1 **2** 3 4

PAIN: 1 2 **3** 4

SUFFERING: 1 2 **3** 4

FATAL: Yes No **Maybe**

...or you might have
ERYTHROPOIETIC PORPHYRIA

WHAT IT IS: Characterized by extreme sensitivity to sunlight. Caused by overproduction of porphyrins in blood, which are toxic in abundance. Neurological complications, as well as severe skin problems, result. Decreased life expectancy. Often hereditary, although may occur spontaneously in adults. Also known as Gunther's disease.

SPECIALIST TO SEE: Hematologist, Dermatologist, Neurologist, Ophthalmologist

OTHER SYMPTOMS:
- Sensitivity to light
- Discolored teeth or urine
- Depression or paranoia
- Constipation
- Numbness
- Hallucinations
- Difficulty pronouncing disease name

PROGRESSION: Exposure to sunlight may cause blistering, inflamed skin. Eye damage can lead to blindness, and lesions often leave scars. Low blood pressure and shock are possible.

TREATMENT: Avoidance of sunlight. Eyedrops. Bone-marrow transplant to reduce porphyrin production.

CONTAGION: **1** 2 3 4

PAIN: 1 2 3 **4**

SUFFERING: 1 2 3 **4**

FATAL: **Yes** No Maybe

...or you might have
WANDERING SPLEEN

WHAT IT IS: Ligaments that usually attach spleen to abdomen are replaced by shaft-like tissue filled with blood vessels. Vessels weaken and cannot hold spleen in place. Spleen "wanders" into pelvis or lower abdomen.

SPECIALIST TO SEE: Gastroenterologist

QUOTE | "It's no longer a question of staying healthy. It's a question of finding a sickness you like." —Jackie Mason

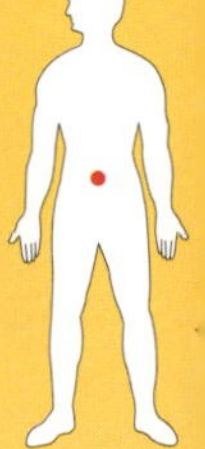

OTHER SYMPTOMS:
- Unidentified abdominal mass
- Vomiting
- Enlarged spleen
- Constipation

PROGRESSION: Arteries surrounding spleen twist, blocking blood supply and severely damaging nearby tissue. Drifting of spleen into lower pelvic region causes extreme stomach pain.

TREATMENT: Splenectomy (surgical removal of spleen). In some cases, reattachment surgery.

CONTAGION:	**1**	2	3	4
PAIN:	1	2	**3**	4
SUFFERING:	1	**2**	3	4
FATAL:	Yes	**No**	Maybe	

...or you might have
WHIPWORM INFECTION

WHAT IT IS: After accidental ingestion of roundworm eggs, parasite infects large intestine. Smaller infestations generally asymptomatic. More serious cases result in bloody diarrhea. Detectable only by stool sample. Worms may reach 2 inches in length.

SPECIALIST TO SEE: Gastroenterologist

OTHER SYMPTOMS:
- Flatulence
- Diarrhea
- Weight loss
- Fatigue
- Bloody stool

PROGRESSION: First, eggs hatch inside small intestine. One end of worm tunnels through intestinal wall to large intestine, while other end remains in small intestine for mating. Blood loss from diarrhea may cause iron deficiency, and rectal prolapse may occur in worst cases.

TREATMENT: Anthelminthic (anti-worm) medication such as mebendazole and albendazole.

CONTAGION:	**1**	2	3	4
PAIN:	1	**2**	3	4
SUFFERING:	1	**2**	3	4
FATAL:	Yes	**No**	Maybe	

If you have abdominal cramping...

...you might have
ALKALOSIS

WHAT IT IS: Balance in blood heavily tilted toward base (or alkali, versus acidity). Causes deficiency of bicarbonate or carbon dioxide in blood possibly resulting from excessive use of diuretics. Respiratory form impairs breathing, while metabolic form affects kidney function.

SPECIALIST TO SEE: Pulmonologist, Gastroenterologist, Nephrologist

OTHER SYMPTOMS:
- Tremors in hand
- Nausea
- Numbness in extremities
- Light-headedness
- Muscle spasms
- Confusion

PROGRESSION: Hyperventilation causes body to lose valuable carbon dioxide, triggering respiratory form. Vomiting can cause blood chloride levels to dip, leading kidneys to hoard bicarbonate, causing confusion and, in severe cases, coma.

TREATMENT: Breathing into paper bag to relieve hyperventilation. Medication to correct chemical loss in kidneys.

CONTAGION:	**1**	2	3	4
PAIN:	1	**2**	3	4
SUFFERING:	1	**2**	3	4
FATAL:	Yes	**No**	Maybe	

...or you might have
CHOLERA

WHAT IT IS: Transmitted through consumption of food or water contaminated with *Vibrio cholerae* bacteria. Spread through fecal matter of infected person. Often occurs in outbreaks, though only 1 in 20 people will present symptoms.

SPECIALIST TO SEE: Infectious Disease Specialist

OTHER SYMPTOMS:
- Fever
- Cramping in legs

VOCAB | **Xenotransplant:** Transplant of an animal organ into a human body.

- Convulsions
- Diarrhea

PROGRESSION: After infection, onset usually occurs within days. Causes body to produce massive amounts of water, leading to severe diarrhea and rapid loss of body fluid. Untreated, up to 50 percent death rate; treated, death rate falls below 1 percent.

TREATMENT: Rehydration through intravenous fluids.

CONTAGION: 1 2 3 4 (1)

PAIN: 1 2 3 4 (4)

SUFFERING: 1 2 3 4 (3)

FATAL: Yes No Maybe (Maybe)

...or you might have
COLON CANCER

WHAT IT IS: Affects both rectum and colon. No single cause; may be associated with diet high in fat and red meat and low in fiber. Second-deadliest cancer overall. Usually detected in later stages, limiting treatment options and decreasing chance of survival.

SPECIALIST TO SEE: Oncologist

OTHER SYMPTOMS:
- Abdominal pain
- Pain or bleeding in rectum
- Weight loss
- Persistent hemorrhoids
- Narrow stool

PROGRESSION: Commonly begins asymptomatically. At onset, unhealthy cells grow inside colon, often forming polyps. If malignant, adenocarcinomas (tumors) line colon tissue. Early detection necessary for complete cure. Often spreads to lymph nodes, requiring rigorous treatment for survival.

TREATMENT: Dietary and lifestyle modifications. Colectomy (surgical removal of colon). Chemotherapy.

CONTAGION: 1 2 3 4 (1)

PAIN: 1 2 3 4 (3)

Don't Let the Bedbugs Bite

Thanks to the pesticide DDT, the meaning of "And don't let the bedbugs bite" was all but lost on people born after the mid-twentieth century. In 1972, however, the ban on DDT in the United States once again created vulnerabilities to the tiny blood-sucking insects. In recent years, *Cimex lectularius* have come back with a vengeance in North American cities, especially in urban dwellings like apartment buildings.

The good news is that bedbugs indicate nothing about filth (they can be found in the best hotels), nor do they carry disease. The bad news is that they suck your blood while you sleep, drawn by body heat and exhaled carbon dioxide, resulting in itchy red welts.

In addition to the DDT ban, experts attribute the resurgence of bedbugs to inexpensive international travel and the popularity of second-hand furniture, both of which are vehicles for the insects. Once they're infested, they're exceedingly difficult to banish, able to live for up to a year without feeding.

Seeing the tiny creatures with the naked eye proves challenging. The most tangible evidence of bedbugs' presence is the dark specks of fecal matter they leave behind, consisting mostly of their hosts' blood.

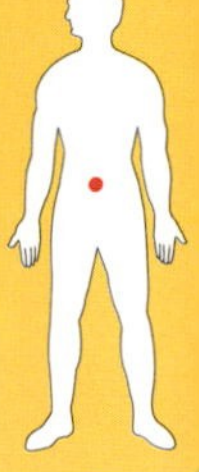

SUFFERING: 1 2 **3** 4

FATAL: Yes No **Maybe**

If your stomach is swollen...

...you might have
KIDNEY CANCER

WHAT IT IS: Malignant kidney growths that develop into renal-cell carcinoma. Risk factors include smoking, obesity, and high blood pressure. Absence of symptoms makes early detection difficult.

SPECIALIST TO SEE: Oncologist

OTHER SYMPTOMS:

- Fatigue
- Weight loss
- Swelling in testicles

PROGRESSION: No symptoms in early stages. Tumor growth may lead to bloody urine, back pain, and abdominal masses. High mortality rate if cancerous cells metastasize to lymph nodes or other organs.

TREATMENT: Chemotherapy, radiation, or immunotherapy. Nephrectomy (surgical removal of kidney). Especially resistant to treatment.

CONTAGION: **1** 2 3 4

PAIN: 1 2 **3** 4

SUFFERING: 1 **2** 3 4

FATAL: Yes No **Maybe**

...or you might have
SHIGELLOSIS

WHAT IT IS: Foodborne illness of large intestine. Results from exposure to contaminated water. Like many parasitical infections, spread by infected stool. Can cause epidemics in overcrowded areas with inadequate sanitation. Accounts for as many as 10 percent of foodborne illness outbreaks in United States.

SPECIALIST TO SEE: Infectious Disease Specialist

OTHER SYMPTOMS:

- Severe diarrhea
- Vomiting
- High fever
- Bloody stool
- Dehydration
- Seizures

PROGRESSION: Bacteria invade intestinal walls, causing uncomfortable swelling and shallow sores. Inflammation of rectal lining. May cause rectal prolapse.

TREATMENT: Fluids to treat dehydration. Antibiotics.

CONTAGION: 1 2 **3** 4

PAIN: 1 2 **3** 4

SUFFERING: 1 **2** 3 4

FATAL: Yes No **Maybe**

If you're bloated...

...you might have
AEROPHAGIA

WHAT IT IS: Greek for "to eat air." Ingestion of too much air, often accompanied by audible swallowing. May result from eating or drinking rapidly, chewing gum, smoking, or wearing loose dentures. In some cases, precipitated by changes in emotional state or increased stress. Sometimes confused with motility disorders (in which food does not move properly through the digestive tract) because of gaseous abdominal distention.

SPECIALIST TO SEE: Gastroenterologist

OTHER SYMPTOMS:

- Belching
- Flatulence
- Abdominal, chest, or back pain

PROGRESSION: Belching relieves most of air in stomach. Excess air moves into small intestine, where some is absorbed. Remaining air travels to large intestine, finally exiting body through flatulence. May exacerbate gastrointestinal disorders.

TREATMENT: Modification of eating habits. Treatment of bloating and belching.

CONTAGION: **1** 2 3 4

PAIN: 1 **2** 3 4

SUFFERING: **1** 2 3 4

FATAL: Yes **No** Maybe

FACT | 11 million cosmetic-surgery procedures were performed in 2006.

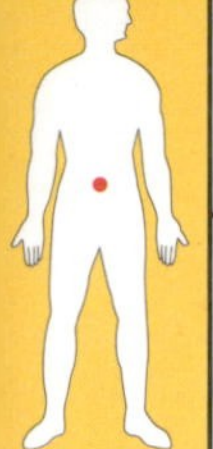

...or you might have

CHRONIC NON-ULCER DYSPEPSIA

WHAT IT IS: Common digestive disorder. Affects esophagus and small intestine, resulting in symptoms typically associated with other ailments. Cause unknown, though eating too quickly and elevated stress are implicated.

SPECIALIST TO SEE: Gastroenterologist

OTHER SYMPTOMS:

- Belching
- Flatulence
- Nausea
- Burning sensation in chest

PROGRESSION: Swift onset. Stomach pain often associated with chronic indigestion. Pain flares and disappears over at least 3 months. Symptoms similar to more serious peptic ulcer, which can lead to perforation of stomach lining.

TREATMENT: Antacids. Lifestyle and dietary modifications.

CONTAGION:	**1**	2	3	4
PAIN:	1	**2**	3	4
SUFFERING:	1	**2**	3	4
FATAL:	Yes	**No**	Maybe	

If you belch excessively...

...you might have

CROHN'S DISEASE

WHAT IT IS: Chronic, incurable inflammation of gastrointestinal tract, causing extreme pain and constant diarrhea. Cause unknown, but can run in families and may be related to immune system attacking perceived virus in intestine. Inexplicably goes into remission then recurs. Carries heightened risk for some cancers.

SPECIALIST TO SEE: Gastroenterologist

OTHER SYMPTOMS:

- Diarrhea
- Weight loss
- Bleeding from rectum
- Abdominal pain
- Constipation

PROGRESSION: Persistent, watery diarrhea is common. Intestinal blockage, ulcerative sores in affected tissue, and nutritional deficiencies possible. May develop arthritis, eye inflammation, and other complications.

TREATMENT: Medication to control inflammation and suppress immune system. Lifestyle and dietary modifications. Surgery to remove damaged or diseased parts of intestine.

CONTAGION:	**1**	2	3	4
PAIN:	1	2	**3**	4
SUFFERING:	1	2	**3**	4
FATAL:	Yes	**No**	Maybe	

...or you might have

GASTRIC ULCER

WHAT IT IS: Sores on stomach lining. Often accompanied by extreme abdominal pain and discomfort. Common ailment affecting millions of people worldwide. Typically caused by *Helicobacter pylori* bacteria. May also develop from excessive stress or stomach cancer.

SPECIALIST TO SEE: Gastroenterologist

OTHER SYMPTOMS:

- Burning sensation in stomach
- Bloody vomit
- Insomnia

PROGRESSION: Overproduction of acids causes stomach lining to erode. Sores may become large enough to inhibit digestive process. Can be exacerbated by aspirin or anti-inflammatory medication.

TREATMENT: Dietary changes. Antacids. Antibiotics in case of infection.

CONTAGION:	**1**	2	3	4
PAIN:	1	**2**	3	4
SUFFERING:	1	**2**	3	4
FATAL:	Yes	**No**	Maybe	

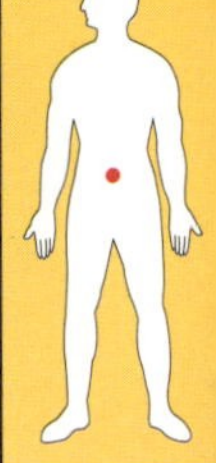

If you have flatulence...

...you might have
GASTROPARESIS

WHAT IT IS: Disease in which weakened stomach takes unusually long to empty contents. Paralysis of stomach muscles hinders full digestion of food. May result in bezoars (solid masses of undigested food) and organ damage. Can affect blood sugar levels and nutrition. Cause unknown. Related to damage of vagus nerve, which controls stomach contractions. Commonly associated with diabetes, anorexia, or hypothyroidism.

SPECIALIST TO SEE: Gastroenterologist

OTHER SYMPTOMS:

- Nausea
- Vomiting
- Weight loss
- Abdominal pain or bloating

PROGRESSION: Food does not break down properly and prevents functioning of small intestine. Later, food may harden into bezoars. Bacterial overgrowth possible due to food fermentation. Feeding tube necessary in extreme cases. Untreated, bezoars may be life-threatening.

TREATMENT: No known cure. Dietary changes (e.g., smaller, more frequent meals). Antibiotics and anti-emetics to treat nausea. Medication to dissolve bezoars if present.

CONTAGION: **1** 2 3 4

PAIN: 1 **2** 3 4

SUFFERING: 1 **2** 3 4

FATAL: Yes **No** Maybe

...or you might have
IRRITABLE BOWEL SYNDROME

WHAT IT IS: Occurs when colon is particularly sensitive to environmental factors. Extremely common and often undiagnosed. Risk factors include high stress, use of laxatives, and low-fiber diet. Accounts for 20 to 50 percent of gastroenterologist visits.

SPECIALIST TO SEE: Gastroenterologist

OTHER SYMPTOMS:

- Constipation
- Diarrhea
- Frequent bowel movements
- Abdominal pain or bloating
- Mucus in stool

PROGRESSION: Certain foods, elevated stress, and excessive serotonin can force bowels to react in spasms, disrupting digestion. Chronic constipation or diarrhea result, often accompanied by pain.

TREATMENT: Stress management. Dietary changes. Stool softeners.

CONTAGION: **1** 2 3 4

PAIN: 1 **2** 3 4

SUFFERING: 1 **2** 3 4

FATAL: Yes **No** Maybe

If you have pain on your side...

...you might have
APPENDICITIS

WHAT IT IS: Inflammation and infection of appendix. Causes intense pain on right side of abdomen. Deadly if not immediately treated surgically, as appendix will burst, spreading infection quickly throughout digestive system. Strikes nearly 10 percent of people.

SPECIALIST TO SEE: Emergency Physician

OTHER SYMPTOMS:

- Chills
- Constipation
- Nausea
- Reduced appetite
- Fatigue

PROGRESSION: Appendix blocked by feces, foreign body, or, rarely, tumor. Typically, pain begins around navel, quickly becoming severe. If appendix bursts, pain may be relieved, but peritonitis (pus accumulation in abdomen) sets in.

TREATMENT: Appendectomy (surgical removal of appendix).

CONTAGION: **1** 2 3 4

PAIN: 1 2 **3** 4

SUFFERING: 1 **2** 3 4

FATAL: Yes **No** Maybe

FACT | Over 22 percent of adult Americans suffer from a diagnosable mental disorder in a given year.

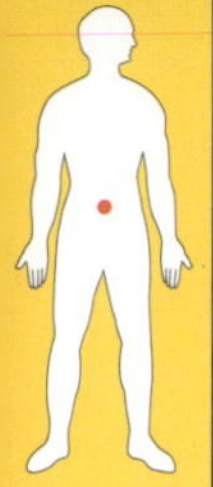

FACT | No 2 tongue prints are alike.

...or you might have

GALLSTONES

WHAT IT IS: Digestive juices high in cholesterol or low in bile salt form pebble-shaped stones in gallbladder. May result in severe pain attacks. Contributing factors include obesity, rapid weight loss, and intolerance of rich, fatty foods. Can range in size from tiny to several centimeters in diameter. Greater risk for older, overweight women.

SPECIALIST TO SEE: Gastroenterologist

OTHER SYMPTOMS:

- Chronic indigestion
- Pain between shoulder blades
- Clay-colored stool
- Nausea

PROGRESSION: Symptoms appear quickly, caused by obstruction of bile duct by large stone. Attack of intense, steadily increasing pain lasts for 30 minutes to several hours. Blocked ducts may lead to severe, potentially fatal damage to gallbladder, liver, or pancreas. Bacteria will possibly grow in bile, causing additional serious complications.

TREATMENT: Oral acids to dissolve stones. Gallbladder flush or cholecystectomy (surgical removal of gallbladder).

CONTAGION:	**1**	2	3	4
PAIN:	1	2	3	**4**
SUFFERING:	1	**2**	3	4
FATAL:	Yes	**No**	Maybe	

...or you might have

KIDNEY STONES

WHAT IT IS: Small, solid masses of crystals form when urine contains high mineral concentration. Notoriously painful. Often undetected until physical distress begins. Four main varieties: calcium, crystine, struvite, and uric acid.

SPECIALIST TO SEE: Urologist

Appendicitis

[Fig. 111]

COMPLICATIONS

Appendix may rupture, allowing leakage of intestinal contents into abdominal cavity and heightening risk of sepsis (bacterial infection of blood) or peritonitis (inflammation of abdominal lining).

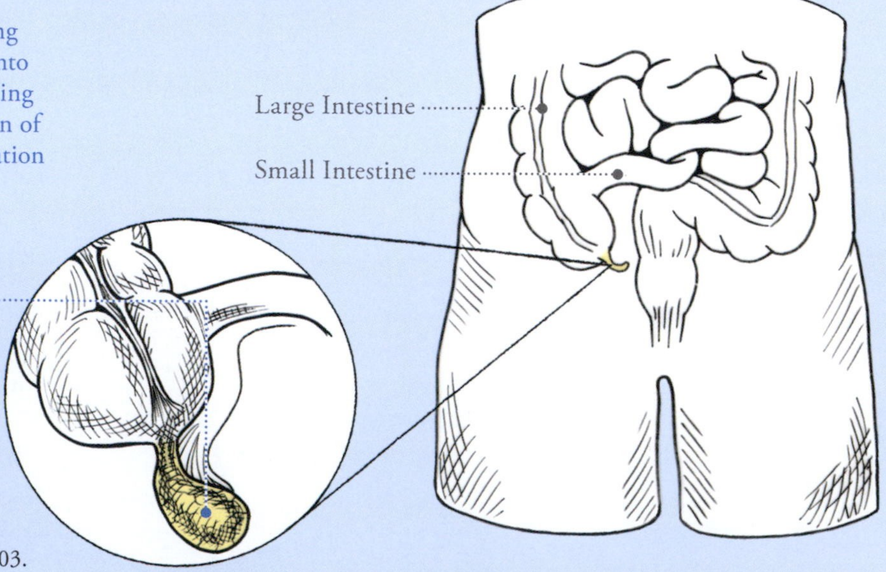

APPENDIX

Due to infection or blockage in intestine, appendix becomes inflamed. Appendectomy almost always necessary.

Large Intestine

Small Intestine

For disease description, see page 103.

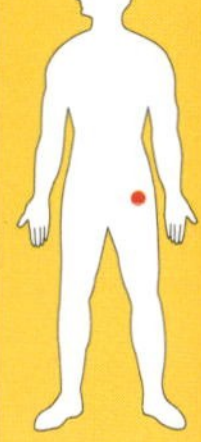

OTHER SYMPTOMS:
- Nausea
- Persistent urge to urinate
- Fever
- Severe pain in lower back

PROGRESSION: Smaller stones usually pass easily in urine. Excruciating pain results as larger stones move to bladder through narrow ureter. May cause vomiting and kidney infection, sepsis (bloodstream infection), or toxic shock.

TREATMENT: Shock-wave therapy to break stone into small pieces. Dietary changes. Minor surgery for severe cases.

CONTAGION: 1 2 3 4 (1)

PAIN: 1 2 3 4 (4)

SUFFERING: 1 2 3 4 (2)

FATAL: Yes No Maybe (No)

...or you might have
PANCREATITIS

WHAT IT IS: Inflammation of pancreas. Often caused by gallstones or excessive alcohol consumption. Digestive enzymes activate inside pancreas instead of small intestine and begin to "digest" pancreas. Rapid onset. Chronic form persists for much longer and causes continual pain or malabsorption.

SPECIALIST TO SEE: Gastroenterologist

OTHER SYMPTOMS:
- Abdominal swelling
- Vomiting
- Tenderness in abdomen
- Hyperventilation
- Constipation
- Weight loss

PROGRESSION: Acute form presents briefly and eventually resolves. Chronic form may lead to gradual destruction of pancreas. In severe cases, bacterial infection spreads to other parts of body, causing organ failure. Pancreatic abscesses, shock, and respiratory failure are also potentially fatal complications.

TREATMENT: Hospitalization. Intravenous fluids.

CONTAGION: 1 2 3 4 (1)

PAIN: 1 2 3 4 (4)

SUFFERING: 1 2 3 4 (3)

FATAL: Yes No Maybe (Maybe)

If you have hip pain...

...you might have
ILIOTIBIAL BAND SYNDROME

WHAT IT IS: Common thigh injury. Results from friction between iliotibial band (tendon-like strip of muscle that runs from hip to knee) and bones in hip or knee. Causes sharp pain on outside of knee, typically felt when running. Often presents in runners, cyclists, hikers, and weight lifters.

SPECIALIST TO SEE: Physical Therapist

OTHER SYMPTOMS:
- Swelling in hip or knee
- Leg pain
- Fatigue

PROGRESSION: Usually begins with dull pain on outside of knee. Pain becomes sharper and, in more severe cases, persists during periods of rest. In extreme cases, difficulty extending lower leg from knee.

TREATMENT: Anti-inflammatory medication. Rest, ice packs, stretching exercises. Corticosteroid injections.

CONTAGION: 1 2 3 4 (1)

PAIN: 1 2 3 4 (2)

SUFFERING: 1 2 3 4 (1)

FATAL: Yes No Maybe (No)

...or you might have
LEGG-CALVÉ-PERTHES DISEASE

WHAT IT IS: Degenerative disease of hip joint. Results from lack of circulation to ball of femur in hip. Leads to avascular necrosis (bone-tissue death) and bone fracture. Eventually, bone is reabsorbed by body and replaced by new bone. Underlying cause unknown; possibly due to injury or abnormal blood clotting. Onset in adulthood rare.

SPECIALIST TO SEE: Orthopedist

QUOTE | "An imaginary ailment is worse than a disease." —Yiddish proverb

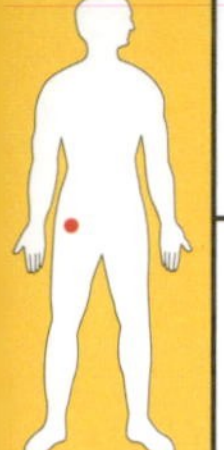

OTHER SYMPTOMS:
- Limping
- Swelling in hip
- Groin pain
- Shortened leg

PROGRESSION: Sharp pain in hip, followed by swelling or tenderness. Limp can develop suddenly. In extreme cases, walking may become too painful, necessitating surgery to shorten muscle or reposition affected bone. Can permanently deform hip joint.

TREATMENT: Anti-inflammatory medication. Physical therapy, crutches, casts, or braces. Tenotomy (surgical removal of part of tendon) or osteotomy (surgical removal of bone fragment).

CONTAGION: **1** 2 3 4
PAIN: 1 2 3 **4**
SUFFERING: 1 2 3 **4**
FATAL: Yes **No** Maybe

...or you might have
OSTEOMYELITIS

WHAT IT IS: Bacterial infection that spreads to bones, usually from another part of body. Can also be caused by open fractures, diabetes, atherosclerosis, or infection of bloodstream from intravenous sources. Chronic or recurrent infection may cause bone death.

SPECIALIST TO SEE: Infectious Disease Specialist

OTHER SYMPTOMS:
- Fever or chills
- Nausea
- Severe bone pain
- Swelling in limbs
- Pus erupting through skin

PROGRESSION: Often begins with general feeling of malaise. Skin around infected bone becomes irritated, red, and full of pus. Can cause abscess or cavity in bone. May lead to blood poisoning or bone deformity. Untreated, can result in death.

TREATMENT: Antibiotics and pain relievers. Surgical cleaning of infected bone, removal of diseased bone, and pus drainage.

CONTAGION: **1** 2 3 4
PAIN: 1 2 3 **4**
SUFFERING: 1 2 **3** 4
FATAL: Yes **No** Maybe

If your hips "catch" or "lock"...

...you might have
OSTEOARTHRITIS

WHAT IT IS: Gradual degeneration of cartilage causes bones to rub together, restricting movement in joints and causing pain. Typically affects hips, arms, fingers, and knees. Most common type of arthritis; accounts for large percentage of visits to primary care doctors in United States.

SPECIALIST TO SEE: Rheumatologist, Orthopedist

OTHER SYMPTOMS:
- Stiff joints
- Inflexibility
- Bony lumps or swelling in joints

PROGRESSION: First, joints and muscles feel stiff. Pain increases as cartilage deteriorates. Bony nodes may appear, causing decreased mobility. If spine is affected, general movement is impaired.

TREATMENT: No known cure. Dietary and lifestyle modifications, physical therapy, and pain relievers to alleviate symptoms.

CONTAGION: **1** 2 3 4
PAIN: 1 2 **3** 4
SUFFERING: 1 **2** 3 4
FATAL: Yes **No** Maybe

...or you might have
TROCHANTERIC BURSITIS

WHAT IT IS: Affliction of hip in which bursa (small, jelly-like sac) becomes inflamed. Causes intense pain in hip, side, or buttocks. Often results from rheumatoid arthritis or injury from falling on upper hip area, but can occur without any known cause.

SPECIALIST TO SEE: Orthopedist

FACT | Measles is the world's most contagious disease. It can be prevented by a vaccine that costs just 26 cents.

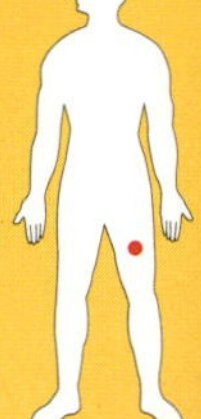

OTHER SYMPTOMS:
- Pain while sitting, walking, or jogging
- Limping
- Swelling in hip

PROGRESSION: Swift onset. Sharp pain in hip or thigh area, followed by tenderness when touched. Can lead to inability to sleep, sit comfortably, or climb stairs without pain.

TREATMENT: Corticosteroids. Anti-inflammatory medication. Physical therapy, use of cane, or ice packs. Surgical removal of bursa.

CONTAGION: 1 2 3 4 (1)

PAIN: 1 2 3 4 (3)

SUFFERING: 1 2 3 4 (3)

FATAL: Yes No Maybe (No)

If you have leg pain...

...you might have
OSTEOSARCOMA

WHAT IT IS: Malignant bone cancer, often found near knee. May metastasize to other bones or to lungs. Many cases misdiagnosed as muscle disorders or cysts. Almost twice as common in men.

SPECIALIST TO SEE: Orthopedist, Oncologist

OTHER SYMPTOMS:
- Fever
- Fatigue
- Limping
- Weight loss
- Swelling in joints

PROGRESSION: Steadily worsening pain at night. Weakened bones may fracture after only minor trauma. Large tumors cause swelling and increasing pain, and interfere with movement. Metastasis is often fatal.

TREATMENT: Surgical removal of tumors, with possible amputation. Chemotherapy.

CONTAGION: 1 2 3 4 (1)

PAIN: 1 2 3 4 (4)

SUFFERING: 1 2 3 4 (3)

FATAL: Yes No Maybe (Maybe)

...or you might have
TROPICAL SPASTIC PARAPARESIS

WHAT IT IS: Progressive, incurable disorder of spinal cord. Caused by HTLV-1 virus, found in tropical regions, although isolated cases have been reported in United States. HTLV-1 also causes leukemia and, like HIV, is spread through blood transfusions and sexual contact.

SPECIALIST TO SEE: Neurologist

OTHER SYMPTOMS:
- Facial paralysis
- Double vision
- Tremors
- Arthritis
- Skin infection

PROGRESSION: Symptoms may not occur for years or even decades after infection. Causes bladder disorders, tingling in feet, and leg pain. Progressive muscle weakness, stiffness, and spasms follow. In rare cases, may result in death.

TREATMENT: No known cure. Corticosteroids and interferon therapy (immune-cell therapy) increase comfort. Treatment of symptoms (e.g., oxybutynin for incontinence).

CONTAGION: 1 2 3 4 (2)

PAIN: 1 2 3 4 (3)

SUFFERING: 1 2 3 4 (3)

FATAL: Yes No Maybe (Maybe)

If you have leg cramping...

...you might have
ATHEROSCLEROSIS

WHAT IT IS: Obstruction of arteries due to plaque buildup on artery walls. May cause narrowing of blood vessels and depletion of blood supply; aneurysm also possible. Affects tissue anywhere, though primarily associated with heart failure and stroke. Risks include obesity, poor diet, stress, advanced age, high blood pressure, and tobacco use.

SPECIALIST TO SEE: Cardiologist

QUOTE | "Health of body and mind is a great blessing, if we can bear it." —John Henry Cardinal Newman

Rise in Disease or Rise in Diagnosis?

Early Detection vs. Increased Survival

With improving diagnostic procedures and treatments, it would seem that we were surviving many ailments longer. On the other hand, as our thresholds for disease identification expand, we declare epidemics and widespread deterioration of health, often attributed to the environment or to lifestyle habits. In reality, however, both survival and incidence rates are generally reported with key variables missing: whether diagnostics have improved, whether the definition of a disease has changed in some way, and whether treatments result in any appreciable improvement in mortality or quality of life.

Increased screening for disease combined with more sensitive testing capabilities inflate both incidence and survival rates. With the advent of CT scans, MRIs, PET scans, and ultrasounds, doctors are able to find small abnormalities that would previously have gone undetected—an excellent illustration of "Seek, and ye shall find." With these diagnoses almost inevitably comes treatment, which for some conditions causes more suffering than the diseases themselves.

When prostate-specific antigen (PSA) tests came into widespread use, diagnoses of prostate cancer increased by 30 percent per year—making it seem, of course, as if cancer rates themselves were increasing, not just diagnosis. Diagnosis occurred at increasingly younger ages, producing 4 times more diagnoses in men under 50 than before the advent of PSA testing. These aren't isolated instances: around 75 percent of men over 50 have been tested, with more than 2 million Americans diagnosed with the ailment over the past decade.

It's not clear that early prostate cancer diagnosis improves prospects for health or longevity. Indeed, in many cases the treatment is worse than living with the affliction, increasingly recognized as a disease men die *with* rather than *from*. Treatment side effects include those associated with chemotherapy and radiation as well as impotence and incontinence from surgical intervention—not to mention the life-altering knowledge that one has cancer. Harvard's Dr. Eric Schneider has called this type of screening, with its potential for false or meaningless positives, "prevention creep": "the notion that we can take strategies designed for public health and large populations and modify them almost at will to be applied in clinical situations to individuals."

New screening for lung cancer has drawn similar criticism. In contrast to the hopes

"Survival is a meaningless statistic."
—Dr. Ned Patz, Duke University Medical Center

that CT scans with increased sensitivity could lead to more effective care, researchers have instead determined that early diagnosis brings only the risks associated with unnecessary surgery and treatment—which in the case of lung cancer are significant. In a *New York Times* article entitled "Researchers Dispute Benefits of CT Scans for Lung Cancer," writer Gina Kolata states, "A person, for example, might die 5 years after symptoms are apparent, no matter what treatment is provided. If the cancer is detected 5 years before symptoms emerge, the person will survive 10 years after diagnosis as opposed to surviving 5 years after diagnosis if the cancer is not found until there are symptoms." Dr. Ned Patz, a professor of radiology at Duke University Medical Center and an investigator in the cited National Cancer Institute lung cancer study, goes on to say, "Survival is a meaningless statistic. What we want to do is reduce the number of people who die from lung cancer. And that is mortality. What we all want to know is mortality."

We are also living through a period in which many previously normal conditions are pathologized—frequently with such nonmedical motivations as formulating drugs that can be prescribed to "prevent" or "manage" conditions (but rarely cure them), thus ensuring ongoing revenue streams for pharmaceutical companies; or feeding the insatiable gloom-and-doom sensationalism of modern media content. "Do you ever feel sad or tired?" query the antidepressant ads, with truisms that apply to all who are human. "Are you at risk?" scream the headlines intended to worry the well. We are experiencing a fundamental shift from treating the sick to examining the healthy for pathology.

Changing disease definitions and awareness also appear to increase incidence. Weights considered healthy in the 1950s are now considered excessive according to currently "acceptable" height-weight ratios. Greater awareness of and expanded criteria for autism make it seem as if that condition were on the rise. Thresholds for type 2 diabetes, osteoporosis, high cholesterol, and hypertension have dropped to the point that over half of the American population either has a disease or is at risk for one.

When people go from healthy to sick in a single early diagnosis, the treatment is worse than the disease, and normal is pathological, perhaps it's time to return to the medical oath, "First, do no harm."

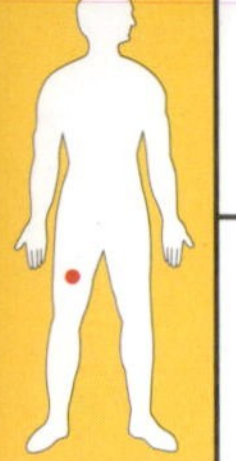

FACT | 35 to 50 million Americans get the flu every year; of those, 100,000 people are hospitalized and 20,000 die.

OTHER SYMPTOMS:
- Muscle weakness
- Fatigue
- Chest pain

PROGRESSION: Often asymptomatic until disruption of blood flow leads to stroke or heart failure. In arms and legs, can cause gangrene and impairment of motor ability.

TREATMENT: Anticoagulants and blood-thinning medication. Reduction of cholesterol. Angioplasty or bypass surgery.

CONTAGION: **1** 2 3 4

PAIN: 1 **2** 3 4

SUFFERING: 1 2 **3** 4

FATAL: Yes No **Maybe**

...or you might have
SPINAL STENOSIS

WHAT IT IS: Compression or blockage in spinal canal. Increased pressure on spinal cord and nerves results from narrowing of spinal column, often as natural process of aging. May lead to severe pain and numbness in multiple limbs.

SPECIALIST TO SEE: Neurologist, Orthopedist

OTHER SYMPTOMS:
- Pain or numbness in buttocks
- Tingling sensation or weakness in leg
- Bladder incontinence
- Erectile dysfunction

PROGRESSION: Initial difficulty with movement. Most cases produce pain while walking, often relieved by sitting. In extreme cases, walking may become impossible.

TREATMENT: Anti-inflammatory medication. Physical therapy and use of back brace. Weight loss and use of cane or walker.

CONTAGION: **1** 2 3 4

PAIN: 1 2 **3** 4

SUFFERING: 1 **2** 3 4

FATAL: Yes **No** Maybe

...or you might have
TARUI DISEASE

WHAT IT IS: Glycogen storage disease. Caused by genetic defect in phosphofructokinase enzyme, which affects breakdown of glucose into energy. Leads to muscle pain and exercise-induced fatigue. Typically resolves with rest; rarely permanently debilitating.

SPECIALIST TO SEE: Endocrinologist

OTHER SYMPTOMS:
- Muscle cramping or weakness
- Rust-colored urine
- Muscle atrophy
- Seizures

PROGRESSION: First, inability to perform any kind of exercise without pain. Intense muscle cramps follow. Cramps later turn into muscle weakness and pain that can make exercise virtually intolerable.

TREATMENT: No known cure. Dietary changes to reduce severe manifestations. Liver transplant to eliminate biochemical abnormalities in severe cases.

CONTAGION: **1** 2 3 4

PAIN: 1 2 **3** 4

SUFFERING: 1 **2** 3 4

FATAL: Yes **No** Maybe

If you feel tingling in your legs...

...you might have
BUERGER'S DISEASE

WHAT IT IS: Inflammation and severe clotting obstruct blood vessels in hands and feet. Causes discomfort and may lead to tissue destruction. Occurs most often in men. Possibly linked to tobacco use; rarely presents in individuals who do not smoke or chew tobacco.

SPECIALIST TO SEE: Hematologist

OTHER SYMPTOMS:
- Enlarged veins
- Pain or tenderness in feet or hands
- Skin ulcers
- Numbness in legs or arms

PROGRESSION: Often misdiagnosed initially. First, diminished blood flow to hands and feet. Exposure to cold temperatures worsens symptoms. If tobacco use continues, infected skin ulcers may develop. Amputation necessary if gangrene sets in.

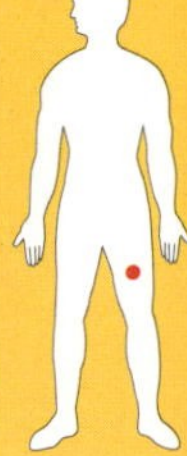

TREATMENT: No known cure. Cessation of tobacco use. Surgery to remove affected tissue in severe cases.

CONTAGION: 1 2 3 4

PAIN: 1 2 3 4

SUFFERING: 1 2 3 4

FATAL: Yes No Maybe

...or you might have
RESTLESS LEGS SYNDROME

WHAT IT IS: Discomfort in legs, such as itching, crawling, or aching, when sitting or lying down creates powerful, uncontrollable urge to move legs. Need to get out of bed may lead to sleep deprivation. Cause unknown, may be due to dopamine imbalance Hereditary cases may present at early age. Risk factors include anemia, nerve damage, pregnancy, drug and tobacco use, and kidney failure.

SPECIALIST TO SEE: Neurologist

OTHER SYMPTOMS:

- Pain or other uncomfortable sensation in legs
- Increased discomfort at night
- Nighttime leg twitching

PROGRESSION: Symptoms may appear gradually, sometimes worsening with advanced age. Symptoms temporarily resolve when leg or foot is moved.

TREATMENT: If appropriate, treatment of underlying condition. Muscle relaxants and sleep aids.

CONTAGION: 1 2 3 4

PAIN: 1 2 3 4

SUFFERING: 1 2 3 4

FATAL: Yes No Maybe

If your legs are numb...

...you might have
CELIAC DISEASE

WHAT IT IS: Immune-system cells react adversely to gluten, found in wheat, oats, and barley. Causes destruction of villi (hairlike projections) in small intestine, decreasing ability to absorb nutrients. Results in malnourishment and vitamin deficiency. Untreated, may develop into cancer, osteoporosis, anemia, or seizures. Hereditary, but can also be triggered by surgery, childbirth, or extreme stress.

SPECIALIST TO SEE: Gastroenterologist

OTHER SYMPTOMS:

- Flatulence
- Weight loss
- Foul smelling, floating stool
- Muscle cramping
- Irritability
- Mild anemia
- Fatigue

PROGRESSION: Typically slow onset results in vitamin deficiencies, leading to scaly skin, muscle spasms, or blood in urine. Causes increased risk of bowel cancer and ulcer formation in small intestine.

TREATMENT: Elimination of gluten from diet. Treatment of resulting complications, such as osteopenia (low bone mass) and osteoporosis.

CONTAGION: 1 2 3 4

PAIN: 1 2 3 4

SUFFERING: 1 2 3 4

FATAL: Yes No Maybe

...or you might have
LERICHE SYNDROME

WHAT IT IS: Plaque builds up in iliac arteries (which stem from aortic arteries) and interferes with blood flow to lower body. Causes include smoking, high blood pressure, and high cholesterol. Found more often in men. May result in range of lower body problems, including pain, numbness, sexual impotence, and difficulty walking.

SPECIALIST TO SEE: Cardiologist

OTHER SYMPTOMS:

- Fatigue
- Muscle cramping
- Frequent urination
- Erectile dysfunction

PROGRESSION: Aching and cramping in buttocks, thighs, and legs during exercise. Absent or diminished femoral pulse (in groin). In extreme cases, degeneration of leg muscle, sores on lower legs and feet, and gangrene.

FACT | Though President John Garfield was shot by an assassin, he died from a nosocomial infection.

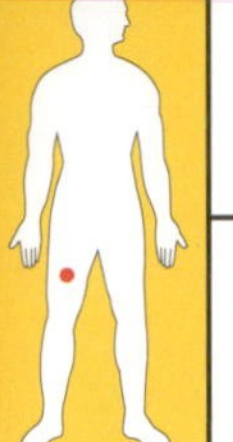

TREATMENT: Weight reduction, regular exercise. Medication to lower cholesterol levels and blood pressure. Specialized foot hygiene and protective footwear.

CONTAGION: 1 2 3 4 (1)

PAIN: 1 2 3 4 (3)

SUFFERING: 1 2 3 4 (3)

FATAL: Yes No Maybe (No)

If you have enlarged veins in your legs...

...you might have
BEHÇET'S SYNDROME

WHAT IT IS: Veins throughout body become inflamed and damaged. Cause unknown; likely combination of inherited and environmental factors. Often more severe in men. Symptoms mimic those of other diseases, so frequently misdiagnosed.

SPECIALIST TO SEE: Rheumatologist

OTHER SYMPTOMS:

- Skin sores
- Mouth ulcers
- Genital sores
- Inflammation in eyes
- Arthritis
- Meningitis

PROGRESSION: Symptoms gradually increase in severity. Most debilitating effects present months or years after onset, flaring and disappearing regularly.

TREATMENT: No known cure. Corticosteroids. Immunosuppressants.

CONTAGION: 1 2 3 4 (1)

PAIN: 1 2 3 4 (3)

SUFFERING: 1 2 3 4 (3)

FATAL: Yes No Maybe (No)

If your legs are swollen...

...you might have
DEEP VEIN THROMBOSIS

WHAT IT IS: Thrombus (blood clot) forms inside vein, most often in thighs or lower legs. Clot disrupts flow of blood. Catalysts for clot formation include obesity, use of oral contraceptives, and air travel. Chronic inactivity heightens risk.

SPECIALIST TO SEE: Emergency Physician

OTHER SYMPTOMS:

- Cramping
- Swelling in bodily tissue
- Warm sensation in leg
- Discoloration in skin

PROGRESSION: Typically, clot formation occurs suddenly. Leg pain and swelling may be extreme. If clot breaks apart and travels to lungs, brain, or heart, can cause pulmonary embolism, stroke, or heart attack.

TREATMENT: Blood-thinning medication. Surgical removal of thrombus with balloon angioplasty or catheter-directed thrombolysis (procedure to break down blood clot).

CONTAGION: 1 2 3 4 (1)

PAIN: 1 2 3 4 (4)

SUFFERING: 1 2 3 4 (2)

FATAL: Yes No Maybe (Maybe)

...or you might have
ELEPHANTIASIS

WHAT IT IS: Round, threadlike parasitic filarial worms transmitted via mosquitoes invade lymphatic system. Results in enlargement and swelling of tissue in arms, legs, breasts, and genitals. Affects more than 120 million people worldwide. Also known as lymphatic filariasis.

SPECIALIST TO SEE: Infectious Disease Specialist

OTHER SYMPTOMS:

- Fever
- Frequent infections
- Inflammation in skin or lymph nodes

Lipedema

[Fig. 112]

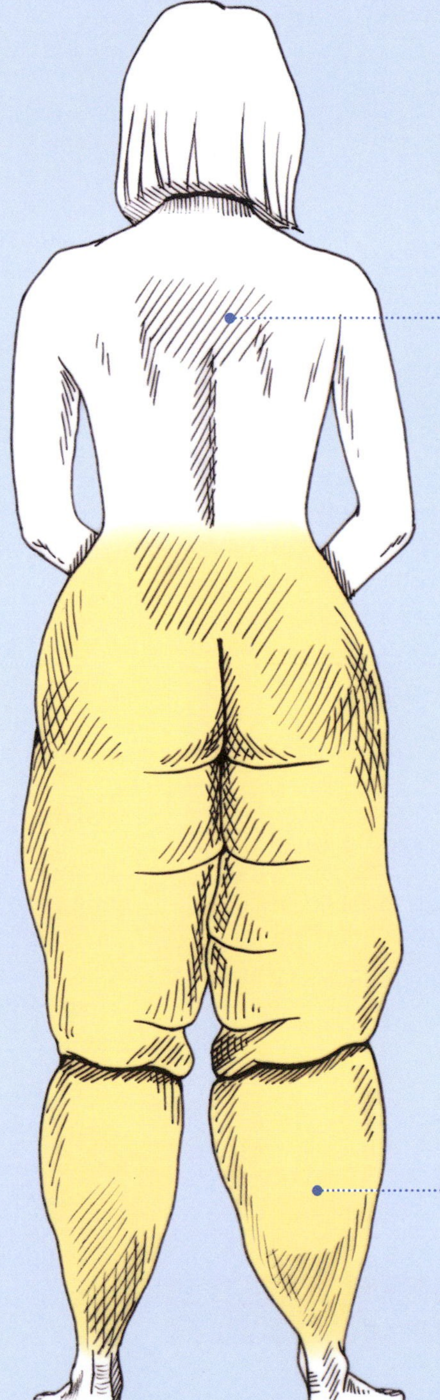

PSYCHOLOGICAL IMPACT
Social stigmatization from abnormal weight gain causes severe emotional distress and may lead to eating disorders. Disease also known as "painful fat syndrome."

PROGRESSION
Fat accumulates in both legs from hip to ankles and cannot be lost. Difficulty with movement and obesity-induced health complications result.

TREATMENT
No known cure. Water exercises to ease strain on joints. Manual lymphatic drainage, compression, and bandaging to reduce swelling. Dieting doesn't reduce lower-body fat.

UPPER BODY
Commonly, weight is maintained from waist up, remaining slender as lower body balloons.

COMPLICATIONS
Painful swelling may result after prolonged sitting or standing. Can cause skin to lose elasticity. Fluid buildup in leg tissue may occur.

NODULES
In early stages, nodules (small fatty lumps) appear near skin surface. Later, lobules (fat deposits larger than nodules) develop.

For disease description, see page 114.

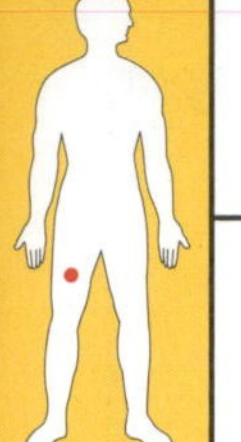

PROGRESSION: Commonly starts with bacterial infections in skin and lymphatic system. Skin may thicken and harden. Results in chronic pain, permanent disability, and, due to drastically inflamed limbs, social ostracism.

TREATMENT: Antipyretic (lowers fever) and antiphlogistic (anti-inflammatory) medication reduce circulation of larvae and worms. Daily elevation and washing of swollen areas.

CONTAGION: **1** 2 3 4

PAIN: 1 2 3 **4**

SUFFERING: 1 2 3 **4**

FATAL: Yes **No** Maybe

...or you might have
LIPEDEMA

WHAT IT IS: Genetic disorder usually arising around puberty or after pregnancy. From hips to lower legs, fats and fluids accumulate in tissue under skin. More common in women. Does not respond to dietary changes or exercise, unlike fat associated with obesity.

SPECIALIST TO SEE: Endocrinologist

OTHER SYMPTOMS:
- Sensitivity to touch
- Bruising under skin

PROGRESSION: During early stages, upper body tends to remain slimmer. Often results in infections and scar-like tissue, known as fibrosis. Leads to obesity-induced stresses on all body systems, as well as immobility.

TREATMENT: Compression clothing and manual lymphatic drainage. Aquatic therapy.

CONTAGION: **1** 2 3 4

PAIN: 1 **2** 3 4

SUFFERING: 1 2 3 **4**

FATAL: Yes **No** Maybe

If you're limping...

...you might have
PAGET'S DISEASE

WHAT IT IS: Second most common bone disease in United States. Accelerates breakdown and reforming of bone tissue, resulting in weak, dense, and structurally unsound bone. Cause unknown; possibly results from viral infection.

SPECIALIST TO SEE: Endocrinologist, Orthopedist, Rheumatologist

OTHER SYMPTOMS:
- Bone pain
- Easily broken bones
- Hearing loss
- Swelling in head
- Deformed bones

PROGRESSION: Bone pain is common. Headaches, loose teeth, and hearing and vision loss may occur when skull is affected. If disease attacks limbs, joint pain may be widespread.

TREATMENT: No known cure. Bisphosphonate increases bone density and slows rate of bone turnover. Pain relievers. Aquatic therapy and walking.

CONTAGION: **1** 2 3 4

PAIN: 1 2 3 **4**

SUFFERING: 1 2 **3** 4

FATAL: Yes **No** Maybe

...or you might have
RICKETS

WHAT IT IS: Softening and weakening of bones due to malnutrition or severe vitamin D deficiency. Without adequate amounts of vitamin D, calcium and phosphate levels become so low that body leeches these minerals from existing bones. Vegetarians or vegans may be vulnerable.

SPECIALIST TO SEE: Orthopedist

OTHER SYMPTOMS:
- Bone pain
- Tooth decay
- Deformed bones
- Muscle cramping

PROGRESSION: Absence of vitamin D causes malabsorption of calcium, leading to dental and skeletal complications. In children, can lead to bowed legs. Increases risk of seizures.

TREATMENT: Supplemental vitamin D and calcium. Special braces or surgery if skeleton has been permanently disfigured.

VOCAB | Previvor: A person with either precancerous cells or a cancer-causing genetic mutation.

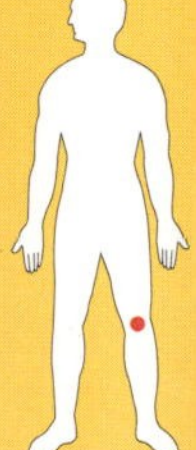

CONTAGION:	1	2	3	4
PAIN:	1	2	3	4
SUFFERING:	1	2	3	4
FATAL:	Yes	No	Maybe	

If you have knee pain...

...you might have

CHONDROMALACIA PATELLAE

WHAT IT IS: Kneecap misaligns, sliding over thigh bone. Women at higher risk; frequently affects runners, cyclists, tennis and soccer players, and those with flat feet. Most common cause of knee pain. Also known as CMP or runner's knee.

SPECIALIST TO SEE: Orthopedist

OTHER SYMPTOMS:
- Discomfort during physical activity
- Tightness in knee
- Swelling
- Loss of muscle control in thigh

PROGRESSION: Pain most noticeable during physical activity or prolonged sitting with bent knees. If treated correctly, pain can usually be reduced and use of joint regained.

TREATMENT: Rehabilitation therapy. Strength training. Anti-inflammatory medication.

CONTAGION:	1	2	3	4
PAIN:	1	2	3	4
SUFFERING:	1	2	3	4
FATAL:	Yes	No	Maybe	

FACT | 80 percent of infections are spread by the hands.

5 Seconds Too Long

While no one knows the origins of the phrase "5-second rule" (or "3-second rule," or "7-second rule," depending on one's timing), it's recently been debunked. In 2003, high school senior Jillian Clarke set out to test the hypothesis that dropped food left on the ground for mere seconds was safe to eat. In 2004, her results made her the youngest-ever winner of the Ig Nobel Award, from Harvard University's Annals of Improbable Research.

When Clarke swabbed high-traffic floors and examined the samples under a microscope, she failed to find a countable number of bacteria. She then dropped food onto tiles painted with *Salmonella* and discovered that the food indeed picked up the bacteria, and the quantity of bacteria increased with the amount of time the food kept contact with the tested surface. In under 5 seconds, however, the food had picked up more than enough bacteria to make someone sick. Whether or not dropped food is dangerous to eat depends not on time, but on the invisible, unknowable presence of bacteria.

Floors aren't the worst culprit, however: most sickness-causing germs are passed via hands. According to University of Arizona researcher Dr. Charles Gerba, the common office desk is 400 times more bacteria-laden than the average toilet seat—and the telephone 700 times more.

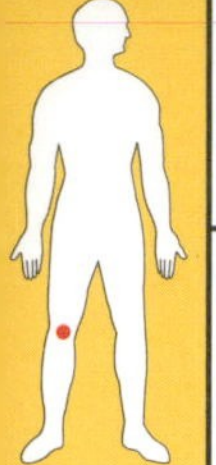

FACT | A single bacteria cell can multiply by 8 million in 24 hours.

...or you might have
HEMOCHROMATOSIS

WHAT IT IS: Inherited disease that causes over-absorption of iron. Excess iron accumulates in tissue throughout body, especially liver, heart, and pancreas. Failure to treat promptly may lead to organ failure, possibly death. More common in men. Also known as iron-overload disorder.

SPECIALIST TO SEE: Gastroenterologist, Hematologist

OTHER SYMPTOMS:
- Fatigue
- Persistent abdominal pain
- Lethargy
- Decreased libido

PROGRESSION: Untreated, iron buildup may cause liver disease, heart complications, diabetes, and arthritis. Symptoms often misattributed to other diseases.

TREATMENT: Phlebotomy (replacement of blood). Elimination of alcohol, vitamin C, and red meat from diet.

CONTAGION:	**1**	2	3	4
PAIN:	1	2	**3**	4
SUFFERING:	1	**2**	3	4
FATAL:	Yes	No	**Maybe**	

If you have a stiff knee...

...you might have
CELLULITIS

WHAT IT IS: Rapidly spreading bacterial infection. Causes inflammation of skin, commonly on face and legs. Risks include advanced age, compromised immune system, obesity, varicose veins, and use of shared hygiene facilities and close living quarters. Severe debilitation and death if untreated.

SPECIALIST TO SEE: Primary Care Physician, Dermatologist

OTHER SYMPTOMS:
- Swelling
- Redness or warm sensation in skin
- Fever or chills
- Headache

PROGRESSION: Bacteria enter through open wound or insect bite. Rash appears and may resolve quickly. Untreated, can spread to subcutaneous tissue, lymph nodes, and bloodstream.

TREATMENT: Antibiotics. Surgery to remove affected tissue in rare cases.

CONTAGION:	**1**	2	3	4
PAIN:	1	2	**3**	4
SUFFERING:	1	2	**3**	4
FATAL:	Yes	No	**Maybe**	

...or you might have
OSTEOCHONDRITIS DISSECANS

WHAT IT IS: Bone or cartilage fragment in joint breaks off. Caused by reduced blood supply to affected area, due to injury or artery blockage. Teens and young adults especially at risk. May develop into osteoarthritis.

SPECIALIST TO SEE: Orthopedist

OTHER SYMPTOMS:
- Clicking sound during joint movement
- Sticking or locking sensation in joint
- Limping
- Swelling
- Pain in joint

PROGRESSION: Starts as pain and soreness in affected joint, followed by inability to fully extend. Usually resolves within weeks or months. Persistent problems may require surgery.

TREATMENT: Painkillers. Anti-inflammatory medication. Abstention from physical activity, especially sports. Surgery in extreme cases.

CONTAGION:	**1**	2	3	4
PAIN:	1	**2**	3	4
SUFFERING:	1	**2**	3	4
FATAL:	Yes	**No**	Maybe	

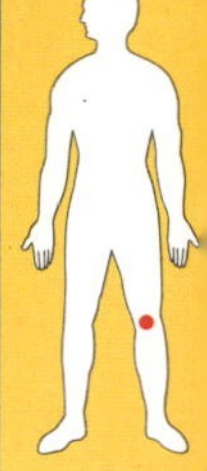

If your knee is numb...

...you might have

TRANSIENT ISCHEMIC ATTACK

WHAT IT IS: Temporary decrease in blood supply to brain causes weakness and slurred speech. Attack lasts only minutes. Symptoms resemble those found at onset of stroke, though no brain injury results. Repeated attacks may increase risk of stroke.

SPECIALIST TO SEE: Neurologist

OTHER SYMPTOMS:

- Facial paralysis
- Slurred speech
- Weakness or numbness on one side of body
- Dizziness
- Sudden blindness

PROGRESSION: Sudden onset of symptoms, usually sudden weakness or partial paralysis. Immediate treatment required. Most symptoms resolve within 1 hour.

TREATMENT: Aspirin. Surgery. Angioplasty in some cases.

CONTAGION: **1** 2 3 4

PAIN: 1 **2** 3 4

SUFFERING: 1 2 **3** 4

FATAL: Yes **No** Maybe

If your knee is swollen...

...you might have

BAKER'S CYST

WHAT IT IS: Arthritis or knee injury, such as cartilage tear, causes excess fluid to build up, forming fluid-filled sac, or cyst, behind knee. Common and easily treated.

SPECIALIST TO SEE: Orthopedist

FACT | 1 in 12 men are color-blind.

Baker's Cyst

[Fig. 113]

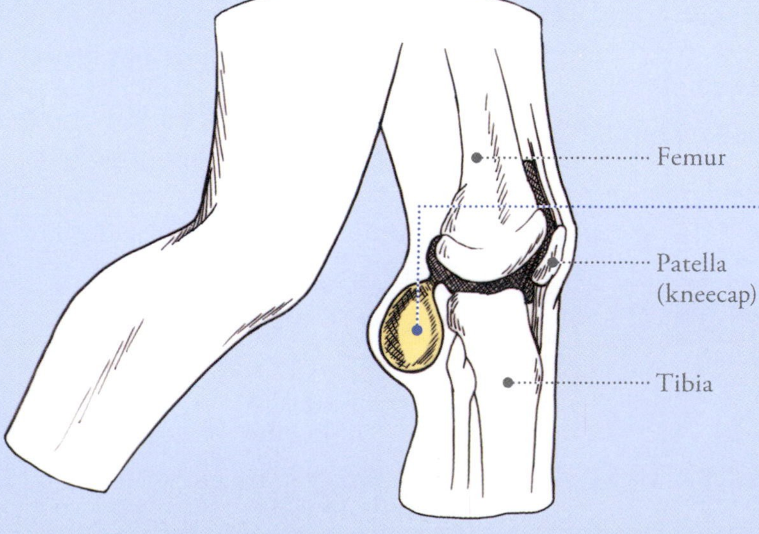

TREATMENT
Drainage of cyst, physical therapy, and pain relievers. Treatment of underlying cause to prevent recurrence.

CYST
Saclike buildup of fluid behind knee. May be caused by knee injury or arthritis. Blood clot or fluid leakage into leg tissue can result.

For disease description, see above.

Top 10 Types of Medical Errors

10 More Reasons to Be an Informed Patient

The National Coordinating Council for Medication Error Reporting and Prevention reports that 1.3 million people are harmed every year by medical error, caused by surgeons, anesthesiologists, Primary Care Physicians, nurses, and pharmacists. Even patient error plays into that figure, resulting from such oversights as miscommunication of special needs and failure to follow medication and recuperation regimens. These mistakes result in as many as 98,000 deaths annually in the United States (including 7,000 who die merely from being prescribed the wrong medication), more than double the number of people who die in car accidents.

1. **Incorrect and Delayed Diagnoses**
   40 percent of all medical errors.

2. **Medication Mistakes**
   Includes wrong medicine prescribed, missed dose, adverse reaction; 28 percent.

3. **Infections and Procedural Errors**
   Includes nosocomial infections, administrative error, mistakes by ill-equipped or ill-trained medical staff; 22 percent.

4. **Treatment Errors**
   Includes damaging self-treatment, post-surgery errors made by doctor or patient, premature discharge; 5 percent or less.

5. **Surgery Errors**
   Strictly surgery mistakes, such as leaving sponge inside patient, removing wrong kidney, anesthesia mistakes; 5 percent or less.

6. **Prevention Errors**
   Includes such scenarios as infectious disease not being properly isolated and then spreading to others, patient with immunity problems placed in same room as someone with contagious ailment; 5 percent or less.

7. **Pharmacist Mistakes**
   Includes wrong prescription filled, wrong dosage; 5 percent or less.

8. **Lab Errors**
   Includes false positives or negatives, mixing up patient reports, incorrectly identifying results; 5 percent or less.

9. **Equipment Malfunction**
   5 percent or less.

10. **Unnecessary Procedures**
    5 percent or less.

*Top 10 medical errors ranked in terms of gravity, according to the National Patient Safety Foundation.

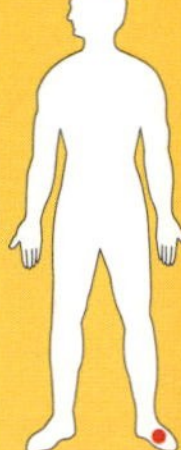

OTHER SYMPTOMS:

- Knee pain
- Tightness in knee
- Swelling in lower leg

PROGRESSION: Dull and aching pain can worsen with prolonged walking and standing. Without treatment, cyst may rupture, leaking fluid into leg tissue.

TREATMENT: Cortisone injections. Removal of fluid from knee. Painkillers.

CONTAGION: **1** 2 3 4

PAIN: 1 **2** 3 4

SUFFERING: 1 **2** 3 4

FATAL: Yes **No** Maybe

...or you might have

PIGMENTED VILLONODULAR SYNOVITIS

WHAT IT IS: Rare joint disorder. Benign tumor grows in lining of joints. Damage to surrounding bone may occur as tumor spreads, resulting in pain and swelling. Joint lining produces extra fluid, exacerbating pain. Cause unknown; occurs most often in middle age. Typically affects only one joint, usually knee, but also hands, hips, and ankles.

SPECIALIST TO SEE: Rheumatologist, Orthopedist

OTHER SYMPTOMS:

- Stiffness
- Popping sensation in joint

PROGRESSION: Swelling and stiffness in joint appear gradually and may flare and disappear.

TREATMENT: Surgery to remove tissue mass. Radiation. Joint replacement.

CONTAGION: **1** 2 3 4

PAIN: 1 2 **3** 4

SUFFERING: 1 **2** 3 4

FATAL: Yes **No** Maybe

...or you might have

SEPTIC BURSITIS

WHAT IT IS: Inflammation of bursa, fluid-filled sacs that protect soft tissue (e.g., muscles, tendons, and skin) from bones. Usually caused by bacterial infection, but may also result from injury, repetitive strain on affected joint, or gout.

SPECIALIST TO SEE: Rheumatologist, Orthopedist

OTHER SYMPTOMS:

- Fever
- Redness or warm sensation in skin
- Swollen glands
- Decreased mobility

PROGRESSION: Minor pain and stiffness progress to significant swelling. Usually accompanied by fever; glands near affected joint may swell. Symptoms can last weeks or months.

TREATMENT: Anti-inflammatory medication. Antibiotics. In rare cases, surgery to drain bursa.

CONTAGION: **1** 2 3 4

PAIN: 1 **2** 3 4

SUFFERING: 1 **2** 3 4

FATAL: Yes **No** Maybe

If you have foot pain...

...you might have

INFECTIOUS ARTHRITIS

WHAT IT IS: Infection spreads through bloodstream to joint. Can be caused by rheumatoid arthritis, intravenous drug use, HIV, untreated Lyme disease, or gonorrhea.

SPECIALIST TO SEE: Rheumatologist

OTHER SYMPTOMS:

- Fever or chills
- Nausea
- Burning sensation in skin
- Headache

PROGRESSION: Swelling and soreness in joint. Diagnosis confirmed through arthrocentesis (syringe inserted into joint to obtain fluid). If infection spreads, fatal septic shock (severe bloodstream infection) likely.

TREATMENT: Hospitalization and antibiotics to prevent further infection. Surgery to drain infected area.

FACT | If two-thirds of your liver were removed, it would grow back within 4 weeks.

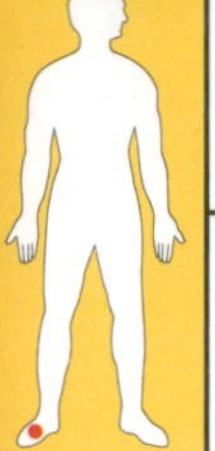

CONTAGION:	1	2	3	4
PAIN:	1	2	3	4
SUFFERING:	1	2	3	4
FATAL:	Yes	No	Maybe	

...or you might have
PLANTAR FASCIITIS

WHAT IT IS: Inflammation of plantar fascia (tissue that runs from heel to arch), resulting in heel pain. Can be caused by flat feet, obesity, excessive or insufficient exercise, or wearing uncomfortable shoes.

SPECIALIST TO SEE: Podiatrist

OTHER SYMPTOMS:
- Sharp pain in heel
- Aching in calves or shins
- Limping

PROGRESSION: Commonly begins with mild pain in heel. Untreated, tissue in heel may tear, causing chronic inflammation and pain.

TREATMENT: Cortisone and anti-inflammatory medication. Ice packs, stretching feet and calves, night splints, and orthotics. Orthopedic surgery in extreme cases.

CONTAGION:	1	2	3	4
PAIN:	1	2	3	4
SUFFERING:	1	2	3	4
FATAL:	Yes	No	Maybe	

If you feel tingling in your foot...

...you might have
TARSAL TUNNEL SYNDROME

WHAT IT IS: Painful foot condition caused by compression of posterior tibial nerve. Nerve runs beneath ligament of ankle and can become inflamed due to arthritis, trauma, obesity, excessive exercise, or flat feet. Symptoms occur anywhere along pinched nerve, from ankle into foot.

SPECIALIST TO SEE: Podiatrist, Orthopedist

OTHER SYMPTOMS:
- Numbness in limbs
- Warm or cold sensation in foot
- Swelling in ankle or foot

PROGRESSION: Initial symptoms occur suddenly. Tapping ankle bone causes tingling that radiates from ankle to big toe. Usually subsides with rest. Untreated, pain will worsen. May cause permanent nerve damage.

TREATMENT: Anti-inflammatory medication and cortisone injections. Orthotics to treat fallen arches. Surgery to release compression.

CONTAGION:	1	2	3	4
PAIN:	1	2	3	4
SUFFERING:	1	2	3	4
FATAL:	Yes	No	Maybe	

If your foot feels cold...

...you might have
PERIPHERAL ARTERIAL DISEASE

WHAT IT IS: Common circulation disorder in which constriction of arteries leads to restricted blood flow to legs. May also affect blood flow to arms and brain. Usually signals extensive accumulation of fatty deposits in arteries. May lead to heart attack or stroke.

SPECIALIST TO SEE: Cardiologist

OTHER SYMPTOMS:
- Numbness in toes
- Back pain
- Erectile dysfunction
- Persistent infections

PROGRESSION: Frequently manifests as sharp pain in leg during exercise. In extreme cases, blocked blood flow results in tissue death, necessitating amputation. Coronary artery disease may also develop.

TREATMENT: Cholesterol and blood pressure medication. Angioplasty to open blocked arteries.

CONTAGION:	1	2	3	4
PAIN:	1	2	3	4
SUFFERING:	1	2	3	4
FATAL:	Yes	No	Maybe	

VOCAB | Mucus trouper: An employee who shows up for work with a cold or the flu.

Gangrene

[Fig. 114]

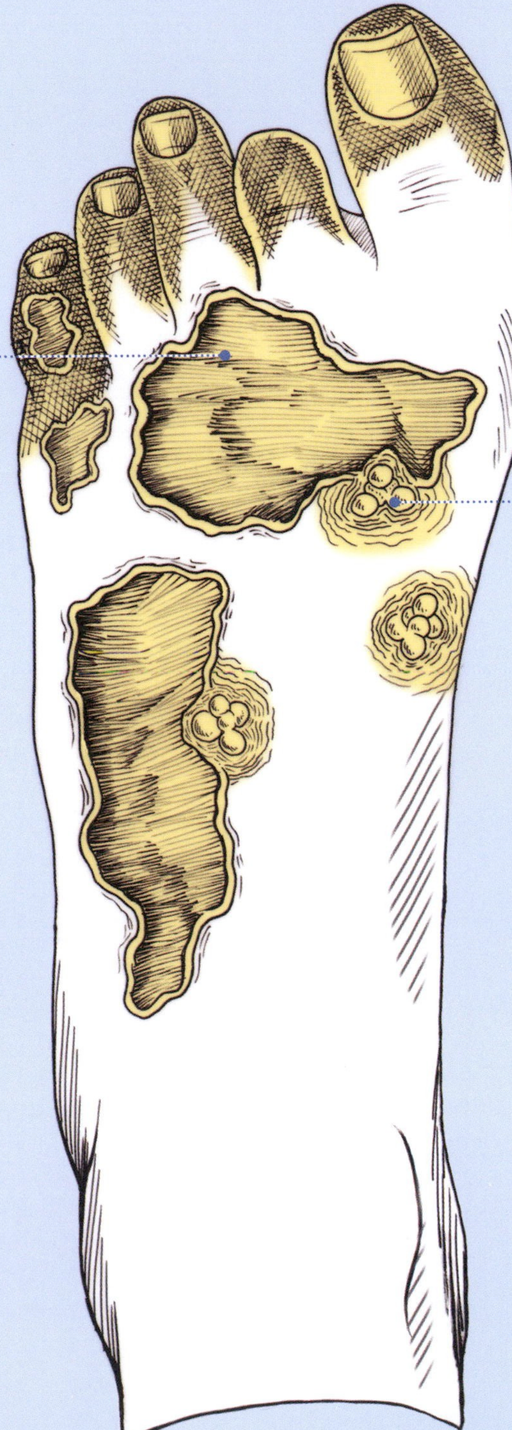

TISSUE DEATH
Necrosis (tissue death) caused by infection or decreased blood flow. Tissue may become infected after surgery or trauma. Blood vessel disorders (e.g., atherosclerosis) and diabetes also increase risk. Causes severe, often irreparable damage.

SYMPTOMS
Skin appears bruised, discolored, or shriveled, and may produce putrid odor or discharge. Often accompanied by pain, numbness, or gas buildup beneath skin.

TYPES
Gangrene types include: wet, due to burns, freezing, or injury; dry, caused by insufficient blood flow through arteries; gas, from bacterial infection; and internal, resulting from interrupted blood flow to abdominal organs.

TREATMENT
Debridement (removal of affected tissue), either surgically or through maggot therapy. Amputation in severe cases.

For disease description, see page 123.

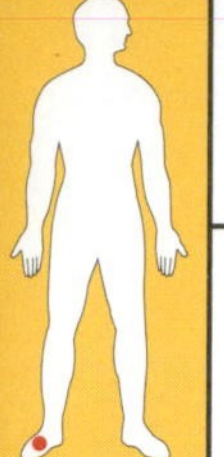

If your foot is numb...

...you might have
CHARCOT-MARIE-TOOTH DISEASE

WHAT IT IS: Common hereditary genetic disorder affecting nerves in brain and spinal cord. Due to lack of stimulation, muscles in legs and arms weaken and atrophy, leading to loss of sensation. May produce characteristic storklike shape in legs.

SPECIALIST TO SEE: Neurologist

OTHER SYMPTOMS:

- Unsteady gait
- Difficulty breathing
- Hearing loss
- Severe pain in limbs

PROGRESSION: Muscle deterioration in arms and legs. Eventually, difficulty distinguishing hot and cold sensations. In severe cases, loss of all feeling in hands and feet can lead to unnoticed injury.

TREATMENT: Exercise. Leg braces, orthotics, or surgery to correct foot problems. Adaptive hand devices for eating and writing.

CONTAGION:	**1**	2	3	4
PAIN:	1	2	**3**	4
SUFFERING:	1	2	**3**	4
FATAL:	Yes	**No**	Maybe	

...or you might have
OLIVOPONTOCEREBELLAR ATROPHY

WHAT IT IS: Degeneration of certain areas in brain, especially those that control balance, voluntary movement, and speech. Can be hereditary. Symptoms similar to Parkinson's disease. More common in men. Life expectancy of approximately 15 years after diagnosis.

SPECIALIST TO SEE: Neurologist

OTHER SYMPTOMS:

- Muscle tremors
- Slurred speech
- Rapid, involuntary eye movements
- Difficulty swallowing
- Erectile dysfunction
- Dementia
- Unsteady gait

PROGRESSION: Initial symptoms include urinary dysfunction, muscle spasms, and clumsiness. Later, bladder and bowel difficulties, hypotension, and persistent tremors. Over time, muscle deterioration may lead to permanent physical disability. Difficulty swallowing poses greatest danger; feeding tube may be necessary in terminal stages.

TREATMENT: Physical and speech therapy. Home care.

CONTAGION:	**1**	2	3	4
PAIN:	1	2	**3**	4
SUFFERING:	1	2	3	**4**
FATAL:	**Yes**	No	Maybe	

If your foot is swollen...

...you might have
GOUT

WHAT IT IS: Form of arthritis. Usually affects big toe, though ankles, feet, and other joints may also be affected. Leads to swelling, discoloration, tenderness, and extreme pain. Caused by uric acid deposits between bones or inside connective tissue. Accumulation of urate crystals causes inflammation. Can be induced by alcohol or drug use.

SPECIALIST TO SEE: Rheumatologist

OTHER SYMPTOMS:

- Redness in skin
- Reduced appetite
- Peeling skin
- Extreme tenderness

PROGRESSION: No symptoms while uric acid accumulates. Then, mild to severe pain attacks flare up, but may disappear for weeks or months. In chronic stage, joints rapidly become inflamed and warm to touch. Kidney damage, kidney stones, and hypertension may result.

TREATMENT: No known cure. Anti-inflammatory medication, corticosteroid injections, and dietary restrictions to alleviate pain.

CONTAGION:	**1**	2	3	4
PAIN:	1	2	**3**	4
SUFFERING:	1	**2**	3	4
FATAL:	Yes	**No**	Maybe	

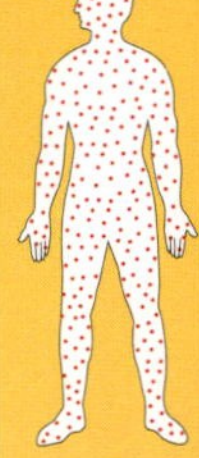

If your toes are discolored...

...you might have
CAROTENEMIA

WHAT IT IS: Yellow or orange skin discoloration, primarily on soles of feet and palms of hands. Usually caused by excessive ingestion of beta carotene in foods such as carrots. May be sign of underlying conditions, including hypothyroidism, lipoproteinemia, diabetes, or renal disease. Most frequently found in toddlers and vegetarians.

SPECIALIST TO SEE: Dermatologist

OTHER SYMPTOMS:

- Craving for more carrots, especially steamed

PROGRESSION: Skin becomes yellow. Untreated, color darkens to orange.

TREATMENT: Elimination from diet of foods containing beta carotene (e.g., carrots, broccoli, mangoes, cantaloupe, spinach).

CONTAGION: **1** 2 3 4

PAIN: **1** 2 3 4

SUFFERING: 1 **2** 3 4

FATAL: Yes **No** Maybe

...or you might have
GANGRENE

WHAT IT IS: Death and decay of body tissue. May arise from blood-vessel disorders, diabetes, injury, or complications from surgery. Four types: wet, due to burns, freezing, or injury; dry, caused by insufficient blood flow through arteries; gas, from bacterial infection; and internal, resulting from interrupted blood flow to abdominal organs.

SPECIALIST TO SEE: Infectious Disease Specialist

OTHER SYMPTOMS:

- Discolored skin
- Loss of sensation
- Discharge in wound
- Pain throughout body
- Fever
- Septic shock

PROGRESSION: Redness, pain, or numbness, often followed by heavy sensation in affected area, skin discoloration, gas bubbles beneath skin, odd-smelling discharge in affected tissue, and necrosis (tissue death). Neurological complications may present in later stages. Can result in death within hours if untreated.

TREATMENT: Antibiotics. Skin graft to replace damaged tissue. Amputation.

CONTAGION: **1** 2 3 4

PAIN: 1 2 **3** 4

SUFFERING: 1 2 **3** 4

FATAL: Yes No **Maybe**

If you have acne...

...you might have
CUSHING'S SYNDROME

WHAT IT IS: Endocrine disorder caused by chronic excess amounts of the hormone cortisol. Commonly associated with use of medication to treat inflammatory illnesses such as rheumatoid arthritis, lupus, or asthma; or excess amounts of cortisol may be produced naturally (e.g., in case of benign tumor of pituitary gland).

SPECIALIST TO SEE: Endocrinologist

OTHER SYMPTOMS:

- Upper body obesity
- Excessive neck fat
- Fragile skin
- Stretch marks on buttocks, arms, breasts, thighs, or abdomen
- Back pain while bending or lifting

PROGRESSION: First, unusual infections, kidney stones, and bone loss may occur. Women experience excessive hair growth and irregular menstrual cycles; men may have diminished fertility and libido. Untreated, can increase risk of heart disease and death.

TREATMENT: Medication to lower cortisol levels. Removal of tumor.

CONTAGION: **1** 2 3 4

PAIN: 1 **2** 3 4

SUFFERING: 1 2 **3** 4

FATAL: Yes **No** Maybe

FACT | One-third of the world's population is infected with tuberculosis, which kills 8,000 people every day.

Dying for Love
Sexually Transmitted Diseases

It's now a forgone conclusion that the carefree, hedonistic 1960s and 1970s were brought to a screeching halt with the fear-laden, latex-wrapped emergence of AIDS in the 1980s. Due to the pandemic's severity and contagion, awareness of HIV/AIDS has since eclipsed that of many other sexually transmitted diseases (STDs)—few of them fatal, perhaps, but none of them pleasant. Although condoms and microbicide gels do offer some protection, they have a 10 to 20 percent failure rate, and STDs can also be contracted from activities other than intercourse. Previously known as venereal diseases (named after Venus, the Roman goddess of love), the ailments are especially contagious because they pass via direct exchange of fluids and mucous membranes, which are more permeable than outer skin. In the United States alone, 15.3 million new cases of STDs are reported annually, and more than half the population will contract an STD in their lifetime.

Chlamydia

The most commonly diagnosed STD in the United States, chlamydia affects 2.8 million people annually. While symptoms can include painful discharge, because chlamydia is frequently asymptomatic, it's known as the "silent epidemic." Though easily treated with antibiotics, undiagnosed it can lead to pelvic inflammatory disease, arthritis in men, and infertility in both sexes.

Gonorrhea

The second most prevalent STD in the United States, gonorrhea infects over 700,000 people a year and has the same symptoms—and non-symptoms—as chlamydia. Gonorrhea can also have the same end results as chlamydia, and, like its companion STD, increases the risk of HIV infection. When diagnosed, "the clap" is treatable with antibiotics, though drug-resistant strains are developing.

Syphilis

Though the incidence of this bacterial infection declined 90 percent from 1990 to 2000, it's on the rise once again. Syphilis presents in three stages: first, one or

More than 50 percent of all Americans will contract an STD in their lifetime.

more sores appear on the genitals, anus, or mouth; second, rashes develop on the hands, feet, mouth, and genitals; and finally, up to a decade following infection, syphilis can result in tumors, blindness, insanity, and death. Called "the great imitator" because its symptoms mimic other diseases, syphilis responds to antibiotics.

Genital Herpes

The Centers for Disease Control estimates that 1 in 5 Americans has genital herpes, but as many as 90 percent don't know they have it because their symptoms are too mild. These carriers can, nonetheless, pass the virus to others. While outbreaks can be treated with antiviral medications, there's no cure for herpes, and the virus will never leave an infected person's body.

Human Papillomavirus (HPV)

Also known as genital warts, sexually transmitted HPV refers to 30 different types of virus and can lead to cervical cancer. Spread by skin-to-skin contact rather than through bodily fluids, HPV infects 6.2 million Americans per year, accounting for over one-third of all newly contracted STDs. At least 50 percent of sexually active men and women will be infected during their lifetime—and most will exhibit no symptoms. When visible, the virus causes clusters of soft, flesh-colored warts on the genitals or anus. To remove the warts, treatments include topical creams, liquid nitrogen, and electrical current. A vaccine to protect against certain types of HPV was recently approved.

Hepatitis B

Causing inflammation of the liver, the hepatitis B virus (HBV) is spread via sexual activity and blood exchange. HBV infects 1 out of 20 Americans, and 5,000 die from resulting illnesses every year. When it's not asymptomatic, HBV can present with flu-like symptoms and jaundice. While HBV can't be cured, the hepatitis B vaccine is an effective prophylactic. HBV can lead to chronic liver infection, cirrhosis, and liver cancer.

Crabs

Highly contagious and maddeningly itchy, crabs are pubic lice, parasitic insects that look like crustaceans under a microscope and prefer the warm, furry shelter provided by the nether regions. Crabs are easily treated with over-the-counter shampoos or with a prescription cream, though one must also be sure to wash all clothing and bed linens in hot water to prevent reinfestation.

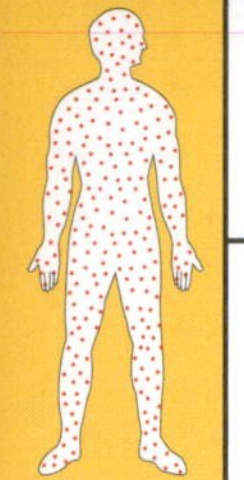

FACT | The human jaw exert 200 pounds of pressure when chewing.

...or you might have

DERMATOMYOSITIS

WHAT IT IS: Connective tissue disorder characterized by inflammation of skin and muscles. May result from viral infection or immune response; often indicates presence of cancer. Can develop quickly or over weeks or months. Women at higher risk.

SPECIALIST TO SEE: Rheumatologist, Dermatologist

OTHER SYMPTOMS:

- Patchy blue or purple rash
- Hard bumps under skin
- Muscle pain or weakness
- Difficulty swallowing
- Fatigue

PROGRESSION: Initially, shortness of breath, weight loss, and fever. Related medical issues include acute renal failure and cardiac, pulmonary, or abdominal complications. Can also lead to pneumonia or malnutrition.

TREATMENT: Corticosteroid or immunosuppressants. Physical therapy to preserve muscle function.

CONTAGION: **1** 2 3 4

PAIN: 1 2 **3** 4

SUFFERING: 1 2 **3** 4

FATAL: Yes No **Maybe**

If you have warts...

...you might have

CORNU CUTANEUM

WHAT IT IS: Type of tumor most often seen on sun-exposed skin. Hard, pointy growth of keratin (protein found in skin and nails) resembles tiny horn. May grow anywhere, but commonly appears on face, ear, nose, forearms, and hands. Tenderness at base of growth may indicate malignancy.

SPECIALIST TO SEE: Dermatologist, Exorcist

OTHER SYMPTOMS:

- Inflammation or sensitivity around growth

PROGRESSION: Unless removed, horn will grow continuously. Largest horn on record was 9 centimeters long. Usually benign, but may also become malignant squamous-cell carcinoma.

TREATMENT: Surgical removal of horn. Radiation and chemotherapy.

CONTAGION: **1** 2 3 4

PAIN: 1 2 **3** 4

SUFFERING: 1 2 **3** 4

FATAL: Yes No **Maybe**

...or you might have

KERATOSIS FOLLICULARIS

WHAT IT IS: Genetic disorder characterized by yellowish, greasy papules (conical, warty bumps). May appear on face, scalp, upper back, neck, chest, and areas of natural skin folds. Also called Darier's disease or Darier-White disease.

SPECIALIST TO SEE: Dermatologist

OTHER SYMPTOMS:

- Foul odor from papules
- Bacterial infection
- Fingernails may show striping, splitting, or v-shaped nicks

PROGRESSION: Usually emerges in late teens but can occur at any age. Rash presents slowly and has distinct odor. Grows darker with time. Can be aggravated by humidity and exposure to sunlight.

TREATMENT: Moisturizer, sunscreen, and topical retinoid (vitamin-A derivative) to improve skin. Antibiotics for infections. Oral contraceptives for women. Dermabrasion.

CONTAGION: **1** 2 3 4

PAIN: 1 **2** 3 4

SUFFERING: 1 2 **3** 4

FATAL: Yes **No** Maybe

...or you might have

SEBORRHEIC KERATOSIS

WHAT IT IS: Benign wartlike growths develop on skin, commonly on chest or back, though growths may appear anywhere. Sometimes called "barnacles of wisdom." Often characterized by "pasted on" or "stuck on" appearance. Coloration varies; typically occur in large numbers.

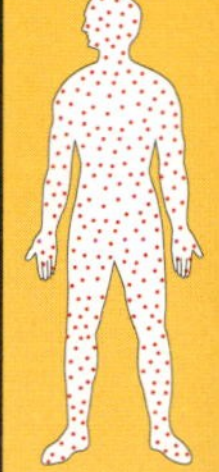

SPECIALIST TO SEE: Dermatologist

OTHER SYMPTOMS:

- Inflammation
- Itchy skin

PROGRESSION: Though painless, growths may become itchy and irritated. Quantity tends to increase with age.

TREATMENT: Cryosurgery (freezing), curettage (tissue scraping), or electrosurgery (burning tissue away with electric current).

CONTAGION: **1** 2 3 4

PAIN: **1** 2 3 4

SUFFERING: 1 **2** 3 4

FATAL: Yes **No** Maybe

If you have a rash...

...you might have ANTHRAX

WHAT IT IS: Acute infectious bacterial disease (though not contagious between humans). May cause hemorrhaging and, even with treatment, death. *Bacillus anthracis* spores live in soil and are generally passed to humans via infected livestock and animal products. Three forms: cutaneous, inhalation, and gastrointestinal.

SPECIALIST TO SEE: Primary Care Physician, Infectious Disease Specialist

OTHER SYMPTOMS:

- Black skin ulcer
- Sore throat
- Fever
- Muscle aches
- Difficulty breathing
- Nausea
- Reduced appetite
- Diarrhea

PROGRESSION: Cutaneous form begins as small, itchy bump on skin that becomes ulcer. Untreated, 20 percent fatality rate. Inhalation form marked by flu-like symptoms that lead to breathing difficulties and usually death. Gastrointestinal form causes vomiting of blood and severe diarrhea; fatal in 25 to 60 percent of cases.

TREATMENT: Antibiotics.

CONTAGION: **1** 2 3 4

PAIN: 1 **2** 3 4

SUFFERING: 1 2 **3** 4

FATAL: Yes No **Maybe**

...or you might have LYME DISEASE

WHAT IT IS: Bacterial illness caused by bite of infected deer tick. Difficult to diagnose; early symptoms are mild and mimic other disorders. If bacteria spread, skin, nerves, heart, muscles, and joints may become infected. Chronic cases commonly result in constant fatigue, psychiatric symptoms, and severely painful joints.

SPECIALIST TO SEE: Primary Care Physician, Infectious Disease Specialist, Rheumatologist

OTHER SYMPTOMS:

- Fever, headache, and fatigue
- Muscle spasms
- Joint pain
- Ringing in ears
- Tingling sensation in skin
- Double vision
- Depression

PROGRESSION: Three stages. Begins with red, ringlike rash, followed by flu-like symptoms. Leads to fatigue and malaise, accompanied by joint pain. Often, droopy eyelids or difficulty smiling occur. Then, multiple organ systems affected, with severe headaches, cardiac damage, hearing loss, and arthritis. Though rarely fatal, can be persistent and very debilitating.

TREATMENT: Antibiotics for up to 4 years. Relapses often occur.

CONTAGION: **1** 2 3 4

PAIN: 1 2 **3** 4

SUFFERING: 1 2 **3** 4

FATAL: Yes **No** Maybe

...or you might have WEST NILE VIRUS

WHAT IT IS: Infectious virus transmitted by mosquitoes. Majority of cases occur in summer or early fall. Most people exhibit no symptoms; 20 percent

QUOTE | "Etymologically, 'patient' means sufferer." —Susan Sontag

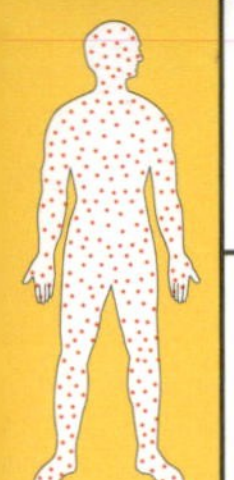

develop flu-like illness. Rarely, progresses into serious condition of high fever, disorientation, convulsions, and coma. Death may result, or permanent neurological damage.

SPECIALIST TO SEE: Infectious Disease Specialist

OTHER SYMPTOMS:

- Fever
- Swollen lymph nodes
- Headache
- Muscle aches

PROGRESSION: With fever syndrome, symptoms appear between 3 and 8 days after infection and self-resolve within 10 days. With West Nile meningitis or encephalitis (brain inflammation), similar early symptoms occur then disease escalates.

TREATMENT: No known cure. Painkillers, intravenous fluids, and supplemental oxygen in severe cases.

CONTAGION: 1 **2** 3 4

PAIN: 1 **2** 3 4

SUFFERING: 1 2 **3** 4

FATAL: Yes No **Maybe**

If you have blisters...

...you might have
FLESH-EATING BACTERIA

WHAT IT IS: Life-threatening bacterial infection most often caused by *Streptococcus pyogenes.* Destroys skin and underlying soft tissue by releasing toxins. Weakened immune systems or diabetes may increase risk. Known as one of fastest-spreading infections.

SPECIALIST TO SEE: Emergency Physician, Infectious Disease Specialist

OTHER SYMPTOMS:

- Redness or swelling in skin
- Difficulty breathing

FACT | Bacteria can double every 20 minutes.

Flesh-Eating Bacteria

[Fig. 115]

STREPTOCOCCUS BACTERIUM
Enters body following surgery or trauma. Also responsible for such infections as strep throat, impetigo, and scarlet fever.

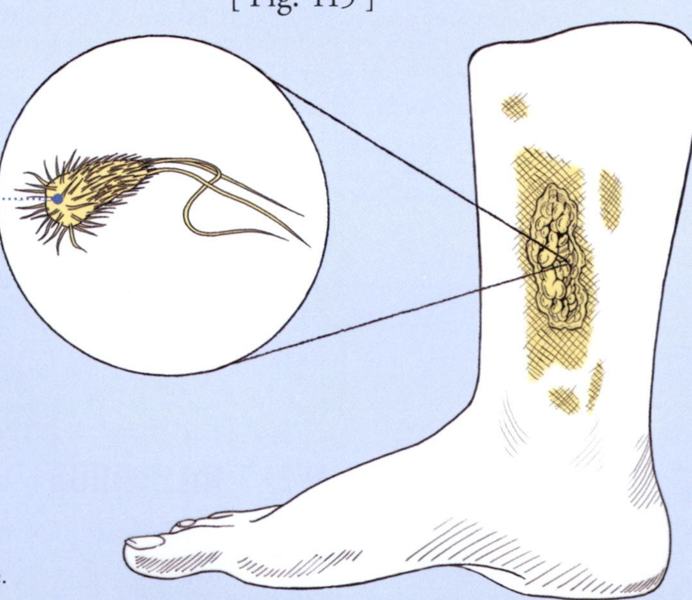

WHAT IT IS
Infection caused when bacteria release toxin that rapidly destroys skin and soft tissue (e.g., fat, muscle, tendons, blood vessels). Mortality rate is 30 percent.

For disease description, see above.

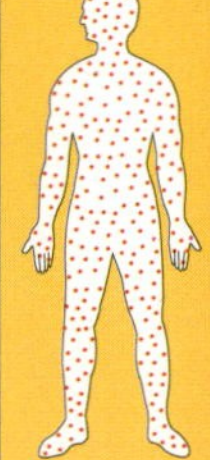

- Red or bluish rash
- Warm sensation in skin
- Sore throat

PROGRESSION: Often begins with sore throat. Then, progresses to sensitive, painful, swollen skin tissue within hours; necrosis occurs at rapid rate. May lead to shock or kidney failure.

TREATMENT: Intravenous antibiotics. Surgery to remove infected dead tissue.

CONTAGION: 1 2 3 **4**

PAIN: 1 2 **3** 4

SUFFERING: 1 2 **3** 4

FATAL: Yes No **Maybe**

...or you might have

HAND-FOOT-AND-MOUTH DISEASE

WHAT IT IS: Highly contagious viral infection caused by Coxsackievirus A. Easily spread from person to person through direct contact with infected feces or mucus. Typically occurs in small epidemics. Most recent fatal outbreak occurred in 2006 in Malaysia, killing 7 people.

SPECIALIST TO SEE: Primary Care Physician

OTHER SYMPTOMS:

- Sore throat
- Fever
- Fatigue
- Headache
- Sores on palms or soles of feet

PROGRESSION: First, small sores develop in throat, and rash appears on hands and feet. Remains contagious even after symptoms resolve. Rare complications include possibly life-threatening viral meningitis and encephalitis (brain inflammation).

TREATMENT: Fluids, rest, and painkillers.

CONTAGION: 1 2 3 **4**

PAIN: 1 **2** 3 4

SUFFERING: 1 2 **3** 4

FATAL: Yes No **Maybe**

...or you might have

PEMPHIGUS VULGARIS

WHAT IT IS: Chronic autoimmune disorder in which immune system produces antibodies that cause separation of epidermal cells. Results in blistering of skin and mucus membranes. Blisters do not itch, but are painful. Can be fatal.

SPECIALIST TO SEE: Primary Care Physician, Dermatologist

OTHER SYMPTOMS:

- Skin lesions that ooze and detach
- Fever or chills

PROGRESSION: Blistering tends to begin in mouth and spreads to skin. Sometimes, blisters erupt in genital area. Large amount of body fluid may be lost through sores. Fatal if untreated, usually resulting from systemic infection.

TREATMENT: Replacement of lost body fluids. Corticosteroids, immunosuppressants, antibiotics, and antifungal medication.

CONTAGION: **1** 2 3 4

PAIN: 1 2 **3** 4

SUFFERING: 1 2 **3** 4

FATAL: Yes No **Maybe**

If you have boils...

...you might have

BUBONIC PLAGUE

WHAT IT IS: Most common form of plague disease among humans. Caused by bite from infected flea or rat. Following initial infection, bacteria travel through lymphatic system and invade lymph nodes, producing buboes (swollen lymph glands) in groin, armpits, or neck.

SPECIALIST TO SEE: Emergency Physician, Infectious Disease Specialist

OTHER SYMPTOMS:

- Sudden fever
- Chills

FACT | Pneumonia kills more people in the United States than any other infectious disease.

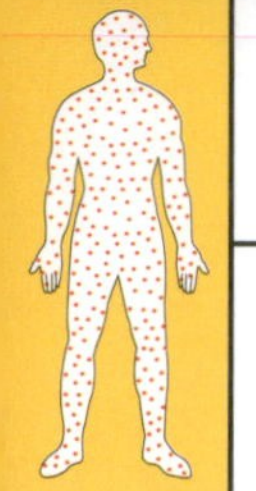

- Muscle pain
- Headache
- Fatigue

PROGRESSION: Symptoms present within 7 days of infection. Diarrhea and high fever emerge. Complications include shock, gangrene in fingers and toes, severe respiratory complications, blood infections, meningitis, and death.

TREATMENT: Hospitalization. Intravenous antibiotics for at least 10 days.

CONTAGION: 1 2 3 **4**

PAIN: 1 2 **3** 4

SUFFERING: 1 2 **3** 4

FATAL: Yes No **Maybe**

...or you might have
PHOTODERMATITIS

WHAT IT IS: Abnormal skin response to ultraviolet rays, especially those produced by the sun. Also known as sun poisoning. Itchy blisters, bumps, and discoloration of skin may occur. Cause can often be traced to photosensitizers, such as certain fragrances, PABA (found in some sunscreens), tetracycline antibiotics, and excessive consumption of figs, limes, or carrots.

SPECIALIST TO SEE: Dermatologist

OTHER SYMPTOMS:

- Redness
- Swelling
- Peeling skin
- Discolored or darkened skin

PROGRESSION: Sun exposure may lead to burning sensation, swelling, and severely inflamed, raw skin. Most cases resolve without treatment; in some instances, reaction may continue for years.

TREATMENT: Steroid and antibacterial cream. Aloe to soothe inflamed skin.

CONTAGION: **1** 2 3 4

PAIN: 1 2 **3** 4

SUFFERING: 1 **2** 3 4

FATAL: Yes **No** Maybe

...or you might have
SEPTICEMIA

WHAT IT IS: Bacterial infection of the bloodstream. Serious, life-threatening condition that may quickly deteriorate into septic shock (lack of blood flow to organs, causing organ failure) and death. Certain conditions increase risk: recent infection, immune-system disease, diabetes, long-term use of antibiotics, and recent medical procedure or surgery.

SPECIALIST TO SEE: Emergency Physician

OTHER SYMPTOMS:

- Purple spots or rash
- Light-headedness
- Agitation
- Lethargy
- Pale skin

PROGRESSION: May begin with chills, spiking fever, and elevated breathing and heartbeat. Then, blood pressure falls, leading to destruction and possible failure of heart, brain, liver, and kidneys. Death occurs in high percentage of cases.

TREATMENT: Intravenous fluids and sympathomimetic medication to maintain blood pressure. Antibiotics. Oxygen therapy. In some cases, treatment for clotting abnormalities.

CONTAGION: **1** 2 3 4

PAIN: 1 2 **3** 4

SUFFERING: 1 2 **3** 4

FATAL: Yes No **Maybe**

If you have open or oozing sores...

...you might have
MYIASIS

WHAT IT IS: Infestation of flesh fly (*Cordylobia anthropophaga*) larvae or maggots. Larvae may be located in or beneath skin or travel through tissue, causing swelling and severe itching. Larvae may enter through body cavity, wound, or orifice.

FACT | 200,000 to 300,000 Americans are infected with hepatitis B every year.

Travel Diseases

Venturing Beyond Theme Parks

Hodophobia is fear of traveling, and it turns out there's good reason. There are nearly 60 travel-related diseases recognized by the Centers for Disease Control, ranging from African sleeping sickness to meningitis to SARS. When exotic diseases strike the traveler, they encounter an immune system that's never been exposed to the illness and occur at the worst possible times and places—beyond the comforts of home and family, sometimes without access to 1quality care, and with the added hurdle of managing in a foreign language.

Cholera

Rare in industrialized countries, cholera is still common in parts of the developing world. This diarrheal illness is spread by contaminated food and water. In severe cases, if rehydration treatment is not administered, death can occur within hours.

Malaria

Spread by mosquitoes, malaria afflicts the red blood cells and is one of the world's biggest killers. Drug and insecticide resistance have increased over the last few decades, and lack of immunity leaves travelers highly vulnerable.

Tetanus

Often called lockjaw, tetanus is a nervous-system disease caused by bacteria, resulting in muscle spasms and seizures. Tetanus spores enter the body via a wound, as when an injury is washed with contaminated water.

Typhoid Fever

The *Salmonella typhi* bacterium is transmitted through food and water and presents as high fever, abdominal pain, diarrhea, and sometimes a rash. If not treated, it's fatal.

Yellow Fever

A viral disease spread by mosquitoes, yellow fever derives its name from the jaundice that can occur. It starts with flu-like symptoms but can progress into liver failure.

Traveler's Diarrhea

By far the most common, whether called turista, Montezuma's revenge, Aztec two-step, Delhi belly, Turkey trot, Hong Kong dog, Rangoon runs, Cairo curse, or Dakar dash.

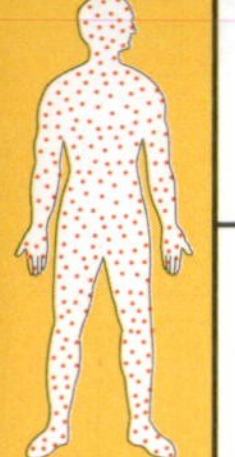

SPECIALIST TO SEE: Infectious Disease Specialist, Dermatologist

OTHER SYMPTOMS:

- Boils
- Moving sensation beneath skin

PROGRESSION: Flesh flies lay eggs directly onto skin or in open wound. Eggs hatch into larvae that burrow deeper into body. Itchy sores develop into boil-like lesions. Maggots may migrate to brain and feed upon brain tissue, possibly causing fatal meningitis.

TREATMENT: Petroleum jelly to suffocate maggots. Excision of infected area in extreme cases.

CONTAGION:	**1**	2	3	4
PAIN:	1	2	**3**	4
SUFFERING:	1	2	**3**	4
FATAL:	Yes	No	**Maybe**	

...or you might have

YAWS

WHAT IT IS: Chronic infection of skin, bones, and joints. Characterized by skin sores and resulting nodule scars. Bone lesions may also lead to complications such as osteomyelitis. Caused by *Treponema pertenue*, closely related to bacteria that cause syphilis. Contracted through person-to-person contact. Nearly eradicated in 1950s; recent rise in cases worldwide.

SPECIALIST TO SEE: Infectious Disease Specialist

OTHER SYMPTOMS:

- Fever
- Reduced appetite
- Swollen glands
- Malaise

PROGRESSION: Within 2 to 8 weeks after exposure, painless bump ("mother yaw") appears. Additional ulcers follow, often oozing and pus-filled. Inflammation of bones and fingers can develop. If untreated, final stage consists of disease, deformity, and disability.

TREATMENT: Penicillin G (antibiotic).

CONTAGION:	1	2	3	**4**
PAIN:	1	2	**3**	4
SUFFERING:	1	2	**3**	4
FATAL:	Yes	**No**	Maybe	

If you have cysts...

...you might have

CIRRHOSIS

WHAT IT IS: Chronic liver disorder characterized by cell damage and tissue scarring throughout liver. Disrupts normal blood flow and leads to gradual liver failure. Most commonly caused by alcoholism and hepatitis C. Generally irreversible. Third most common cause of death in United States between ages 45 and 65.

SPECIALIST TO SEE: Hepatologist

OTHER SYMPTOMS:

- Itching skin
- Abdominal pain
- Jaundice
- Fatigue
- Swelling on breast tissue in men
- Shrunken testicles
- Bloating
- Spidery veins around navel

PROGRESSION: As scar tissue forms, liver function decreases. Capacity to remove toxins becomes impaired, blood flow is hindered, and high levels of toxins accumulate in body. Complications may include fluid buildup in abdomen, blood disorders, and neurological degeneration. Untreated, leads to liver failure.

TREATMENT: No known cure. Medication to stem deadly complications. Liver transplant if disease becomes life threatening.

CONTAGION:	**1**	2	3	4
PAIN:	1	2	**3**	4
SUFFERING:	1	2	3	**4**
FATAL:	**Yes**	No	Maybe	

If you have irregularly shaped moles...

...you might have

MELANOMA

WHAT IT IS: Deadliest form of skin cancer. Develops in melanocytes (pigment-producing cells). Numerous causes, including genetic

QUOTE | "It is dainty to be sick if you have leisure and convenience for it." —Ralph Waldo Emerson

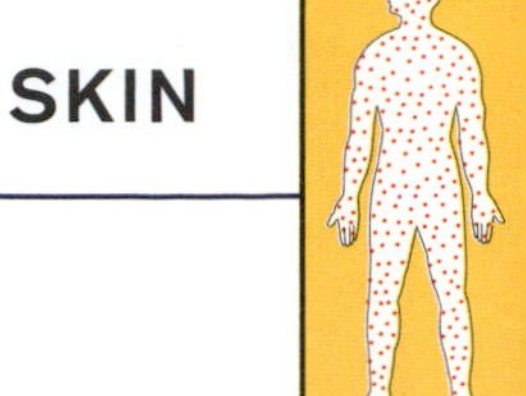

predisposition, sun exposure, and advanced age. Most common in fair-skinned people who sunburn easily.

SPECIALIST TO SEE: Dermatologist, Oncologist

OTHER SYMPTOMS:

- Itching skin
- Vision obstruction
- Discolored fingernails

PROGRESSION: Can develop on any part of body. May appear on normal skin, but often occurs in preexisting moles. Change in size, color, or texture of moles indicates cancer. Can spread to other organs.

TREATMENT: Excision of lesion. With metastasis, chemotherapy, radiation, and removal of nearby lymph nodes.

CONTAGION: **1** 2 3 4

PAIN: 1 **2** 3 4

SUFFERING: 1 2 **3** 4

FATAL: Yes No **Maybe**

...or you might have

VITILIGO

WHAT IT IS: Skin disorder characterized by destruction of melanocytes (pigment-producing cells) Depigmentation appears on mouth, nose, retinas, hands, face, and genitals. Often occurs symmetrically. Hair in affected area can turn white as well. Exact cause unknown. Immune diseases such as pernicious anemia and thyroid disorders may increase risk.

SPECIALIST TO SEE: Dermatologist, Mental Health Professional

OTHER SYMPTOMS:

- Premature graying of hair
- Depression

PROGRESSION: Commonly begins with small depigmented patches. Regions may grow gradually or rapidly. Blemished appearance may lead to significant psychological effect.

TREATMENT: No known cure. Topical steroid therapy. Grafts and dyes for skin. Restricted sun exposure. Skin may be depigmented in extreme cases.

CONTAGION: **1** 2 3 4

PAIN: 1 2 **3** 4

SUFFERING: 1 2 **3** 4

FATAL: Yes **No** Maybe

If you have bruises...

...you might have

EHLERS-DANLOS SYNDROME

WHAT IT IS: Genetic disorder that disrupts production of collagen (fiber that connects bones and tissue). Causes very loose joints and hyperelastic, easy-to-pull skin. There are 6 varieties, all with different symptoms. Complications, such as early-onset arthritis and slow-healing wounds, may occur.

SPECIALIST TO SEE: Rheumatologist

OTHER SYMPTOMS:

- Vision loss
- Joint pain
- Overly flexible joints
- Gum disease
- Fragile skin
- Sunken chest

PROGRESSION: Nearsightedness is common. Osteoporosis may occur. Vascular form carries high risk for rupturing organs, including eyeballs and intestines.

TREATMENT: Varies according to symptoms and form of disease. Vitamin C to aid collagen maintenance.

CONTAGION: **1** 2 3 4

PAIN: 1 2 **3** 4

SUFFERING: 1 2 **3** 4

FATAL: Yes **No** Maybe

...or you might have

HEMOPHILIA

WHAT IT IS: Hereditary condition in which blood's ability to clot properly is impaired by absent or low clotting factor (blood proteins that aid platelets in coagulating blood), resulting in excessive bleeding, both external and internal.

SPECIALIST TO SEE: Hematologist

FACT | One-third of persons who travel abroad experience a travel-related illness.

Yaws

[Fig. 116]

PROGRESSION
"Mother yaw" appears 2 to 8 weeks after exposure, followed by multiple ulcers on hands, feet, and face. Can cause destruction of skin, bones, and joints.

CAUSE
Caused by *Treponema pertenue* bacteria, in same family as bacteria responsible for syphilis.

CONTAGION
Highly contagious through direct contact with open sore.

TREATMENT
Single dose of penicillin is usually sufficient. Recurrence unlikely.

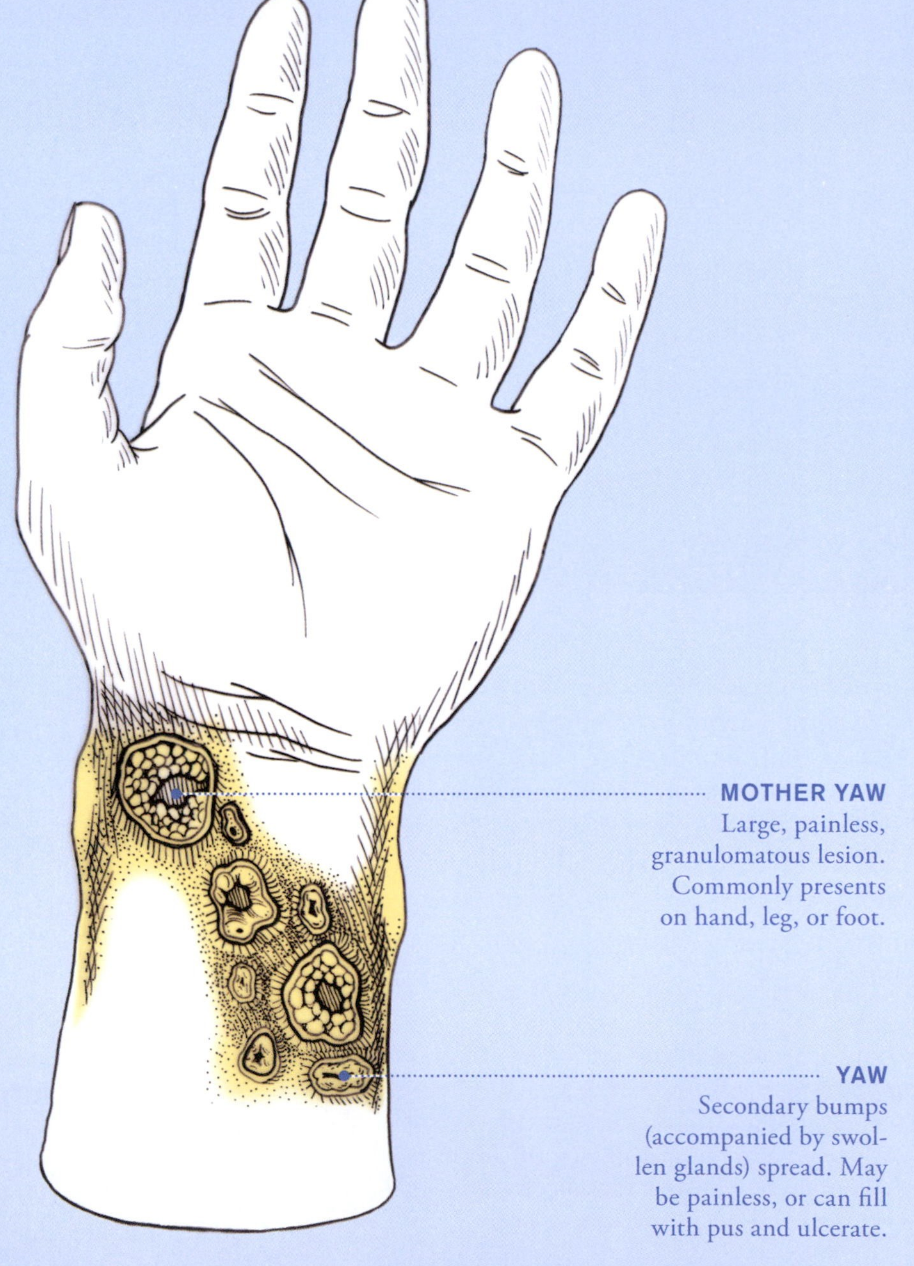

MOTHER YAW
Large, painless, granulomatous lesion. Commonly presents on hand, leg, or foot.

YAW
Secondary bumps (accompanied by swollen glands) spread. May be painless, or can fill with pus and ulcerate.

For disease description, see page 132.

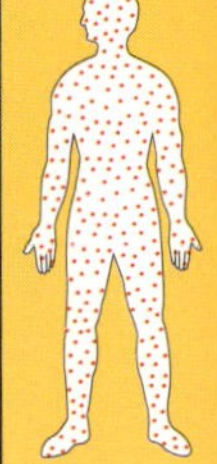

OTHER SYMPTOMS:

- Prolonged bleeding from wounds
- Spontaneous bleeding
- Bloody urine or stool
- Joint pain

PROGRESSION: Commonly presents through surface bruising. Internal bleeding strains nerves, causing severe pain, deadened sensation, and inflexibility. In some cases, permanent nerve damage may occur.

TREATMENT: Intravenous replacement of clotting factor. For milder cases, other medication (e.g., desmopressin).

CONTAGION: **1** 2 3 4

PAIN: 1 **2** 3 4

SUFFERING: 1 2 **3** 4

FATAL: Yes No **Maybe**

If you feel burning on your skin...

...you might have
CIGUATERA POISONING

WHAT IT IS: Most common marine-borne infection worldwide. Poisoning due to consumption of tropical fish that contain toxins from algae. Toxins are "heat-stable"; i.e., fish remains contaminated even after cooking. Affects both gastrointestinal and neurological systems. Symptoms usually appear within hours of consuming contaminated fish.

SPECIALIST TO SEE: Infectious Disease Specialist

OTHER SYMPTOMS:

- Vomiting
- Tingling sensation throughout body
- Joint or muscle pain
- Dizziness
- Excessive sweating
- Hallucinations

PROGRESSION: As body absorbs poison, extremities go numb. Cold objects may feel hot, and vice versa. Symptoms typically resolve in weeks, but can last years.

TREATMENT: Mannitol (sugar alcohol used in foods) to reduce neurological symptoms.

CONTAGION: **1** 2 3 4

PAIN: 1 2 **3** 4

SUFFERING: 1 2 **3** 4

FATAL: Yes **No** Maybe

...or you might have
TOXIC SHOCK SYNDROME

WHAT IT IS: Deadly bacterial infection. Can be caused by minor skin wounds, surgery, recent childbirth, or respiratory ailment. May lead to kidney failure. Potentially fatal within 2 days. Became well-known after 1981 epidemic related to tampon use.

SPECIALIST TO SEE: Emergency Physician

OTHER SYMPTOMS:

- Muscle pain
- Nausea
- Redness in eyes, mouth, or throat
- Confusion
- Seizures
- Sunburn-like rash

PROGRESSION: Typically presents with high fever accompanied by low blood pressure and general fatigue or discomfort. After 1 week, skin can begin to peel. May lead to multi-organ failure or coma. Nearly 50 percent death rate. Known to recur.

TREATMENT: Antibiotics. Blood pressure medication. Intravenous fluids. Dialysis to treat kidney complications.

CONTAGION: **1** 2 3 4

PAIN: 1 **2** 3 4

SUFFERING: 1 2 **3** 4

FATAL: Yes No **Maybe**

If your skin is discolored...

...you might have
PELLAGRA

WHAT IT IS: Deficiency of vitamin B3 (niacin) and tryptophan in diet causes red skin lesions, diarrhea, skin inflammation, dementia, and possibly death. Common where corn, low in niacin and tryptophan, is dietary staple.

VOCAB | Sicker and quicker: Situation in which a patient is released from a hospital before having completely recovered.

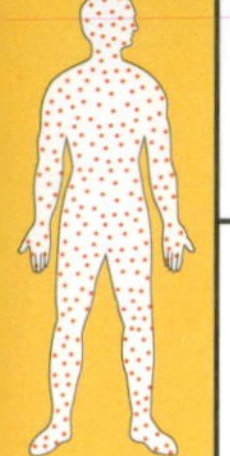

SPECIALIST TO SEE: Dietitian

OTHER SYMPTOMS:

- Reduced appetite
- Abdominal pain
- Inflammation in skin
- Weight loss
- Irritability or aggression
- Sensitivity to light
- Insomnia
- Confusion

PROGRESSION: First, skin blistering and thickening occurs. Psychiatric symptoms such as depression, irritability, and possibly delirium set in. Untreated, may result in coma and death within 5 years.

TREATMENT: Intravenous or oral niacin supplements. Addition of protein and vitamins to diet.

CONTAGION: 1 2 3 4 (**1**)

PAIN: 1 2 3 4 (**3**)

SUFFERING: 1 2 3 4 (**3**)

FATAL: Yes No Maybe (**Maybe**)

If you have pale spots on your skin...

...you might have LEPROSY

WHAT IT IS: Chronic, infectious disease caused by *Mycobacterium leprae* bacteria. Characterized by skin nodules that can lead to severe disfigurement, especially on face. Also accompanied by nerve damage and muscle weakness. Infected areas, such as fingers and toes, lose sensation, resulting in unnoticed (and potentially untreated) injuries. Spread through respiratory droplets of untreated infected persons. Also known as Hansen's disease.

SPECIALIST TO SEE: Infectious Disease Specialist

OTHER SYMPTOMS:

- Numbness
- Skin lesions
- Bloody nose
- Loss of body hair
- Blindness
- Paralysis

PROGRESSION: Long incubation period of 4 to 8 years. Then, large, damaging nodules develop on skin, impairing skin's sensitivity. May result in permanent nerve damage and disfigurement. Severe cases can lead to gangrene and loss of infected limbs.

TREATMENT: Multidrug regimen of dapsone, rifampicin, and clofazimine. Physical therapy. Prosthetics.

CONTAGION: 1 2 3 4 (**2**)

PAIN: 1 2 3 4 (**3**)

SUFFERING: 1 2 3 4 (**4**)

FATAL: Yes No Maybe (**Maybe**)

...or you might have PROTEUS SYNDROME

WHAT IT IS: Complex condition involving multiple organ systems. Affects body randomly, causing overgrowth of skin, bone, and tissue. Commonly presents as hemihyperplasia (asymmetric enlargement of head, face, or limbs). Nerve impairment often leads to cognitive disability. Exact cause unknown; may be linked to deep vein thrombosis and other disorders. Vascular destruction can result in death.

SPECIALIST TO SEE: Orthopedist, Dermatologist, Neurologist, Psychologist

OTHER SYMPTOMS:

- Skin growths or inflammation
- Tingling sensation
- Numbness
- Difficulty breathing
- Depression

PROGRESSION: Growths are accompanied by tumors that eventually cover much of body. Nerve and blood-vessel malformations develop. Frequently affects lungs. Extreme disfigurement often occurs.

TREATMENT: Surgery to remove tumors. Medication to relieve physical and neurological complications.

CONTAGION: 1 2 3 4 (**1**)

PAIN: 1 2 3 4 (**4**)

SUFFERING: 1 2 3 4 (**4**)

FATAL: Yes No Maybe (**Maybe**)

QUOTE | "Be careful about reading health books. You may die of a misprint." —Mark Twain

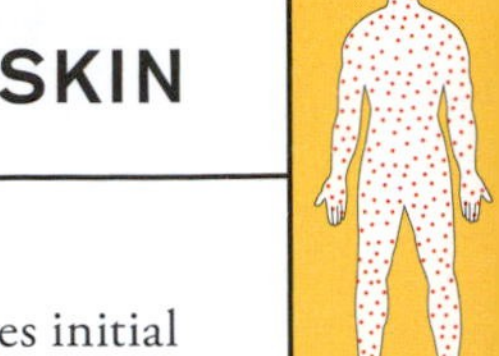

If you have thickened skin...

...you might have

DUPUYTREN'S CONTRACTURE

WHAT IT IS: Rare hand deformity. Causes thickening and scarring of fascia (connective tissue) under palms. Knots form and force one or more fingers into contracted position; fingers cannot be straightened. Most commonly affects ring and little fingers. Cause unknown; may be associated with biochemical irritants. Occurs more frequently in men.

SPECIALIST TO SEE: Primary Care Physician, Orthopedist

OTHER SYMPTOMS:

- Visible chord stretching from palm to fingertips
- Lumps on palm
- Discomfort in affected hand

PROGRESSION: First, firm lumps appear in palm. Then, one or more fingers begin to curl. May become difficult to complete everyday tasks such as shaking hands. Can recur.

TREATMENT: No known cure. Surgery to improve hand function. Radiation to inhibit development of finger contracture.

CONTAGION: **1** 2 3 4

PAIN: 1 **2** 3 4

SUFFERING: 1 2 **3** 4

FATAL: Yes **No** Maybe

...or you might have

LYMPHEDEMA

WHAT IT IS: Condition of localized fluid retention. Causes blockage of lymphatic system in arms or legs. Fluid is unable to drain, resulting in swelling. Degree of swelling ranges from barely noticeable to immense; may prevent use of limbs.

SPECIALIST TO SEE: Primary Care Physician

OTHER SYMPTOMS:

- Limited range of motion
- Infections
- Heavy sensation in limbs
- Discolored skin

PROGRESSION: Severe fatigue often accompanies initial symptoms. Affected limb swells, causing skin discoloration and, eventually, deformity (i.e., elephantiasis). May trigger serious infections such as cellulitis and lymphangitis.

TREATMENT: Exercise, massage, and compression garments.

CONTAGION: **1** 2 3 4

PAIN: 1 2 **3** 4

SUFFERING: 1 2 **3** 4

FATAL: Yes **No** Maybe

...or you might have

SCLERODERMA

WHAT IT IS: Disorder that causes progressive tightening and hardening of skin and connective tissue. Widespread rash may indicate extensive internal organ damage. Can cause painful ulcers on toes and fingers, arthritis, or damage to kidneys, heart, or lungs.

SPECIALIST TO SEE: Rheumatologist

OTHER SYMPTOMS:

- Loss of skin elasticity
- Finger curling
- Joint pain
- Muscle weakness
- Swelling in hands or feet

PROGRESSION: First, skin on hands and face becomes reddened and hardened. Condition moves up arms (and possibly feet and legs) to upper arms, thighs, abdomen, and chest. Eventual possibility of organ damage.

TREATMENT: No known cure. Nonsteroidal anti-inflammatory medication, immunosuppressants to treat symptoms.

CONTAGION: **1** 2 3 4

PAIN: 1 2 3 **4**

SUFFERING: 1 2 3 **4**

FATAL: Yes No **Maybe**

FACT | Approximately 5.3 million Americans between the ages of 18 and 54 have a social phobia.

Genetic Testing for Disease
Do You Want to Know?

In 2003, the Human Genome Project was declared complete, a 13-year effort that resulted in the successful identification of the 20,000 to 25,000 genes in human DNA. For years before that watershed moment in scientific history, however, issues were being raised about how best to use the genetic information and prowess that was to come.

In the 1960s, the first genetic testing was administered to newborn infants to determine whether the babies had inherited rare diseases, starting with phenylketonuria, which causes mental retardation but which can be prevented with a special diet if identified early. In the 1970s, genetic tests could be performed on prospective parents to ascertain whether they were both carriers of genes such as Tay Sach's. By the 1980s, prenatal genetic testing was common practice to identify abnormalities like Down syndrome in fetuses. In the 1990s, disease-causing genes were identified, including those that indicate susceptibility—but not certainty—of developing diseases.

With scientific knowledge growing at ever faster rates, we stand at the threshold of a genetic era of medicine. Scientists predict that our medical treatment will soon be customized to suit our genetic profile and those of our diseases, using molecular diagnostic tests to provide doctors with information in unprecedented detail. No longer will different types of chemotherapy be given in trial-and-error, blitzkrieg fashion; instead, medications will target the exact type of illness and the isolated site of a tumor. Another new arena for treatment would consist of altering the problematic genes themselves, whether turning them on or off or inserting or removing genetic material.

In advance of these treatments, however, one of the most heated current medical controversies is whether individuals should be tested to determine if they carry genes that either increase the likelihood or positively assure that they will develop a disease, especially in scenarios where there's nothing practical the information can provide—no earlier treatment, no changes to lifestyle, no guarantees either way whether the disease will strike or not. The result is often no more than a dark cloud lurking over a long—or short—life.

In cases where genetic analysis definitively determines that a disease will develop but there is no advance treatment, as with Huntington's disease—one of the worst fates possible, with its extreme physical and mental deterioration—the results may be clear-cut

“Don’t order a test if you lack the facts to know how to interpret the result.”
—Bernadine Healy, former NIH director

but the issues aren’t. You will or you won’t. You do or you don’t. With the knowledge of such impending doom and genetic anomaly, perhaps the only major life change would be a decision not to marry or procreate.

The grayer areas lie with those conditions for which genes indicate only susceptibility: various cancers, Alzheimer’s disease, type 2 diabetes, even depression, impulsivity, and violent tendencies. In an editorial in the *New England Journal of Medicine*, former National Institutes of Health director Bernadine Healy summed it up perfectly: “It is too early to use [breast cancer] gene testing in everyday clinical practice, because it violates a common-sense rule of medicine: don’t order a test if you lack the facts to know how to interpret the result.”

In response to testing for genes implicated in heritable breast cancer (known as BRCA1 and BRCA2), for example, some women, after watching family members ail and die from the disease, have elected to undergo prophylactic bilateral mastectomies. Some 90 percent of all breast cancer cases, however, are what’s known as “sporadic”—occurring with no genetic predisposition. BRCA1 and BRCA2 do not assure that a woman will get breast cancer, nor is it certain that prophylactic mastectomies remove all tissue at risk. On the other hand, in the case of familial adenomatous polyposis, an inherited colorectal cancer syndrome, genetic identification enables monitoring for and extraction of polyps as well as eventual removal of the colon.

Genetic testing also carries with it the risk of discrimination, most acutely with medical insurance and employment—including the disturbing possibility of testing conducted without subjects’ knowledge or approval. For this reason, many who undergo testing opt to pay for it themselves and don’t report the results to their carriers (and many such tests aren’t covered by insurance).

As one might expect, this brave new genetic world is spawning modern-day snake-oil hawkers, including the new phenomenon of unregulated direct-to-consumer testing options that bypass professional medical care and genetic counseling completely. Some claim to tailor diet, supplements, and lotions and potions to an individual’s genetic makeup, while others deliver potentially devastating information that has yet to prove useful. While potential regulation and study are under way, in the meantime, caveat DNA—let the gene carrier beware.

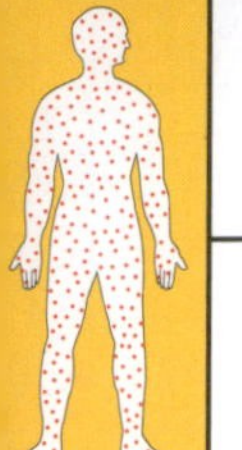

FACT | There are over 690,000 doctors in the United States licensed by the American Medical Association.

If your skin is peeling...

...you might have
TOXIC EPIDERMAL NECROLYSIS

WHAT IT IS: Life-threatening skin disorder in which large sections of epidermis (top layer of skin) separate from layers below. High risk of profound dehydration and systemic infection due to extensive skin loss. Usually caused by severe drug reaction. Complications can lead to hemorrhage or respiratory failure. Up to 40 percent mortality rate.

SPECIALIST TO SEE: Emergency Physician, Dermatologist

OTHER SYMPTOMS:
- Flesh that appears scalded or raw
- Fever

PROGRESSION: Swift onset; typically presents within 3 days. Starts with fever and cough. Then, raw, red lesions appear on skin, which soon detach. In severe cases, may lead to loss of entire epidermis.

TREATMENT: Hospitalization (typically, burn unit). Isolation. Bandages, intravenous fluids, and antibiotics.

CONTAGION:	**1**	2	3	4
PAIN:	1	2	3	**4**
SUFFERING:	1	2	3	**4**
FATAL:	Yes	No	**Maybe**	

If you have bone pain...

...you might have
GAUCHER'S DISEASE

WHAT IT IS: Inherited metabolic disorder. Large amounts of glucocerebrosides (fatty lipids) accumulate in spleen, liver, lungs, bone marrow, and, in some cases, brain. Caused by deficiency of enzyme glucocerebrosidase, which can break down fatty lipid. May be fatal.

SPECIALIST TO SEE: Hematologist, Neurologist, Orthopedist

OTHER SYMPTOMS:
- Bruising
- Fatigue
- Bleeding from nose or gums
- Enlarged liver or spleen
- Deformed bones

PROGRESSION: Lung and kidney damage may occur. Bone pain and fractures that can interfere with bone's blood supply develop, causing painful bone death in hip or shoulder. Abdominal complications related to massive organ enlargement may arise.

TREATMENT: No known cure. Enzyme replacement therapy.

CONTAGION:	**1**	2	3	4
PAIN:	1	2	3	**4**
SUFFERING:	1	2	3	**4**
FATAL:	Yes	No	**Maybe**	

...or you might have
OSTEOGENESIS IMPERFECTA

WHAT IT IS: Rare genetic disorder characterized by easily broken bones, often with little or no pressure. Results from inability to produce collagen (protein for connective tissue), cartilage, and bone. Also known as brittle-bone disease.

SPECIALIST TO SEE: Orthopedist

OTHER SYMPTOMS:
- Blue, purple, or gray color in whites of eyes
- Brittle teeth
- Loose joints
- Muscle weakness
- Hearing loss

PROGRESSION: First, broken ribs from repeated coughing and leg fractures from rolling in bed may occur. Eventually, rib cage becomes barrel-shaped, and spinal curvature may develop. Respiratory difficulties and tooth loss can also occur.

TREATMENT: Abstention from physical activity. Surgical procedures such as rodding (internal splinting of long bones) to stabilize bones and prevent deformity.

CONTAGION:	**1**	2	3	4
PAIN:	1	2	3	**4**
SUFFERING:	1	2	3	**4**
FATAL:	Yes	**No**	Maybe	

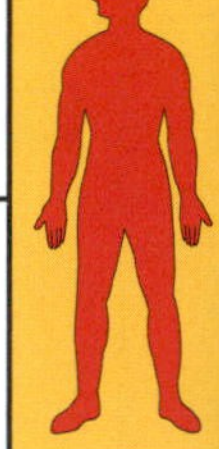

If your muscles are weak...

...you might have
ADDISON'S DISEASE

WHAT IT IS: Rare endocrine disorder. Due to attacks by immune system on adrenal cortex or pituitary gland, body produces inadequate supply of cortisol and aldosterone (both hormones). Adrenal failure, known as Addisonian crisis, may cause convulsions, vomiting, diarrhea, and loss of consciousness.

SPECIALIST TO SEE: Endocrinologist

OTHER SYMPTOMS:
- Salt cravings
- Diarrhea
- Fainting
- Darkened skin
- Nausea

PROGRESSION: Symptoms vary widely and may develop for several months. Fatigue, weakness, altered eating habits, and hyperpigmentation (darkened skin). Life-threatening Addisonian crisis may arise suddenly.

TREATMENT: Hormone-replacement therapy. Intravenous sugar, hydrocortisone, and saline solution.

CONTAGION:	**1**	2	3	4
PAIN:	1	2	**3**	4
SUFFERING:	1	2	**3**	4
FATAL:	Yes	No	**Maybe**	

...or you might have
MENINGITIS

WHAT IT IS: Infection causing inflammation of meninges (membranes surrounding brain and spinal cord). Diagnosed through lumbar puncture (spinal tap). Most cases acute, with bacteria passing from bloodstream to space around meninges. Chronic cases caused by fungal infection or slow-growing organisms may also occur.

SPECIALIST TO SEE: Infectious Disease Specialist, Neurologist

OTHER SYMPTOMS:
- Lethargy
- Nausea
- Stiff neck
- Sensitivity to light
- Back pain
- Inability to straighten legs in front of body

PROGRESSION: Swift and fierce onset, requiring emergency medical attention. Often subsides within 10 days of first presentation. Inflammation increases pressure around brain, limiting amount of blood and oxygen to brain cells. Untreated, can be fatal.

TREATMENT: Fluids and pain relievers for viral form. Hospitalization and antibiotics for bacterial form. Intravenous therapy for fungal form.

CONTAGION:	1	2	**3**	4
PAIN:	1	2	**3**	4
SUFFERING:	1	2	**3**	4
FATAL:	Yes	No	**Maybe**	

...or you might have
MULTIPLE SCLEROSIS

WHAT IT IS: Degenerative autoimmune disease that affects central nervous system. Immune system attacks myelin (fatty material surrounding nerve fibers) on neurons in brain and spinal cord. Leads to loss of muscle coordination, strength, sensation, and vision. May result in permanent disability or, in severe cases, death.

SPECIALIST TO SEE: Neurologist

OTHER SYMPTOMS:
- Muscle weakness, numbness, or tremors
- Double vision
- Clumsiness
- Loss of short-term memory
- Erectile dysfunction
- Difficulty speaking

PROGRESSION: Commonly begins with minor symptoms. Can eventually lead to cognitive impairment and loss of muscle function. Severe dehydration, malnutrition, or kidney failure may result in death.

TREATMENT: Interferon medication, steroids, and muscle relaxants. Physical therapy. Brain surgery to reduce muscle tremors.

CONTAGION:	**1**	2	3	4
PAIN:	1	2	**3**	4
SUFFERING:	1	2	3	**4**
FATAL:	Yes	No	**Maybe**	

QUOTE | "If I'd known I was going to live so long, I'd have taken better care of myself." —Leon Eldred

The World's Most Expensive Pee
Unnecessary Supplements

Though 70 percent of the American population spends a total of $23 billion annually on vitamin, mineral, and herbal supplements, there's little scientific evidence to support their positive impact. Unlike drugs, dietary supplements do not require FDA testing or approval; instead, manufacturers and distributors are responsible for ensuring that the supplements are safe and the claims on the label are true, but only when challenged. Because there are so few valid medical studies on herbal remedies, those who ingest them act as guinea pigs for their safety and efficacy. Many assert that the supplements are "natural," as if everything in nature were safe—like arsenic, which is also "all natural." Most educated health-care professionals will advise that the best way to get enough vitamins and minerals is to eat a balanced, diverse diet high in fruits and vegetables. Beyond that, some supplements—especially in high doses or when combined with certain medical conditions or prescription drugs—will do more harm than good. In 2004 alone, 60,000 vitamin overdoses resulted in 3 deaths.

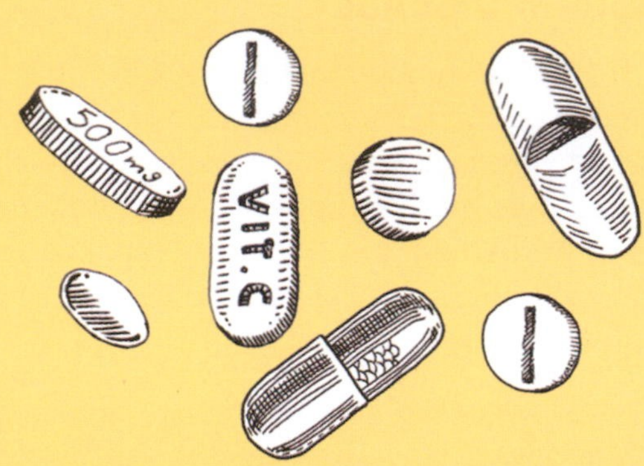

Vitamin A
Vitamin A can be toxic in high doses, potentially causing diarrhea, blurred vision, headaches, nausea, and liver and bone damage.

Vitamin C
Vitamin C is no more or less effective above daily doses of 100 mg. Anything over 500 mg per day is flushed from the body and may cause stomachaches and diarrhea.

Vitamin D
Excess vitamin D intake may cause kidney damage, calcium deposits, brain lesions, and high blood pressure.

Vitamin E
Vitamin E has been linked to heart failure and can increase the risk of bleeding, including hemorrhagic stroke.

Multi-Vitamins
Researchers at the National Cancer Institute found that men who took too many vitamins increased their risk of advanced cancer—especially prostate cancer—by 30 percent.

Iron
High doses of iron can result in kidney damage, impair calcium and zinc absorption, and increase the risk for heart disease.

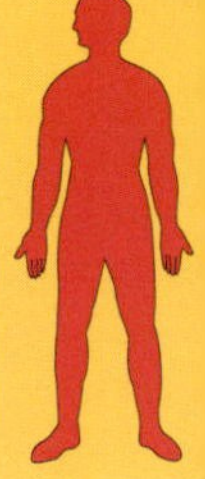

If you're trembling…

…you might have
HUNTINGTON'S DISEASE

WHAT IT IS: Genetic neurodegenerative disorder. Brain cells slowly die, causing personality change, dementia, and progressively uncontrollable muscle movement, beginning in legs. Typically presents in middle age. More rapid progression in younger adults. Often described as combination of Alzheimer's and Parkinson's diseases.

SPECIALIST TO SEE: Neurologist

OTHER SYMPTOMS:
- Muscle spasms
- Muscle rigidity
- Difficulty walking
- Slurred speech
- Dementia
- Drastic personality changes

PROGRESSION: Usually deteriorates over 10 to 15 years. Difficulty walking, swallowing, speaking, and eating develop and intensify. Eventually, severe cognitive and physical disability occur. Ultimately fatal.

TREATMENT: Antidepressants, tranquilizers, and antipsychotics. Physical therapy. Long-term home care.

CONTAGION: **1** 2 3 4

PAIN: 1 2 3 **4**

SUFFERING: 1 2 3 **4**

FATAL: **Yes** No Maybe

…or you might have
MERCURY POISONING

WHAT IT IS: Overexposure to mercury causes widespread effects on central nervous system, endocrine system, kidneys, and mouth. May be acute or chronic. Exposure comes from environment, usually through fertilizers and wastewater disposal. Inhaled mercury is most dangerous, followed by mercury absorbed through skin. Exposure duration dictates outcome, ranging from no effects to death.

SPECIALIST TO SEE: Primary Care Physician, Toxicologist

OTHER SYMPTOMS:
- Vomiting
- Difficulty breathing
- Metallic taste in mouth
- Chronic coughing

PROGRESSION: Depends on type and length of exposure. Mild exposure may result in no symptoms. High exposure may lead to incurable lung impairment, followed by brain damage and sometimes death.

TREATMENT: Suctioning of lungs to remove mercury. Intravenous fluids. Breathing tubes.

CONTAGION: **1** 2 3 4

PAIN: 1 2 **3** 4

SUFFERING: 1 2 **3** 4

FATAL: Yes No **Maybe**

…or you might have
TOXOPLASMOSIS

WHAT IT IS: Infectious disease caused by parasite *Toxoplasma gondii*. Typically found in infected cat feces or dirty cat litter; may also be contracted from undercooked meat. Pregnancy and weakened immune systems increase risk. Severe cases can entail brain or eye damage.

SPECIALIST TO SEE: Infectious Disease Specialist

OTHER SYMPTOMS:
- Swollen lymph nodes
- Muscle aches
- Extreme fatigue

PROGRESSION: May remain asymptomatic. Slow onset of symptoms; often mistaken for flu or other viral infections. Often persists for one month or longer. Not fatal in adulthood, but can cause infant death if passed from mother to fetus.

TREATMENT: If otherwise healthy, may self-resolve within weeks to months. Sulfadiazine (antibiotic) and pyrimethamine (antiprotozoal) for compromised immune system.

CONTAGION: **1** 2 3 4

PAIN: 1 **2** 3 4

SUFFERING: 1 **2** 3 4

FATAL: Yes **No** Maybe

FACT | The state of Florida has the highest malpractice insurance premiums in the United States.

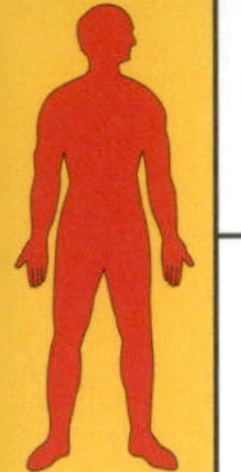

FACT | About 54 million Americans are pre-diabetic.

If you have fever and chills...

...you might have
BACILLARY ANGIOMATOSIS

WHAT IT IS: Infection caused by *Bartonella* bacteria, often transmitted through cat scratch or bite. Blood cells clump together beneath skin and other organs, forming tumorlike masses or lesions. Fatal if not treated promptly.

SPECIALIST TO SEE: Infectious Disease Specialist, Dermatologist

OTHER SYMPTOMS:
- Purple skin lesions
- Firm nodules under skin
- Reduced appetite
- Nausea
- Vomiting

PROGRESSION: First, tiny, purple or red lesions form on skin. Then, firm nodules develop and may be accompanied by fever, sweats, chills, and tender lymph nodes. Without timely treatment, causes death.

TREATMENT: Antibiotics for up to 4 weeks. Wound drainage.

CONTAGION: 1 **2** 3 4

PAIN: 1 **2** 3 4

SUFFERING: 1 2 **3** 4

FATAL: Yes No **Maybe**

...or you might have
BRUCELLOSIS

WHAT IT IS: Infection caused by *Brucella* bacteria, found in contaminated dairy products from diseased cows. Bacteria may also be inhaled or contracted through open wound. Sheep, goats, deer, and pigs can spread bacteria; person-to-person transmission is rare.

SPECIALIST TO SEE: Infectious Disease Specialist

OTHER SYMPTOMS:
- Weakness throughout body
- Joint pain
- Headache
- Arthritis

PROGRESSION: First, rising and falling fever, followed by systemic weakness, joint pain, and fatigue. Finally, if untreated, can spread throughout body and cause long-term debilitating effects.

TREATMENT: Antibiotics.

CONTAGION: 1 **2** 3 4

PAIN: 1 **2** 3 4

SUFFERING: 1 2 **3** 4

FATAL: Yes **No** Maybe

...or you might have
CYSTITIS

WHAT IT IS: Bladder infection or inflammation. Results in frequent painful, burning urination. Caused when bacteria enters urinary tract and multiplies. Occurs more often in women, due to shorter urethra. May lead to pain during sexual intercourse.

SPECIALIST TO SEE: Urologist, Gynecologist

OTHER SYMPTOMS:
- Dark, cloudy, or foul-smelling urine
- Bloody urine
- Abdominal pain
- Shoulder pain

PROGRESSION: May start as mild discomfort, pressure, or intense bladder pain. Often accompanied by confusion if pain becomes severe. Untreated, can lead to kidney infection.

TREATMENT: Antibiotics such as amoxicillin and ciprofloxacin. Increased fluid intake to flush out urinary system.

CONTAGION: **1** 2 3 4

PAIN: 1 **2** 3 4

SUFFERING: 1 **2** 3 4

FATAL: Yes **No** Maybe

...or you might have
DENGUE FEVER

WHAT IT IS: Mosquito-borne flu-like viral infection that poses worldwide public health problems. Cannot be spread from person to person. Characterized by fever and significant pain; known as "break-bone fever." No specific treatment.

SPECIALIST TO SEE: Infectious Disease Specialist

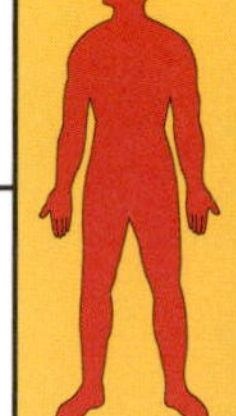

OTHER SYMPTOMS:

- Headache
- Joint or muscle pain
- Reduced appetite
- Vomiting
- Cold or clammy skin
- Pain behind eyes
- Rash

PROGRESSION: Typically presents as high fever, rash, and headache. Joint pain and migraines may follow, in addition to nausea and vomiting. Commonly, rash appears 3 to 4 days later. Symptoms typically persist for 7 to 10 days.

TREATMENT: No known cure. Intravenous fluids.

CONTAGION: **1** 2 3 4

PAIN: 1 2 3 **4**

SUFFERING: 1 2 **3** 4

FATAL: Yes No **Maybe**

...or you might have GUINEA WORM

WHAT IT IS: Parasitic infection caused by consumption of water contaminated with fleas carrying *Dracunulus* worm larvae. Once full-grown, worm may measure 3 feet long. Not fatal, though may result in long-term effects, including permanent paralysis if untreated.

SPECIALIST TO SEE: Infectious Disease Specialist

OTHER SYMPTOMS:

- Swelling, pain, or burning sensation
- Blisters
- Oozing skin lesions
- Locking sensation in joints
- Nausea, vomiting, or diarrhea
- Dizziness

PROGRESSION: As worms spread throughout body, symptoms emerge. Oozing skin lesions present when adult worms surface, confirming diagnosis.

TREATMENT: Removal of worm from open lesion. Worm is wrapped around thin strip of wood until completely expelled. May take several days or weeks for complete removal.

CONTAGION: **1** 2 3 4

PAIN: 1 2 **3** 4

SUFFERING: 1 2 3 **4**

FATAL: Yes **No** Maybe

...or you might have MALARIA

WHAT IT IS: Infectious disease contracted from parasite-carrying mosquitoes. Spreads throughout body, producing severe flu-like illness; without medication, death likely. Pregnant women and international travelers are particularly susceptible. Leading cause of death worldwide. Mosquito repellent can help prevent infection.

SPECIALIST TO SEE: Emergency Physician, Infectious Disease Specialist, Pathologist

OTHER SYMPTOMS:

- Excessive sweating
- Fatigue
- Headache
- Diarrhea

PROGRESSION: Symptoms typically occur within 2 weeks following mosquito bite, but may take up to 1 year. Most cases resolve with medication. Untreated, some cases can be fatal within hours.

TREATMENT: Antimalarial medication (e.g., chloroquine, mefloquine, primaquine).

CONTAGION: 1 **2** 3 4

PAIN: 1 **2** 3 4

SUFFERING: 1 2 **3** 4

FATAL: Yes No **Maybe**

...or you might have TYPHOID FEVER

WHAT IT IS: Potentially life-threatening infection by *Salmonella typhi* bacteria, found in sewage, contaminated food, and water. After ingestion, bacteria travel through bloodstream and multiply in intestines and liver. Easily acquired during international travel.

SPECIALIST TO SEE: Infectious Disease Specialist

OTHER SYMPTOMS:

- Headache
- Fatigue

QUOTE | "If the doctor told me I had 6 minutes to live, I'd type a little faster." —Isaac Asimov

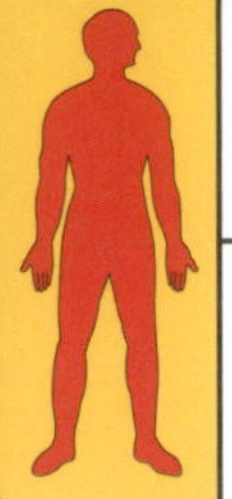

FACT | A taste bud lives for only 10 days.

- Abdominal pain
- Reduced appetite
- Diarrhea

PROGRESSION: First, fever may reach 104 degrees followed by chills, nosebleeds, lethargy, hallucinations, and delirium. Then, small, flat, rose-colored spots appear on abdomen and chest. Intestinal hemorrhage may develop. Untreated, 20 percent likelihood of death.

TREATMENT: Intravenous fluids and electrolytes. Antibiotics.

CONTAGION:	1	**2**	3	4
PAIN:	1	2	**3**	4
SUFFERING:	1	2	**3**	4
FATAL:	Yes	No	**Maybe**	

If you sweat excessively...

...you might have

SPLEEN CANCER

WHAT IT IS: Malignant white blood cell deposits form tumors in spleen. Generally goes undetected unless found in conjunction with another disease, such as non-Hodgkin's lymphoma or ovarian cancer, that has metastasized throughout body.

SPECIALIST TO SEE: Oncologist

OTHER SYMPTOMS:

- Fever
- Diarrhea
- Weight loss
- Jaundice
- Night sweats
- Itching skin
- Rash

Why They're Called Lepers

Until the late 19th century, leprosy was believed to be hereditary, a curse, or evidence of God's wrath on sinners. In 1873, a Norwegian doctor discovered its true cause: *Mycobacterium leprae*. Once the disease was revealed as contagious, sufferers were widely quarantined into lepers' colonies.

A chronic, infectious disease spread in humans via respiratory discharge, leprosy's early manifestations include numbness and hot and cold sensations, while advanced cases result in skin lesions and paralysis. Because it kills nerve endings, lepers repeatedly injure themselves, causing skin deformations and loss of atrophied appendages. Even when allowed to live among the general population, lepers have faced vicious discrimination. So acute was the fear of contracting this disfiguring malady that patients with unrelated skin conditions, such as eczema, were often sent to live with the lepers—and subsequently contracted leprosy.

In the mid-1970s, the success of a drug cocktail consisting of dapsone, rifampicin, and clofazimine signaled the beginning of the end of leprosy. Vestiges of the disease remain, however, with more than 100 cases diagnosed annually in the United States. Globally, 400,000 new infections were reported in 2004, and as many as 2 million people are still permanently disabled from the disease.

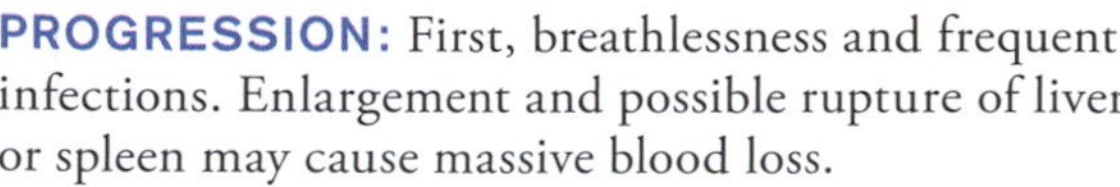

PROGRESSION: First, breathlessness and frequent infections. Enlargement and possible rupture of liver or spleen may cause massive blood loss.

TREATMENT: Splenectomy (total or partial surgical removal of spleen). Chemotherapy.

CONTAGION: **1** 2 3 4

PAIN: 1 2 **3** 4

SUFFERING: 1 2 **3** 4

FATAL: Yes No **Maybe**

If you have night sweats...

...you might have

ENDOCARDITIS

WHAT IT IS: Bacterial or fungal infection of endocardium (inner lining of heart or heart valves). Bacteria from mouth and respiratory system enter bloodstream and spread to heart, lodging in lining of blood vessels. Prior heart disease increases risk. Fatal if not treated promptly.

SPECIALIST TO SEE: Cardiologist

OTHER SYMPTOMS:

- Irregular heartbeat
- Fever or chills
- Reduced appetite
- Fatigue
- General discomfort

PROGRESSION: Bacteria enter heart and multiply. Sudden onset of fever and chills. Infection may spread to other parts of body, causing enlarged spleen or heart failure. May result in death.

TREATMENT: Antibiotics over several weeks. Surgery to repair damaged heart valves.

CONTAGION: **1** 2 3 4

PAIN: 1 2 **3** 4

SUFFERING: 1 2 **3** 4

FATAL: Yes No **Maybe**

...or you might have

HYPERHIDROSIS

WHAT IT IS: Excessive sweating due to overactive sweat glands. Cause is unclear, but acute cases may be triggered by food, drink, certain smells, hyperthyroidism, tuberculosis, or low blood sugar. Not life-threatening, but embarrassing. Severe cases lead to emotional distress and interfere with daily life.

SPECIALIST TO SEE: Primary Care Physician

OTHER SYMPTOMS:

- Excessive sweating
- Body odor
- Anxiety
- Warts

PROGRESSION: Acute instances sparked by spicy food, stress, or heat usually resolve once causal factor is removed. With chronic cases, excessive sweating and strong odor persist. Fungal infections, jock itch, and bacterial infections may develop.

TREATMENT: No known cure. Botox injections to paralyze nerves that control sweat glands. Surgical removal of sweat glands.

CONTAGION: **1** 2 3 4

PAIN: **1** 2 3 4

SUFFERING: 1 2 **3** 4

FATAL: Yes **No** Maybe

If you're excessively thirsty...

...you might have

CHRONIC KIDNEY DISEASE

WHAT IT IS: Slow and progressive loss of kidney function. Results in inability to remove waste from blood. Sometimes hereditary, but can be caused by injury, high blood pressure, or diabetes complications. Chest tightness, heart inflammation, and poor blood clotting may occur. Waste-product accumulation in brain can cause cognitive disorders.

SPECIALIST TO SEE: Nephrologist

FACT | Every year in the United States, there are 44,000 to 98,000 medical error–related deaths.

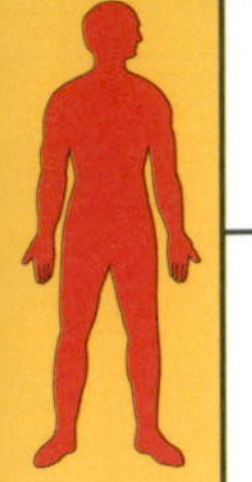

FACT | 1 in 5 Americans have genital herpes, but 90 percent don't know it.

OTHER SYMPTOMS:
- Headache
- Fatigue
- Weakness throughout body
- Reduced appetite
- Nausea
- Fluid retention

PROGRESSION: Initially, often asymptomatic. Gradually progresses through 5 stages, from accrual of excess protein to total renal failure, which may result in death.

TREATMENT: Dialysis or organ transplant.

CONTAGION:	**1**	2	3	4
PAIN:	1	2	**3**	4
SUFFERING:	1	2	3	**4**
FATAL:	Yes	No	**Maybe**	

...or you might have HYPOKALEMIA

WHAT IT IS: Low concentration of potassium in blood leads to weakness and heart abnormalities. May be caused by low potassium intake, prolonged diarrhea or vomiting, or use of diuretics. Can also be associated with various underlying conditions, such as liver disease and heart failure.

SPECIALIST TO SEE: Primary Care Physician

OTHER SYMPTOMS:
- Irregular heartbeat
- Weakness or fatigue
- Muscle cramping
- Constipation

PROGRESSION: First presents with weakness and fatigue. Can result in cardiac arrhythmia, leading to cardiac arrest and death. May also affect nerve activity and multiple organ systems.

TREATMENT: Increase potassium in diet. Intravenous potassium in severe cases.

CONTAGION:	**1**	2	3	4
PAIN:	1	**2**	3	4
SUFFERING:	1	2	**3**	4
FATAL:	Yes	No	**Maybe**	

If you have overwhelming body odor...

...you might have HYPERTHYROIDISM

WHAT IT IS: Also known as overactive thyroid. Caused by overproduction of hormone thyroxine, which regulates metabolism and heart rate. Excess amounts can cause rapid weight loss and, in serious cases, heart failure. Most people respond well once diagnosed and treated. If ignored, may be fatal.

SPECIALIST TO SEE: Endocrinologist

OTHER SYMPTOMS:
- Rapid or irregular heartbeat
- Heart palpitations
- Anxiety
- Excessive sweating

PROGRESSION: Goiter (enlarged thyroid gland) may appear as swelling at base of neck. Heat intolerance and fatigue during regular activities occur. Light sensitivity combined with blurry or double vision also possible. May lead to congestive heart failure.

TREATMENT: Antithyroid medication and radioactive iodine to slow hormone production. Thyroidectomy (surgical removal of thyroid).

CONTAGION:	**1**	2	3	4
PAIN:	1	**2**	3	4
SUFFERING:	1	2	**3**	4
FATAL:	Yes	No	**Maybe**	

...or you might have TRIMETHYLAMINURIA

WHAT IT IS: Rare genetic disorder consisting of inability to break down dietary trimethylamine (TMA), causing excess of chemical in urine, sweat, breath, and bodily secretions. Powerful aroma derives from same chemical as present in rotting fish, resulting in objectionable, overpowering body odor. Often called "fish-odor syndrome."

SPECIALIST TO SEE: Endocrinologist

OTHER SYMPTOMS:
- High blood pressure
- Rapid heartbeat
- Depression

PROGRESSION: First, strong fishy odor becomes noticeable. Then, hypertension and rapid heart rate may develop. Can lead to social ostracism, clinical depression, and suicidal tendencies.

TREATMENT: No known cure. Low doses of antibiotics to reduce bacteria in intestines.

CONTAGION:	**1**	2	3	4
PAIN:	1	**2**	3	4
SUFFERING:	1	2	3	**4**
FATAL:	Yes	**No**	Maybe	

If you're drowsy...

...you might have

NARCOLEPSY

WHAT IT IS: Chronic neurological disorder characterized by brain's inability to normally regulate sleep-wake cycles. Leads to overwhelming excessive daytime sleepiness (EDS), even after adequate nighttime sleep. Napping at inappropriate times and places may occur. Typically diagnosed 10 to 15 years after onset of initial symptoms. Cause unknown.

SPECIALIST TO SEE: Neurologist

OTHER SYMPTOMS:

- Persistent fatigue
- Frequent, brief napping
- Muscle weakness
- Hallucinations

PROGRESSION: Abnormal sleep patterns and EDS are primary symptoms. Cataplexy (loss of muscle tone), temporary paralysis, hallucinations, and erratic behavior also possible.

TREATMENT: No known cure. Antidepressants and stimulants to alleviate symptoms.

CONTAGION:	**1**	2	3	4
PAIN:	**1**	2	3	4
SUFFERING:	1	2	**3**	4
FATAL:	Yes	**No**	Maybe	

...or you might have

SLEEP APNEA

WHAT IT IS: Repeated breathing stoppage while sleeping, often hundreds of times overnight. Brain frequently instigates awakening to prompt resumption of breathing, resulting in poor sleep quality. Very common, especially among overweight males over age 40. Potentially life-threatening if accompanied with underlying heart disease; low blood oxygen incites cardiac event. Requires immediate medical attention.

SPECIALIST TO SEE: Sleep Specialist

OTHER SYMPTOMS:

- Excessive fatigue
- Loud snoring
- Headaches
- Dry mouth
- Confusion

PROGRESSION: First, may cause hypertension and other cardiovascular complications due to drop in blood-oxygen levels. Then, memory problems, weight gain, and gastroesophageal reflux disease occur. Worsens with age, and potentially fatal.

TREATMENT: Weight loss and sleeping on side. Mouth devices to keep airways open.

CONTAGION:	**1**	2	3	4
PAIN:	**1**	2	3	4
SUFFERING:	1	2	**3**	4
FATAL:	Yes	No	**Maybe**	

If you're tired...

...you might have

ANEMIA

WHAT IT IS: Common blood disorder. Red blood cell count or hemoglobin level is too low, caused by blood loss, iron or vitamin deficiency, infections, and some types of cancer. Can be temporary or long-term, mild or severe.

SPECIALIST TO SEE: Hematologist

FACT | Almost 4 percent of hospitalizations lead to adverse medical reactions.

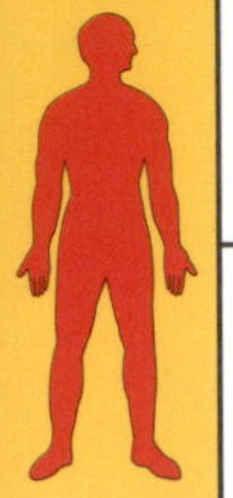

OTHER SYMPTOMS:

- Headache
- Pale skin or nails
- Numbness or coldness in hands and feet
- Decreased libido
- Difficulty sleeping

PROGRESSION: Early symptoms may be mild and unnoticeable. Eventually, cognitive difficulties result. Untreated, can cause rapid or irregular heartbeat, congestive heart failure, or enlarged spleen.

TREATMENT: Vitamin B12 or iron supplements for deficiencies. In severe cases, blood transfusion to boost red blood cell count.

CONTAGION:	**1**	2	3	4
PAIN:	1	**2**	3	4
SUFFERING:	1	**2**	3	4
FATAL:	Yes	**No**	Maybe	

...or you might have

BOWEL TUMOR

WHAT IT IS: Benign or malignant mass that grows in wall of colon. Crohn's disease and intestinal polyps increase risk. Recovery dependent on severity of disease and likelihood of successful surgical resection.

SPECIALIST TO SEE: Gastroenterologist, Oncologist

OTHER SYMPTOMS:

- Diarrhea
- Constipation
- Abdominal pain
- Vomiting
- Anemia

PROGRESSION: Usually starts without symptoms, often leading to misdiagnosis. Bloody stool and gastrointestinal bleeding develop. Blockage created by growth can cause sudden rupture of colon, resulting in severe pain and dangerous drop in blood pressure.

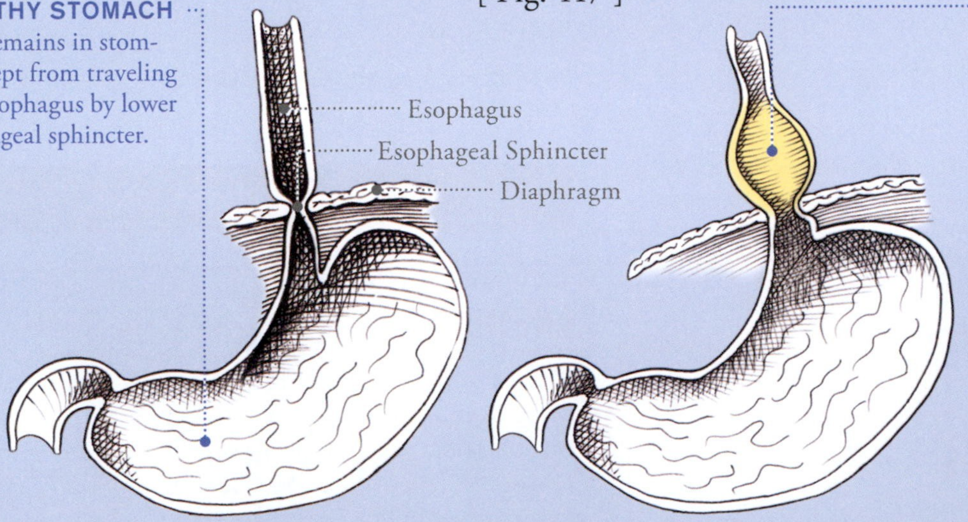

Hiatal Hernia

[Fig. 117]

For disease description, see page 153.

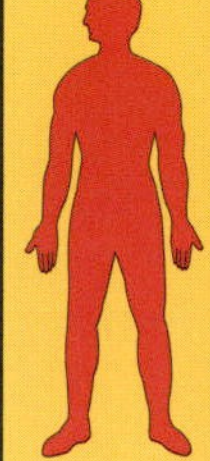

TREATMENT: Surgery. Radiation or chemotherapy.

CONTAGION: 1 2 3 4

PAIN: 1 2 3 4

SUFFERING: 1 2 3 4

FATAL: Yes No Maybe

...or you might have

TOXIC HEPATITIS

WHAT IT IS: Metabolism of chemicals found in drugs, cleaning solvents, or industrial pollutants can produce unstable, toxic by-products that attack liver, causing inflammation and scarring. Frequent sources of toxicity include dry cleaning products, pain and fever medication, and anabolic steroids, though nearly all drugs have been implicated. Excessive alcohol consumption increases drug toxicity.

SPECIALIST TO SEE: Toxicologist, Hepatologist

OTHER SYMPTOMS:

- Fatigue
- Dark-colored urine
- Nausea, vomiting, or diarrhea
- Reduced appetite
- Jaundice

PROGRESSION: Can develop abruptly or over several months or years following exposure to toxic substance. Symptoms often clear after removal of toxin; however, may cause irreversible cirrhosis (scarring of liver tissue) or liver failure. Closely resembles other forms of liver disease.

TREATMENT: Prevention of further exposure to chemical.

CONTAGION: 1 2 3 4

PAIN: 1 2 3 4

SUFFERING: 1 2 3 4

FATAL: Yes No Maybe

If you have insomnia...

...you might have

FIBROMYALGIA

WHAT IT IS: Chronic condition characterized by extreme fatigue and pain throughout body. Occurs more often in women. Typically diagnosed in middle age. May be caused by hypersensitive nerve cells or neurotransmitter imbalance.

SPECIALIST TO SEE: Rheumatologist

OTHER SYMPTOMS:

- Weakness in limbs
- Stiff joints
- Irritable bowel syndrome
- Headache
- Heightened skin sensitivity

PROGRESSION: Usually starts following major surgery or physical trauma. Slow onset of symptoms often misdiagnosed in children as "growing pains." Pain eventually spreads throughout body, limiting physical activities.

TREATMENT: No known cure. Acetaminophen, pain relievers, antidepressants, muscle relaxants, and sleep aids to treat symptoms.

CONTAGION: 1 2 3 4

PAIN: 1 2 3 4

SUFFERING: 1 2 3 4

FATAL: Yes No Maybe

...or you might have

HEMORRHOIDS

WHAT IT IS: Enlarged or swollen veins in anus or rectum, resulting in bleeding, pain, and itching. Often caused by obesity, pregnancy, or chronic diarrhea or constipation.

SPECIALIST TO SEE: Gastroenterologist, Proctologist

OTHER SYMPTOMS:

- Itching, burning, or pain in rectum
- Bleeding from rectum
- Mucus in stool

PROGRESSION: First, condition may be fairly unobtrusive. Then, swelling becomes external, causing anal bleeding, mucus discharge, and severe emotional and physical discomfort.

TREATMENT: For mild cases, topical medication and change in dietary and toilet habits. Severe cases require hemorrhoidectomy, rubber-band ligation (binding) to cut off circulation, or stapling to block blood flow.

CONTAGION: 1 2 3 4

PAIN: 1 2 3 4

SUFFERING: 1 2 3 4

FATAL: Yes No Maybe

FACT | Most germs can live on doorknobs and other dry surfaces for 2 to 3 hours; if the surface is wet, it's longer.

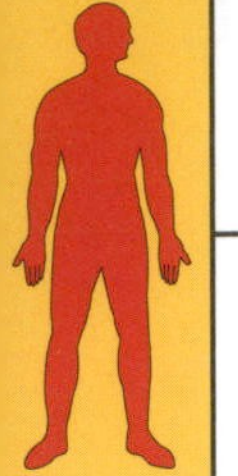

If you have nausea...

...you might have
GIARDIASIS

WHAT IT IS: Common infection caused by parasite *Giardia lamblia*. Spread when water is contaminated with raw sewage. Often contracted from community pools, water parks, and lakes. May be asymptomatic, but usually marked by frequent, watery diarrhea. May recur after treatment.

SPECIALIST TO SEE: Primary Care Physician

OTHER SYMPTOMS:

- Persistent diarrhea
- Cramping
- Weight loss
- Bloating

PROGRESSION: Within weeks after exposure, abdominal cramping and loose stools occur, often accompanied by fever. Symptoms usually resolve in 7 to 10 days, but may persist for months.

TREATMENT: Metronidazole (antibiotic).

CONTAGION: 1 **2** 3 4

PAIN: **1** 2 3 4

SUFFERING: **1** 2 3 4

FATAL: Yes **No** Maybe

...or you might have
HYPONATREMIA

WHAT IT IS: Condition caused by dangerously low levels of sodium in blood. Results from excessive vomiting, diarrhea, extended use of diuretics, and kidney disease. Sodium in blood helps regulate blood pressure; extreme deficiency can be life-threatening, especially in acute cases that develop in 48 hours or less.

SPECIALIST TO SEE: Primary Care Physician, Nephrologist

OTHER SYMPTOMS:

- Vomiting
- Headache
- Reduced appetite
- Fatigue
- Restlessness

PROGRESSION: Onset may be sudden or may span several weeks. Symptoms gradually worsen, moving from vomiting and headache to disorientation and hallucinations. Prompt diagnosis, through blood and urine tests, is critical. Untreated, can lead to coma or even death.

TREATMENT: Intravenous fluids. Reduction of water and salt intake. Supplemental oxygen.

CONTAGION: **1** 2 3 4

PAIN: 1 **2** 3 4

SUFFERING: 1 2 **3** 4

FATAL: Yes No **Maybe**

...or you might have
ROCKY MOUNTAIN SPOTTED FEVER

WHAT IT IS: Infection caused by *Rickettsia rickettsii* bacteria, transmitted by ticks. Occurs primarily during late spring and early summer months. Name derived from characteristic red rash that eventually covers entire body. Benign if treated promptly.

SPECIALIST TO SEE: Primary Care Physician

OTHER SYMPTOMS:

- Fever or chills
- Headache
- Pain throughout body
- Sore throat
- Vomiting
- Full body rash

PROGRESSION: Incubation period of 5 to 10 days follows tick bite. Initial signs are fever, nausea, and headache. Rash appears on ankles and wrists 2 to 5 days after onset of fever, eventually spreading over entire body.

TREATMENT: Antibiotics.

CONTAGION: **1** 2 3 4

PAIN: 1 **2** 3 4

SUFFERING: 1 2 **3** 4

FATAL: Yes **No** Maybe

...or you might have
SALMONELLOSIS

WHAT IT IS: Infection caused by *Salmonella* bacteria, contracted by consuming contaminated water or food such as raw meat, poultry, and egg yolks. Common among HIV-positive persons. Preventable

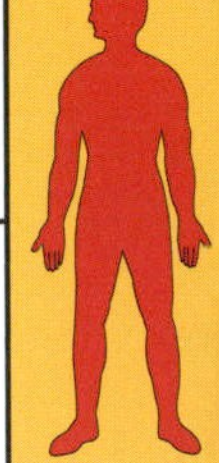

through proper handling and cooking of food. Weakened immune system heightens risk of potentially fatal infection.

SPECIALIST TO SEE: Primary Care Physician

OTHER SYMPTOMS:

- Diarrhea
- Watery stool
- Fever
- Vomiting

PROGRESSION: Symptoms develop within hours or several days after exposure. Vomiting and diarrhea can cause dehydration. May resolve within days, but in some cases, effects continue for up to 3 weeks.

TREATMENT: Antibiotics.

CONTAGION: 1 **2** 3 4

PAIN: 1 **2** 3 4

SUFFERING: 1 **2** 3 4

FATAL: Yes No **Maybe**

If you're vomiting...

...you might have

MELIOIDOSIS

WHAT IT IS: Infection by *Burkholderia pseudomallei* bacteria, usually through contact with contaminated soil or water. May also be spread from person to person through body fluids. Potential biological warfare agent. Fatal in some cases.

SPECIALIST TO SEE: Infectious Disease Specialist

OTHER SYMPTOMS:

- Fever
- Muscle pain
- Headache
- Chest pain
- Dry cough

PROGRESSION: Symptoms may appear within 2 days or up to several years after exposure. Localized infection may spread to respiratory and circulatory systems. Bloodstream infections are most serious and can be fatal.

TREATMENT: Antibiotics.

CONTAGION: 1 **2** 3 4

PAIN: 1 **2** 3 4

SUFFERING: 1 2 **3** 4

FATAL: Yes No **Maybe**

...or you might have

SCHISTOSOMIASIS

WHAT IT IS: Often called "swimmer's itch." Parasitic disease found in tropical regions. Caused by contact with or ingestion of contaminated freshwater. *Schistosomes* (parasitic worms) reproduce in blood vessels, releasing up to 3,000 eggs per day.

SPECIALIST TO SEE: Infectious Disease Specialist

OTHER SYMPTOMS:

- Rash
- Itching skin
- Diarrhea
- Fatigue
- Muscle pain
- Coughing

PROGRESSION: Most eggs lodge in mesenteric veins, which carry blood from intestines to liver. Eggs may become stuck in liver or kidney, causing hepatosplenomegaly (enlarged liver and spleen). In some cases, central nervous system complications occur after eggs are deposited in brain.

TREATMENT: Anthelminthic (anti-worm) medication to reduce worm infections.

CONTAGION: **1** 2 3 4

PAIN: 1 2 **3** 4

SUFFERING: 1 2 **3** 4

FATAL: Yes **No** Maybe

If you lose your appetite...

...you might have

HIATAL HERNIA

WHAT IT IS: Uppermost section of stomach pushes through small opening in diaphragm and enters chest cavity. Acid builds up, causing reflux, heartburn, and other symptoms. Torsion of stomach can occur, completely shutting off blood supply. Obesity and smoking increase risk. Tends to affect women more than men.

FACT | More than 3 billion prescriptions are dispensed each year in the United States.

Your Ailment Resumé

Medical Records Past, Present, and Future

During medical exams, we take for granted that the doctor will consult and update our medical records, comparing current data with previous visits and noting present medications before prescribing new ones. Before the 20th century, however, medical records weren't kept in a systematic way. Ledger books were often used for jotting notes, sequenced chronologically rather than according to patient. In a hospital setting, different departments kept individual ledger books. Unifying a patient's medical history was difficult, if not impossible.

In 1907 at the Mayo Clinic, Dr. Henry Plummer and his assistant, Mabel Root, debuted their innovation in hospital record-keeping: the single-unit record, organized by patient and bringing together all documents, including doctors' notes and test results, in one file. Taking a cue from factories and businesses, Plummer also developed a system of pneumatic tubes and conveyors for transporting the records through the hospital. Simple but effective, the single-unit record was rapidly adopted by medical institutions around the world.

As with so many types of information, the next medical-record innovation was the computer. Though the value of computerized medical records has long been recognized, thus far it's been confined to individual hospitals and providers and used primarily for administrative rather than clinical purposes. Determining which systems to carry across multiple providers for interoperability and if and how to convert existing paper documentation have contributed to the slow implementation, complicated by privacy concerns. Many national governments—whether overseeing a national health service or just engaged in research, persuasion, and legislation—and large health-care providers have promised universal implementation of electronic medical records by around 2015.

Once our medical records are computerized, we'll have the terrifyingly convenient option of implanting radio-frequency identification (RFID) chips containing all our records—already in use by some at-risk patients.

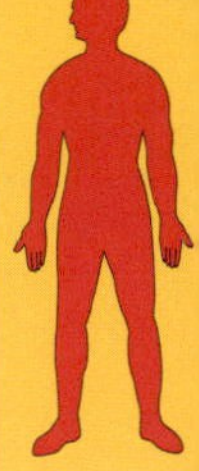

SPECIALIST TO SEE: Gastroenterologist

OTHER SYMPTOMS:

- Indigestion
- Belching
- Chest pain
- Difficulty swallowing

PROGRESSION: First, few symptoms present. Then, mild heartburn and belching may progress into chest pain; often mistaken for heart attack. Complications may arise, including Barrett's esophagus (acid-caused cell damage) and esophageal cancer.

TREATMENT: Antacids, proton-pump inhibitors, and hydrogen blockers to treat overproduction of acid. Surgery if symptoms persist chronically.

CONTAGION: **1** 2 3 4

PAIN: 1 **2** 3 4

SUFFERING: 1 2 **3** 4

FATAL: Yes **No** Maybe

...or you might have

VIRAL HEPATITIS

WHAT IT IS: Infection, usually by hepatitis viruses A, B, or C, targeting liver. Hepatitis A virus often transmitted through fecal-oral route or direct contact with carrier; B virus may be transmitted through sexual contact, contaminated needles, or blood transfusions; C virus can be contracted through contact with infected blood. B and C variants may cause chronic or relapsing complications, frequently necessitating liver transplant, and possibly resulting in fatal liver failure.

SPECIALIST TO SEE: Infectious Disease Specialist, Gastroenterologist, Hepatologist

OTHER SYMPTOMS:

- Fatigue
- Fever
- Dark-colored urine
- Nausea, vomiting, or diarrhea
- Reduced appetite
- Jaundice

PROGRESSION: May develop without symptoms. Fever, arthritis, and edema can present for up to 3 weeks before jaundice sets in. Then, respiratory and gastrointestinal complications arise, often accompanied by dark urine and pale stool coloration. Finally, jaundice and possible skin lesions appear.

TREATMENT: Hospitalization. Antiviral medication. Liver transplant.

CONTAGION: 1 2 **3** 4

PAIN: 1 2 **3** 4

SUFFERING: 1 2 **3** 4

FATAL: Yes No **Maybe**

If you have unintended weight gain...

...you might have

DERCUM'S DISEASE

WHAT IT IS: Rare, progressive condition characterized by lipomas (fatty deposits) covering arms, legs, and torso. Pain and swelling result. Occurs most often in middle-aged women. Cause unknown. Often results in obese appearance.

SPECIALIST TO SEE: Endocrinologist

OTHER SYMPTOMS:

- Pain throughout body
- Stinging pain in fatty tissue
- Hardened skin folds
- Muscle weakness

PROGRESSION: Intensely painful fatty growths remain for months after onset. May disappear, leaving pendulous skin folds. Progressively, more growths appear, with increasing pain. Pulmonary or cardiac complications result if fatty growths reach heart or lungs, often leading to death.

TREATMENT: No known cure or effective treatment.

CONTAGION: **1** 2 3 4

PAIN: 1 2 3 **4**

SUFFERING: 1 2 3 **4**

FATAL: Yes No **Maybe**

If you have unintended weight loss...

...you might have

KRABBE DISEASE

WHAT IT IS: Genetic disorder in which deficiency of galactosylcermidase enzyme causes growths of

FACT | Diabetes is the sixth leading cause of death in the United States.

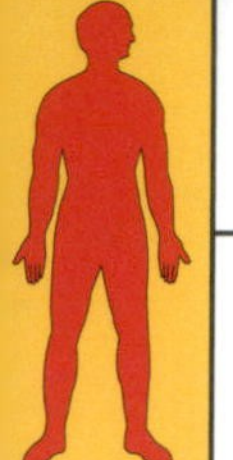

undigested "storage" cells around nerves. Consequent damage to nerves' protective myelin covering leads to various neurological complications. Early onset form is usually fatal before age 2; late onset form may arise in adolescence and cause permanent complications into adulthood.

SPECIALIST TO SEE: Neurologist

OTHER SYMPTOMS:

- Fever
- Seizures
- Vomiting
- Muscle weakness
- Distorted vision
- Blindness

PROGRESSION: Often presents as vision problems that may lead to blindness. Eventual disability likely as muscle weakness impairs mobility and gait. Deafness also likely. Usually fatal.

TREATMENT: No known cure. Bone marrow transplantation in early stages.

CONTAGION: **1** 2 3 4

PAIN: 1 2 **3** 4

SUFFERING: 1 2 3 **4**

FATAL: Yes No **Maybe**

...or you might have

RIFT VALLEY FEVER

WHAT IT IS: Acute infection by Phlebovirus, transmitted through infected mosquitoes and other bloodsucking insects. Commonly spread among animal herds, but can also be spread to humans. First identified in early 1900s. Rarely fatal, but causes high rates of fetal death if infected during pregnancy.

SPECIALIST TO SEE: Infectious Disease Specialist

OTHER SYMPTOMS:

- Fever
- Lethargy
- Dizziness
- Pain in lower back
- Retinal infection
- Irregular heartbeat

PROGRESSION: May be asymptomatic for long period after exposure. Characterized by mild, flu-like symptoms. When present, symptoms persist for 2 to 7 days. Retinal infection may lead to permanent vision loss.

TREATMENT: None; usually self-limiting.

CONTAGION: 1 2 **3** 4

PAIN: 1 **2** 3 4

SUFFERING: 1 **2** 3 4

FATAL: Yes **No** Maybe

If you lose your balance...

...you might have

NAEGLERIA

WHAT IT IS: Infection by *Naegleria fowleri* amoeba, found in lakes, rivers, and under-chlorinated pools. Commonly enters through nose while swimming. Amoeba travels through central nervous system, and ultimately destroys brain tissue. Death likely.

SPECIALIST TO SEE: Neurologist, Infectious Disease Specialist

OTHER SYMPTOMS:

- Headache
- Nausea
- Stiff neck
- Confusion
- Seizures
- Hallucinations

PROGRESSION: Causes encephalitis (brain inflammation) and irreparable destruction of brain tissue. Progresses rapidly and usually results in death within 3 to 7 days.

TREATMENT: No known cure.

CONTAGION: **1** 2 3 4

PAIN: 1 2 3 **4**

SUFFERING: 1 2 **3** 4

FATAL: **Yes** No Maybe

...or you might have

PROGRESSIVE SUPRANUCLEAR PALSY

WHAT IT IS: Debilitating brain disorder that impedes movement and balance. Lesions develop on brain stem, gradually causing tissue destruction. Cause unknown. Symptoms may develop in middle age, though more common after 60.

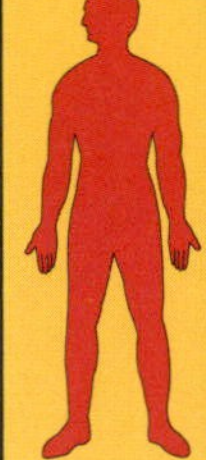

SPECIALIST TO SEE: Neurologist

OTHER SYMPTOMS:
- Decreased mobility
- Irritability
- Difficulty sleeping
- Slurred speech
- Apathy

PROGRESSION: As brain weakens, dizziness, difficulty walking, shakiness, and personality changes may follow. Often necessitates wheelchair usage or permanent bed rest. Aspiration pneumonia caused by impaired swallowing may result in death.

TREATMENT: No known cure. Palliative care to treat symptoms.

CONTAGION: **1** 2 3 4

PAIN: 1 2 **3** 4

SUFFERING: 1 2 3 **4**

FATAL: Yes No **Maybe**

If you're clumsy...

...you might have
BINSWANGER'S DISEASE

WHAT IT IS: Rare, progressive form of dementia characterized by lesions in deep white matter of brain. Typically causes gradual memory loss, cognitive impairment, and personality changes. May coexist with Alzheimer's disease. Symptoms may be transient. Full recovery unlikely.

SPECIALIST TO SEE: Neurologist

OTHER SYMPTOMS:
- Mood swings
- Abnormal blood pressure
- Bladder incontinence
- Facial paralysis
- Difficulty speaking

PROGRESSION: Onset slow, with initial symptoms relatively benign, including minor clumsiness and moderate mood changes. As degeneration continues, intellectual ability diminishes. Ultimately results in paralysis, memory loss, and seizures.

TREATMENT: No known cure. Treatment of symptoms. Long-term home care.

CONTAGION: **1** 2 3 4

PAIN: 1 2 **3** 4

SUFFERING: 1 2 3 **4**

FATAL: Yes No **Maybe**

...or you might have
CREUTZFELDT-JAKOB DISEASE

WHAT IT IS: Degenerative, invariably fatal brain disease. Spongiform lesions (porous holes) develop in brain, causing rapid decrease of mental and physical function. Usually diagnosed in midlife. Variant form similar to "mad cow" disease occurs in younger patients. Can be genetically inherited or acquired through tissue donation.

SPECIALIST TO SEE: Neurologist

OTHER SYMPTOMS:
- Anxiety
- Personality changes
- Hallucinations
- Difficulty speaking
- Muscle spasms or stiffness
- Paralysis

PROGRESSION: Rapid onset and progression. Early symptoms include personality changes and loss of coordination. Quickly graduates to muscle wasting, impaired cognitive ability, aggression, and dementia. Full paralysis may occur in later stages. Death usually occurs within 1 year of onset.

TREATMENT: None. Sedatives and antipsychotics to control aggressive behavior. Full-time caretakers and safe, secure environment.

CONTAGION: **1** 2 3 4

PAIN: 1 2 3 **4**

SUFFERING: 1 2 3 **4**

FATAL: **Yes** No Maybe

...or you might have
SHY-DRAGER SYNDROME

WHAT IT IS: Degenerative disorder of nervous system. Standing up causes blood pressure to drop, leading to dizziness and fainting. Tremors, muscle rigidity, and decreased motor ability resemble Parkinson's disease. Primarily develops in men between ages 40 and 75.

QUOTE | "Health nuts are going to feel stupid someday, lying in hospitals dying of nothing." —Redd Foxx

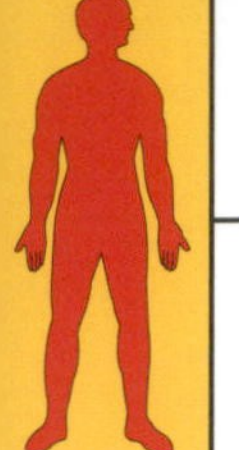

FACT | The average life expectancy of a female born in the United States is 5.4 years longer than that of a male.

SPECIALIST TO SEE: Neurologist

OTHER SYMPTOMS:
- Poor posture
- Difficulty speaking
- Difficulty sleeping
- Reduced sweating
- Constipation
- Erectile dysfunction

PROGRESSION: Degeneration of nerve cells in brain and spinal cord leads to loss of functions controlled by these areas. Death occurs within 10 years due to respiratory or cardiopulmonary failure.

TREATMENT: No known cure. Management of underlying conditions and symptoms.

CONTAGION: **1** 2 3 4

PAIN: 1 2 3 **4**

SUFFERING: 1 2 3 **4**

FATAL: **Yes** No Maybe

...or you might have
TETHERED SPINAL CORD SYNDROME

WHAT IT IS: Neurological disorder in which extra tissue attachments restrict spinal cord movement within spinal column. As column grows, spinal cord becomes abnormally stretched, leading to nerve damage and dysfunction in lower areas of spine. May result from incorrect growth of neural tube during fetal development.

SPECIALIST TO SEE: Neurologist

OTHER SYMPTOMS:
- Weakness in legs or feet
- Lesions on lower back
- Incontinence
- Impaired sensory perception
- Decreased mobility

PROGRESSION: Initial symptoms include fatty masses in lower back, skin lesions, and hairy patches. May cause loss of bowel control. Eventually, orthopedic problems develop, such as difficulty walking, spinal-cord cysts, and numbness in back and legs.

TREATMENT: Neurectomy (surgical removal of nerve) to relieve pain. Surgery to free spine can prevent continued development of spinal cord cysts.

CONTAGION: **1** 2 3 4

PAIN: 1 2 3 **4**

SUFFERING: 1 2 3 **4**

FATAL: Yes **No** Maybe

If you have dizzy spells...

...you might have
HEART ARRHYTHMIA

WHAT IT IS: Irregular beating of heart; may be benign or life-threatening. Can be caused by drug or alcohol use, stress, or preexisting heart disorder. Can lead to stroke or congestive heart failure. About 300,000 people per year die of sudden arrhythmia death syndrome (SADS).

SPECIALIST TO SEE: Cardiologist

OTHER SYMPTOMS:
- Irregular heartbeat
- Loss of consciousness
- Chest pain
- Shortness of breath

PROGRESSION: First, appears as palpitations or pounding in chest, combined with light-headedness, fatigue, and shortness of breath. Repeated or prolonged incidents may indicate underlying, potentially fatal heart disease.

TREATMENT: Anti-arrhythmic medication and anticoagulants. Pacemaker, implanted defibrillator, or electroshock therapy. Heart surgery.

CONTAGION: **1** 2 3 4

PAIN: 1 2 **3** 4

SUFFERING: 1 2 **3** 4

FATAL: Yes No **Maybe**

...or you might have
MÉNIÈRE'S DISEASE

WHAT IT IS: Fluid disorder of inner ear that results in complications with hearing and balance. Characterized by sudden, often severe attacks of vertigo. May occur as isolated incident, but commonly recurs with increasing intensity. Tinnitus (ringing in ears) and hearing loss are possible and may become permanent.

SPECIALIST TO SEE: Neurologist, Otolaryngologist

Hemorrhoids

[Fig. 118]

WHAT IT IS
Swollen or inflamed (varicose) veins in anus or rectum; also known as piles.

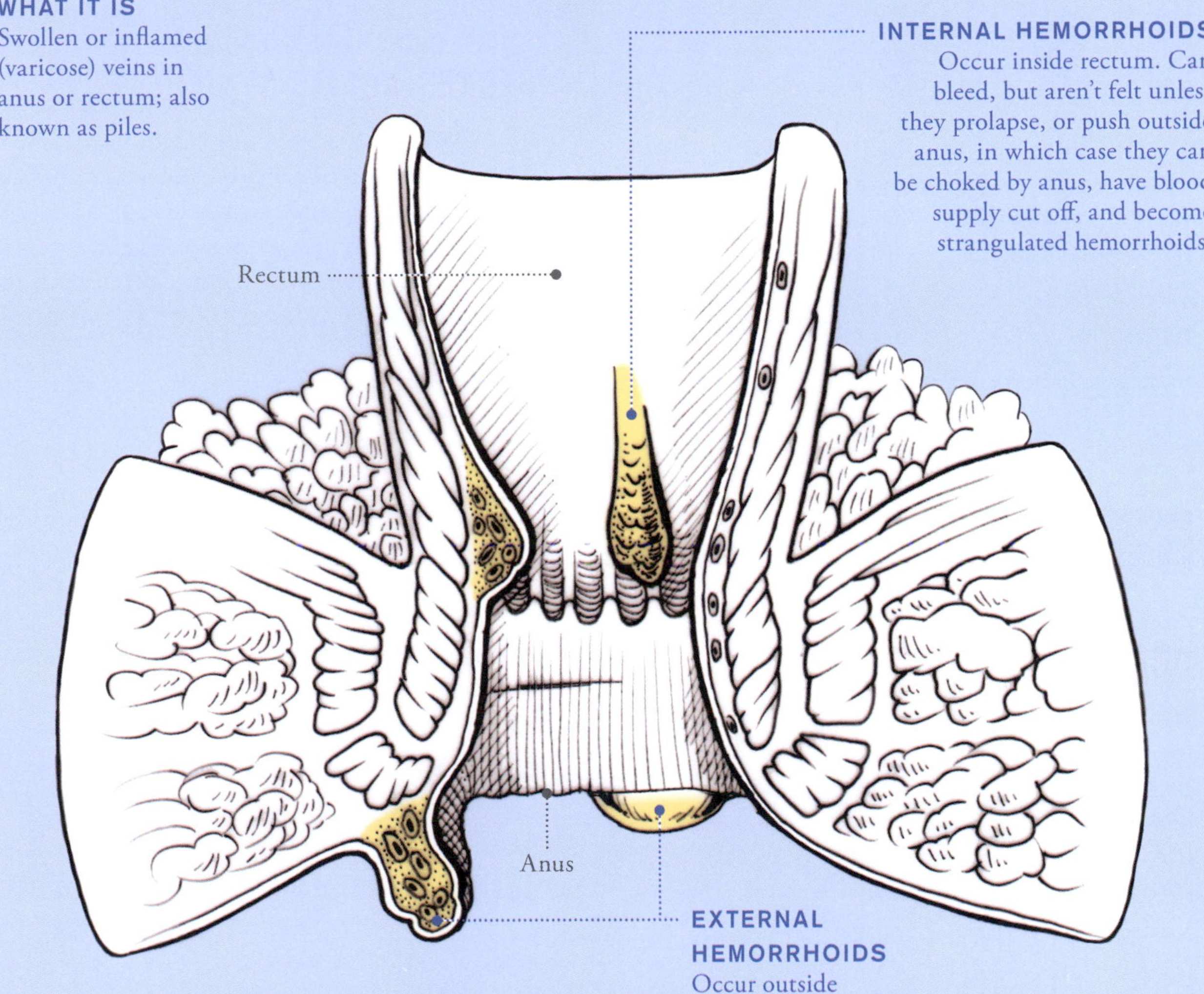

INTERNAL HEMORRHOIDS
Occur inside rectum. Can bleed, but aren't felt unless they prolapse, or push outside anus, in which case they can be choked by anus, have blood supply cut off, and become strangulated hemorrhoids.

EXTERNAL HEMORRHOIDS
Occur outside anal canal; can be painful and itchy.

TREATMENT
Over-the-counter topical medication or warm baths for mild cases. Hemorrhoidectomy (surgical hemorrhoid removal) or other procedures, including rubber-band ligation (rubber band is applied to cut off blood supply to hemorrhoid until it falls off), for problematic cases.

CAUSES
Straining and increased pressure on veins. Can be exacerbated by chronic constipation or diarrhea, obesity, pregnancy, and childbirth.

For disease description, see page 151.

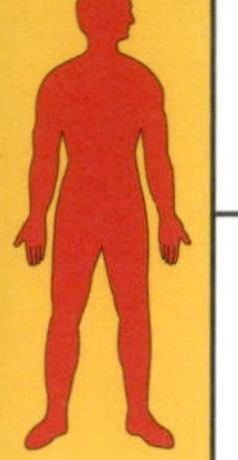

FACT | The second leading cause of unintentional death is poisoning from prescription drugs.

OTHER SYMPTOMS:
- Vertigo
- Inability to hear low-pitched sounds
- Ringing in ears
- Inner-ear pressure
- Nausea
- Vomiting

PROGRESSION: Inconsistent development. Ranges from single episode with minor symptoms to recurring, unpredictable bouts of progressively worsening vertigo over several years.

TREATMENT: Anti-nausea medication and antibiotics to treat symptoms and resulting infections. Surgery in rare cases.

CONTAGION:	**1**	2	3	4
PAIN:	1	**2**	3	4
SUFFERING:	1	2	**3**	4
FATAL:	Yes	**No**	Maybe	

If you have fainting spells...

...you might have
BRADYCARDIA

WHAT IT IS: Abnormally slow heart rate, usually lower than 60 beats per minute. May be caused by disruption of electrical pathways that trigger heartbeat. Linked to aging, heart disease, and excessive use of cold medication and diet pills. Can lead to cardiac arrhythmia (abnormal heart rhythm).

SPECIALIST TO SEE: Cardiologist

OTHER SYMPTOMS:
- Dizziness
- Weakness throughout body
- Lack of energy
- Dehydration
- Shock

PROGRESSION: Can be temporary or persistent depending on underlying cause. In some cases, inability to deliver adequate blood supply to bodily tissue may have fatal consequences.

TREATMENT: Pacemaker to regulate heartbeat. Surgery in certain cases.

CONTAGION:	**1**	2	3	4
PAIN:	**1**	2	3	4
SUFFERING:	1	**2**	3	4
FATAL:	Yes	No	**Maybe**	

...or you might have
STOKES-ADAMS SYNDROME

WHAT IT IS: Temporary stoppage or extreme slowing of pulse due to heart blockage or ventricular fibrillation (abnormal heart muscle contraction). Leads to sudden attacks of unconsciousness and collapse. Rare, but occurs more often over age 40. Untreated, 50 percent mortality rate within 1 year of first episode.

SPECIALIST TO SEE: Cardiologist

OTHER SYMPTOMS:
- Dizziness
- Fixed pupils
- Incontinence
- Warm or flushed sensation
- Convulsions

PROGRESSION: Paleness and slowed pulse, possibly leading to unconsciousness. May recur frequently. Episodes are brief and potentially fatal.

TREATMENT: Pacemaker or medication to regulate heartbeat.

CONTAGION:	**1**	2	3	4
PAIN:	1	**2**	3	4
SUFFERING:	1	2	**3**	4
FATAL:	Yes	No	**Maybe**	

If you have aggressive outbursts...

...you might have
INTERMITTENT EXPLOSIVE DISORDER

WHAT IT IS: Periods of aggressive and violent outbursts arising from often trivial provocation. Episodes may last from minutes to hours and can result in injury or property destruction. Occurs independently of other mental disorders, medical conditions, or drug effects.

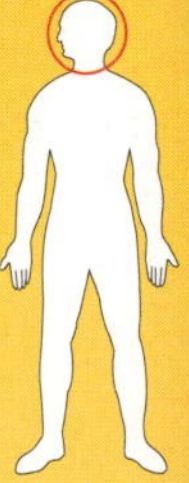

SPECIALIST TO SEE: Psychiatrist

OTHER SYMPTOMS:
- Tingling sensation throughout body
- Tremors
- Distorted hearing
- Irregular heartbeat
- Chest pressure
- Tension

PROGRESSION: Violent outburst occurs, then tapers off, usually followed by deep remorse. May be prefaced by tingling, tremors, chest tightness, or auditory echoes. Can occur in clusters or as separate incidents. May lead to depression, anxiety disorders, and suicide.

TREATMENT: Behavioral therapy and anger management. Antidepressants, mood regulators, and anticonvulsants to reduce attacks.

CONTAGION: **1** 2 3 4

PAIN: **1** 2 3 4

SUFFERING: 1 2 **3** 4

FATAL: Yes **No** Maybe

If you're impulsive...

...you might have
BORDERLINE PERSONALITY DISORDER

WHAT IT IS: Mental illness in which minor provocations tend to trigger extreme emotional responses, and self-identity is often incoherent and uncertain. Splitting (i.e., trait in which people or things are seen as absolutely good or bad) also common. Cause uncertain; thought to be linked to childhood abuse or neglect, inherited characteristics, and brain dysfunctions. Suicide committed in 10 percent of cases.

SPECIALIST TO SEE: Psychiatrist

OTHER SYMPTOMS:
- Extreme mood swings
- Anxiety or depression
- Risky or suicidal behavior
- Difficulty managing relationships, work, or school
- Drug abuse or eating disorder
- Fear of abandonment

PROGRESSION: Flares of intense depression, anger, self-mutilation, and anxiety can last for minutes, hours, or entire days. Difficulty anticipating and controlling emotions and physical behavior arises. Symptoms may diminish with maturity.

TREATMENT: Long-term behavior therapy and psychoanalysis. Antidepressants or anti-anxiety medication.

CONTAGION: **1** 2 3 4

PAIN: **1** 2 3 4

SUFFERING: 1 2 3 **4**

FATAL: Yes **No** Maybe

If you have anxiety...

...you might have
AGORAPHOBIA

WHAT IT IS: Fear of public spaces. Outings generally lead to panic attacks. Usually accompanies history of anxiety. Results in restricted behaviors to avoid potentially anxiety-provoking situations.

SPECIALIST TO SEE: Cognitive-Behavioral Therapist

OTHER SYMPTOMS:
- Avoidance of social situations
- Panic attacks
- Alcohol or drug abuse

PROGRESSION: Commonly starts with panic attack in public place. Then, public situations avoided for fear of recurrent attacks. Finally, marked withdrawal from all outside contacts, and potential social ostracism.

TREATMENT: Therapy. Mood regulators, beta-blockers, and sedatives. Treatment of underlying related problems, such as clinical depression.

CONTAGION: **1** 2 3 4

PAIN: 1 **2** 3 4

SUFFERING: 1 2 3 **4**

FATAL: Yes **No** Maybe

...or you might have
SCHIZOPHRENIA

WHAT IT IS: Psychiatric disorder characterized by paranoid delusions, incoherent thought or speech, and hallucinations. Distorted perception of reality often produces false beliefs of being persecuted or

QUOTE | "I was nauseous and tingly all over. I was either in love or I had smallpox." —Woody Allen

Superbugs
Antibiotic Resistance

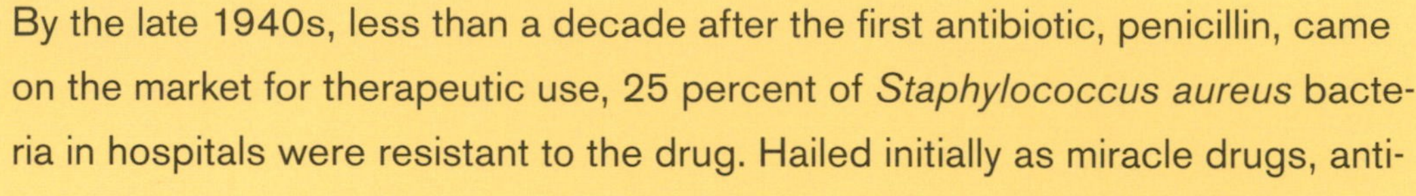

By the late 1940s, less than a decade after the first antibiotic, penicillin, came on the market for therapeutic use, 25 percent of *Staphylococcus aureus* bacteria in hospitals were resistant to the drug. Hailed initially as miracle drugs, antibiotics have since proved weak against bacteria's moving-target ability to mutate quickly and to easily spread immunity, and antibiotic resistance is now, according to the Centers for Disease Control, "one of the world's most pressing health problems."

Resistant bacteria have arisen in part due to misuse and overuse of antibiotics in both humans and animals. Bacteria can develop resistance in a few ways. With natural selection, an antibiotic kills all but a few anomalously resistant bacteria, and they reproduce, forming a resistant strain—this is especially common when people do not finish their prescribed course of antibiotics. One bacterium can pass resistance to another through a process called "plasmid transfer," in which DNA structure is transferred between bacteria. Mutation and evolution can also result in resistance. Patients develop drug-resistant infections either by contracting an already-resistant bug or when a resistant microbe emerges in response to antibiotic treatment. There are now bacteria that are resistant to multiple antibiotics—so-called superbugs.

Superbugs are frequently forms of *S. aureus*, bacteria that spark a variety of diseases, including pneumonia, meningitis, and septicemia, either through infection or by the toxins they produce. Often highly contagious, staph infections can run rampant through hospitals. Other drug-resistant bacteria include those causing tuberculosis, flesh-eating fasciitis, and malaria. When infections become resistant to "first-line" antimicrobials, diseases must be treated with second- and third-line drugs, which are generally more expensive and toxic. According to the World Health Organization, "Most alarming of all are diseases where resistance is developing for virtually all currently available drugs, thus raising the specter of a post-antibiotic era . . . Current trends suggest that some diseases will have no effective therapies within the next 10 years."

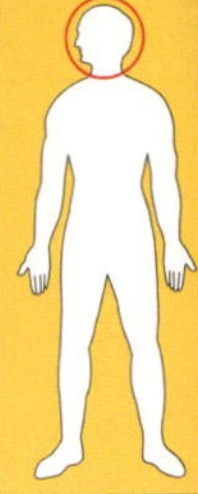

manipulated by others, or hearing voices that others do not hear. Genetics, childhood environment, and neurological dysfunction are important contributing factors. Onset typically occurs in late adolescence or early adulthood. Symptoms are continuous and may progressively worsen.

SPECIALIST TO SEE: Psychiatrist

OTHER SYMPTOMS:

- Aberrant behavior
- Decline in emotional response or motivation
- Difficulty managing relationships, work, or school
- Distorted sensory perception
- Catatonia (muscle rigidity)

PROGRESSION: Commonly starts with odd behavior. Then, psychotic episode follows, including delusions, hallucinations, or paranoia. Chronic condition; worsens with age.

TREATMENT: Antipsychotics. Electroconvulsive therapy, long-term psychotherapy, and rehabilitation therapy.

CONTAGION: **1** 2 3 4

PAIN: 1 **2** 3 4

SUFFERING: 1 2 3 **4**

FATAL: Yes **No** Maybe

If you're paranoid...

...you might have
SCHIZOID PERSONALITY DISORDER

WHAT IT IS: Affliction marked by total indifference to social interaction or norms. Inexpressiveness and lack of interest in social relations lead to isolated lifestyle or preoccupation with fantasy or introspection.

SPECIALIST TO SEE: Psychiatrist

OTHER SYMPTOMS:

- Avoidance of social situations
- Indifference
- Decreased libido
- Aversion to physical contact

PROGRESSION: First, starts with mild introversion and avoidance of social interaction. Becomes more acute over time. Lifelong isolation may occur.

TREATMENT: Treatment rarely sought. Psychotherapy.

CONTAGION: **1** 2 3 4

PAIN: **1** 2 3 4

SUFFERING: 1 2 **3** 4

FATAL: Yes **No** Maybe

...or you might have
WOLFRAM SYNDROME

WHAT IT IS: Progressive neurological disorder caused by recessive gene that interferes with production of wolframin protein. Often presents with diabetes, deafness, and optic atrophy. Leads to behavioral problems, psychiatric complications, and, in some cases, suicide attempts. Typically results in death by age 30.

SPECIALIST TO SEE: Neurologist, Psychiatrist

OTHER SYMPTOMS:

- Vision loss
- Anxiety
- Depression
- Cognitive impairment
- Hallucinations

PROGRESSION: Initially, symptoms similar to diabetes. Then, hearing and vision impairment, peripheral neuropathy, and psychiatric illness. Death can result from complete degeneration of central nervous system or kidney failure.

TREATMENT: No known cure. Thiamin (vitamin B1) to treat diabetes and anemia. Antidepressants.

CONTAGION: **1** 2 3 4

PAIN: 1 2 **3** 4

SUFFERING: 1 2 3 **4**

FATAL: **Yes** No Maybe

If you have mood swings...

...you might have
DEPRESSION

WHAT IT IS: Condition in which persistent disinterest, sadness, hopelessness, and fatigue significantly interfere with daily life. Sometimes triggered by life-changing events, addiction, or

FACT | Human skin regenerates 1,000 times in a lifetime, during which we shed 40 pounds of skin.

You Eat, You Suffer

Foodborne Illnesses

Among the most common ways to contract an illness, bacteria and viruses ingested with food come with little warning and render victims incapacitated for days at a time—and, in some cases, permanently damaged or dead. According to the Centers for Disease Control, there are more than 250 known foodborne illnesses, responsible for 76 million incidents each year in the United States alone. Of those, an estimated 325,000 people will be hospitalized and 5,000 will die. Health-care professionals are legally required to report food poisoning so that outbreaks can be tracked, as with the *E. coli*–tainted spinach of 2006 and the *Salmonella*-infested peanut butter of 2007. However, those outbreaks comprise only a small number of total food-poisoning instances, leaving us with little choice but to eat and hope.

Noroviruses

A group of viruses that cause viral gastroenteritis, the noroviruses, also called calicivirus, are the most common cause of foodborne illness, resulting in at least 23 million cases annually and approximately 50 percent of all outbreaks. Colloquially (but incorrectly) called stomach flu, noroviruses cause sudden-onset episodes of vomiting and diarrhea that last 1 to 2 days, appearing 12 to 48 hours after exposure. They're spread from person to person, or via anything touched by an infected individual. Named after Norwalk, Ohio, following a 1968 outbreak that led to its identification, noroviruses are a particular problem on cruise ships.

Salmonella

Salmonella is a type of bacteria found in the intestines of birds, reptiles, and mammals, spread to humans primarily by raw foods of animal origin, especially eggs. According to the CDC, approximately 40,000 cases of salmonellosis are reported annually, though it is presumed that 30 times that figure go unreported. The symptoms of salmonellosis manifest 1 to 3 days after exposure and include diarrhea, fever, and abdominal cramps. *Salmonella* can cause life-threatening infections in those with weakened immune systems, responsible for 600 deaths a year. A small number of sufferers will develop Reiter's syndrome, a chronic arthritis condition.

More than 250 known foodborne pathogens cause 76 million incidents of illness per year in the United States alone.

Salmonella has nothing to do with salmon—it was named after one of its discovers, Daniel Elmer Salmon.

Campylobacter

One of the most common causes of diarrheal illness in the United States, *Campylobacter* lives in the intestines of birds and is frequently transmitted through raw or undercooked poultry—more than half of the raw chicken in the United States carries the bacteria. Symptoms appear 2 to 5 days after exposure, last under a week, and include diarrhea (sometimes bloody), abdominal pain and cramping, and fever. Campylobacteriosis appears as isolated instances rather than outbreaks; the CDC estimates that it affects over 1 million Americans per year. While the ailment is almost never fatal, in rare cases it leads to Guillain-Barré syndrome, which causes the immune system to attack the body's own nerves and can result in paralysis.

E. Coli

The *Escherichia coli* bacteria, or *E. coli*, live peacefully in human intestines as part of our gut flora, suppressing harmful bacteria and synthesizing vitamins. Some strains, however, cause hemorrhagic colitis in humans by producing toxins that damage the intestinal lining, especially one called O157:H7. Symptoms appear 2 to 8 days after infection and consist of bloody diarrhea, severe stomach cramps, and vomiting. A complication called hemolytic uremic syndrome can arise, especially in children and the elderly, causing hemolytic anemia and renal failure. According to the CDC, *E. coli* O157:H7 was responsible for 73,000 infections and 61 deaths in 1999. It's transmitted by undercooked ground beef, raw milk, unpasteurized fruit juice, and contaminated produce and water, as well as from person to person via fecal matter.

Botulism

Now exceedingly rare, botulism is a serious paralytic illness caused by nerve toxins produced by the bacterium *Clostridium botulinum*. Just over 100 cases are reported annually in the United States, of which only a quarter derive from food. Foodborne botulism occurs when spores are insulated by aluminum and allowed to multiply, and is primarily associated with home-canned or jarred foods that haven't been sealed at high temperatures. Symptoms include double and blurred vision, drooping eyelids, slurred speech, and muscle weakness, leading to full paralysis, and generally begin 18 to 36 hours after exposure. Treatment requires being placed on a ventilator for weeks or months and intensive medical care.

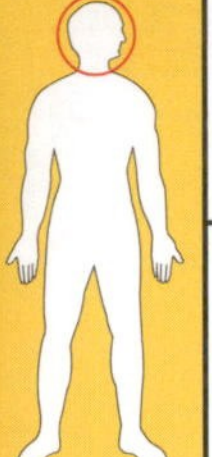

serious underlying medical issue. Believed to be related to serotonin levels in brain. Twice as many women as men affected.

SPECIALIST TO SEE: Psychiatrist

OTHER SYMPTOMS:

- Lethargy
- Irritability
- Uncontrollable crying
- Difficulty sleeping
- Suicidal ideation

PROGRESSION: First, deep lethargy appears, followed by an overwhelming sense of hopelessness. May last indefinitely, requiring supervision and medication. Can lead to suicide attempts.

TREATMENT: Psychotherapy or electroconvulsive therapy. Antidepressants.

CONTAGION: **1** 2 3 4

PAIN: **1** 2 3 4

SUFFERING: 1 2 **3** 4

FATAL: Yes **No** Maybe

...or you might have

EPILEPSY

WHAT IT IS: Recurring seizures due to malfunction of neuron clusters. Can result in abnormal behavior and emotions. Caused by brain tumors, swelling, bleeding, infection, injury, or exposure to toxin such as lead or carbon monoxide. Ascertaining underlying condition essential for treatment.

SPECIALIST TO SEE: Neurologist

OTHER SYMPTOMS:

- Aggression
- Anger
- Irritability
- Muscle tremors
- Hallucinations

PROGRESSION: Can cause spasms, convulsions, incontinence, and loss of consciousness. Seizures increase risk of serious harm. In extreme cases, permanent brain damage and death may occur.

TREATMENT: Anticonvulsants. Brain surgery.

CONTAGION: **1** 2 3 4

PAIN: 1 2 **3** 4

SUFFERING: 1 2 **3** 4

FATAL: Yes No **Maybe**

If your personality changes...

...you might have

PERNICIOUS ANEMIA

WHAT IT IS: Persistent deficiency of intrinsic factor (protein) caused by improper nutrition, bacterial or parasitic infections, drugs, metabolic disorders, or autoimmune dysfunction. Causes inability to adsorb vitamin B12, required for functioning of nerves and red blood cells. Complications may be permanent if not treated.

SPECIALIST TO SEE: Neurologist, Hematologist

OTHER SYMPTOMS:

- Fatigue
- Constipation or diarrhea
- Tingling or burning sensations throughout body
- Inflammation in tongue
- Muscle spasms

PROGRESSION: Develops slowly over months, years, or decades. First, fatigue and appetite loss. As vitamin B12 deficiency worsens, other symptoms emerge, including muscle weakness, color-blindness, and cognitive impairment. Complications can be permanent.

TREATMENT: Monthly injections of vitamin B12. Dietary changes.

CONTAGION: **1** 2 3 4

PAIN: 1 **2** 3 4

SUFFERING: 1 2 **3** 4

FATAL: Yes **No** Maybe

...or you might have

POST-TRAUMATIC STRESS DISORDER

WHAT IT IS: Delayed reaction to traumatic event, such as plane crash, war, earthquake, or rape. Manifests as extreme and prolonged bouts of anxiety, emotional numbness, and other behavioral problems. Three forms: acute, chronic, and delayed-onset. Affects millions of people every year, especially war veterans.

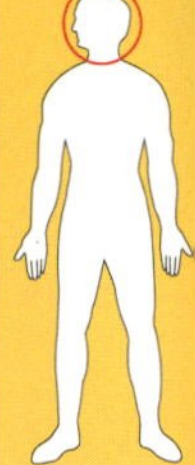

SPECIALIST TO SEE: Psychiatrist

OTHER SYMPTOMS:
- Nightmares or flashbacks
- Anger, guilt, hopelessness, or apathy
- Depression
- High blood pressure
- Muscle tension
- Nausea

PROGRESSION: Often starts with difficulty sleeping, nightmares, or fearful overreaction to simple noises. Physical ailments can include head and body aches, gastrointestinal disorders, vertigo, and chest pain. Untreated, can lead to drug, food, or alcohol abuse; divorce; and possibly suicide.

TREATMENT: Antidepressants. Cognitive and behavioral therapy. Stress-management training.

CONTAGION: **1** 2 3 4

PAIN: 1 **2** 3 4

SUFFERING: 1 2 3 **4**

FATAL: Yes **No** Maybe

If you have spells of confusion...

...you might have
CEREBRAL SPARGANOSIS

WHAT IT IS: *Spirometra mansonoides* tapeworm migrates from intestines to eye or brain, causing cysts that spread and become increasingly debilitating. Contracted by eating raw meat containing larvae. Can grow to 50 feet long and live in host for up to 20 years.

SPECIALIST TO SEE: Neurologist

OTHER SYMPTOMS:
- Headache
- Fatigue
- Fever
- Seizures

PROGRESSION: Symptoms first appear within weeks or months of exposure. Tapeworm moves to brain, causing headaches, encephalitis (cerebral inflammation), disorientation, and seizures. Permanent tissue damage, meningitis, dementia, and death possible.

TREATMENT: Anti-inflammatory steroids or surgery.

CONTAGION: **1** 2 3 4

PAIN: 1 2 **3** 4

SUFFERING: 1 2 3 **4**

FATAL: Yes No **Maybe**

...or you might have
HYPOGLYCEMIA

WHAT IT IS: Dangerously low blood-sugar levels lead to inadequate supply of sugar to brain. Often results from diabetes or other underlying condition. Induces recurrent episodes of disorientation and anxiety that last up to 30 minutes.

SPECIALIST TO SEE: Endocrinologist

OTHER SYMPTOMS:
- Trembling
- Seizures
- Dilated pupils
- Double vision
- Irregular heartbeat
- Slurred speech

PROGRESSION: Commonly starts with disorientation, accompanied by shakes, sweating, anxiety, and impaired vision. Then, fainting spells and coma may occur. Finally, can lead to permanent physical impairment and brain damage.

TREATMENT: Glucose tablets, food, candy, and intravenous glucose to boost blood sugar.

CONTAGION: **1** 2 3 4

PAIN: 1 2 **3** 4

SUFFERING: 1 2 **3** 4

FATAL: Yes **No** Maybe

If you have delusions...

...you might have
BIPOLAR DISORDER

WHAT IT IS: Characterized by manic-depressive cycles of intense emotional highs and lows, possibly leading to irrational, aggressive, or self-destructive behavior. Thought to be defect in brain neurotransmitters.

QUOTE | "If you trust Google more than your doctor, then maybe it's time to switch doctors." —Cristina Cordova

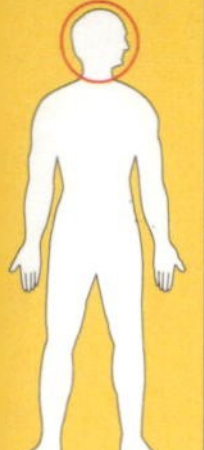

SPECIALIST TO SEE: Psychiatrist

OTHER SYMPTOMS:

- Anxiety
- Reckless behavior
- Increased libido
- Weight loss or gain
- Insomnia
- Psychosis

PROGRESSION: First, cycles of heightened anxiety or euphoria and deep depression appear. Episodes can last for days, weeks, or months. Untreated, symptoms become increasingly more pronounced, resulting in dangerously aggressive behavior and even suicide.

TREATMENT: Mood stabilizers (e.g., lithium). Antidepressants, anticonvulsants, and antipsychotics. Psychiatric and electroconvulsive therapy.

CONTAGION:	**1**	2	3	4
PAIN:	1	**2**	3	4
SUFFERING:	1	2	3	**4**
FATAL:	Yes	**No**	Maybe	

FACT | The human eye sees 7 million colors.

...or you might have

MULTI-INFARCT DEMENTIA

WHAT IT IS: Memory-loss affliction that arises from clots in small blood vessels in brain that create lesions. Believed to be aggravated by high blood pressure and aging. Treatment cannot reverse damage. Survival rate of 40 percent after 5 years. More prevalent among men.

SPECIALIST TO SEE: Neurologist

OTHER SYMPTOMS:

- Confusion
- Loss of memory
- Incontinence
- Wandering
- Emotional changes

PROGRESSION: Commonly starts with mental, emotional, and behavioral changes. Then, progresses over 5 to 10 years, with periods of rapid neurological decline. May

Dental Dangers

Most people don't love the dentist. The perilous trip to the chair. The jaw-aching, lip-numbing, drool-inducing techniques. The needles, the scraper, and worst of all, the drill. And that's before knowing about these potential hazards:

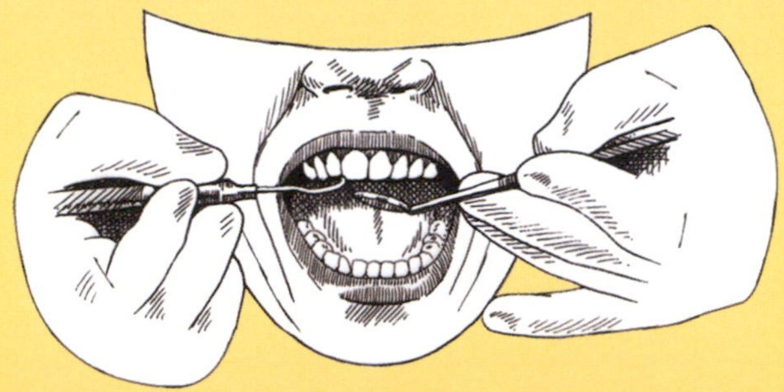

TMJ Damage

Opening the mouth too wide can damage the jaw's temporomandibular joint (TMJ), causing difficulty chewing and lifelong pain and discomfort.

Unneeded Surgery

Wisdom teeth that aren't causing problems don't need to be removed—why be unnecessarily exposed to risks related to surgery?

Mercury

Many dentists still fill cavities with mercury. Though studies establish its safety, it's a toxic chemical known to cause brain damage and kidney failure.

Infection

While dentists immerse their tools in germicides between patients, the system isn't perfect.

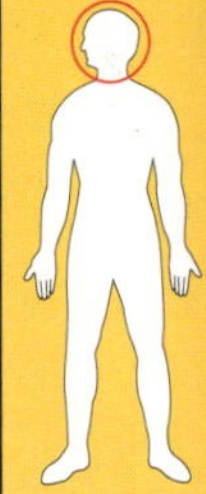

result in death from stroke, heart disease, pneumonia, or other serious complication.

TREATMENT: Medication to control hypertension, diabetes, cholesterol, and heart disease.

CONTAGION: **1** 2 3 4

PAIN: 1 **2** 3 4

SUFFERING: 1 2 3 **4**

FATAL: Yes No **Maybe**

If you have hallucinations...

...you might have

FATAL FAMILIAL INSOMNIA

WHAT IT IS: Very rare inherited disease caused by genetic mutation that affects thalamus, which governs sleep. Characterized by inability to sleep. Worsens over period of 3 years and ultimately leads to death. Reported in only 28 families worldwide. Generally occurs in middle age.

SPECIALIST TO SEE: Neurologist

OTHER SYMPTOMS:

- Panic attacks
- Paranoia
- Weight loss
- Dementia

PROGRESSION: In first months, chronic insomnia engenders panic attacks and phobias. Progresses to full-blown hallucinations and dramatic weight loss. Followed by dementia and eventually death.

TREATMENT: No known cure.

CONTAGION: **1** 2 3 4

PAIN: 1 2 **3** 4

SUFFERING: 1 2 3 **4**

FATAL: **Yes** No Maybe

...or you might have

KLEINE-LEVIN SYNDROME

WHAT IT IS: Rare phenomenon marked by extreme drowsiness and sleeping up to 20 hours per day for several weeks. May result in temporary amnesia or depression following attacks. Four times more prevalent among males. Thought to be malfunction of thalamus, which governs sleep and appetite.

SPECIALIST TO SEE: Neurologist, Sleep Specialist

OTHER SYMPTOMS:

- Binge eating
- Mood swings
- Sensitivity to noise

PROGRESSION: Commonly begins with lethargy almost all day for up to several weeks. In between, overeating, hypersexual behavior, and psychotic episodes occur. Flares and disappears without warning.

TREATMENT: No known cure. Stimulants to treat sleepiness.

CONTAGION: **1** 2 3 4

PAIN: 1 **2** 3 4

SUFFERING: 1 **2** 3 4

FATAL: Yes **No** Maybe

If you're depressed...

...you might have

DYSLEXIA

WHAT IT IS: Neurological disorder affecting reading, writing, speaking, and numeracy in persons of otherwise normal intelligence. Typically manifests as inability to make connection between written symbol and spoken sound. May also cause difficulty following directions, sequencing (putting things in order), and distinguishing right from left. Often attributed to hereditary factors and childhood hearing problems; strongly correlated with left-handedness as well.

SPECIALIST TO SEE: Psychologist, Neurologist

OTHER SYMPTOMS:

- Impaired writing ability
- Careless or bizarre reading and spelling mistakes
- Disorganization
- Low self-esteem
- Difficulty managing relationships, work, or school
- Inability to perform mental arithmetic

PROGRESSION: Signs may present as early as infancy. Slowed vocabulary learning in preschool years, usually followed by difficulty understanding alphabet. Speech

QUOTE | "I've just learned about his illness. Let's hope it's nothing trivial." —Irvin Shrewsbury Cobb

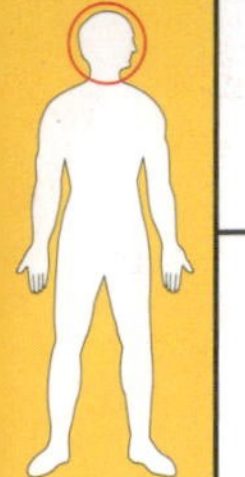

development may also be delayed. Reading and writing difficulties often persist into adulthood.

TREATMENT: Multisensory tutoring to build phonetic decoding skills.

CONTAGION: 1 2 3 4

PAIN: 1 2 3 4

SUFFERING: 1 2 3 4

FATAL: Yes No Maybe

...or you might have

ERGOT POISONING

WHAT IT IS: Poisoning that results from consumption of grain, grain products, or drugs containing *Claviceps purpurea* fungus. Starts in gastrointestinal tract and spreads to brain and nervous system. Also known as St. Anthony's Fire.

SPECIALIST TO SEE: Neurologist

OTHER SYMPTOMS:

- Diarrhea
- Headache
- Nausea
- Vomiting
- Convulsions
- Hallucinations

PROGRESSION: First, begins with gastrointestinal symptoms, quickly followed by seizures, hallucinations, mania, and psychosis. Then, dry gangrene may occur in fingers, toes, and even nose, leading to death of affected tissue.

TREATMENT: No known cure. Vasodilators, anticoagulants, sympathetic nerve blockade, and temporary sedation to relieve symptoms.

CONTAGION: 1 2 3 4

PAIN: 1 2 3 4

SUFFERING: 1 2 3 4

FATAL: Yes No Maybe

...or you might have

SEASONAL AFFECTIVE DISORDER

WHAT IT IS: Subtype of major depressive illness related to shortened daylight in fall and winter, mainly in northern hemisphere. Prolonged time spent in buildings without exposure to daylight can result in year-round suffering. Severe cases may lead to mania or overwhelming enthusiasm during warm months. Believed to be caused by impaired serotonin production.

SPECIALIST TO SEE: Psychiatrist

OTHER SYMPTOMS:

- Lethargy
- Weight gain
- Persistent drowsiness
- Avoidance of social situations

PROGRESSION: As daylight hours diminish, depressive periods and severe fatigue present. Then, malaise impacts work habits and social relationships. Commonly results in sleep disorder. Often misdiagnosed as clinical depression.

TREATMENT: Daily light-box therapy and increased exposure to available daytime light. Antidepressants. Psychotherapy.

CONTAGION: 1 2 3 4

PAIN: 1 2 3 4

SUFFERING: 1 2 3 4

FATAL: Yes No Maybe

...or you might have

SICK BUILDING SYNDROME

WHAT IT IS: Ailments attributable to time spent in building without other cause, alleviated upon leaving. Stems from inadequate ventilation, release of chemicals from building materials, and biological contaminants (e.g., mold). May exist in up to 30 percent of new or renovated buildings.

SPECIALIST TO SEE: Primary Care Physician, Allergist

OTHER SYMPTOMS:

- Headache
- Dizziness
- Fatigue
- Inability to concentrate
- Itching eyes, nose, or throat
- Sensitivity to odors

PROGRESSION: Commonly begins with persistent headache, malaise, inability to concentrate, congestion, skin sensitivity, and nausea. In extreme cases, poor ventilation can result in carbon monoxide poisoning, tuberculosis, or Legionnaires' disease. Untreated, infections may become chronic.

How Long Will I Live?
The Definitive Answer

Only a century ago, the average life expectancy in the United States was just over 47 years. During the 20th century, the average American life span grew one year for every 5 calendar years. Those born at the turn of the new millennium can expect to live to be 78, according to the Centers for Disease Control, while the Social Security Administration's outlook is even rosier: 80.5 for men and 84.6 for women. That's almost double the life in just one century, significantly faster than gains made in any previous century, or even millennium.

Era	Average Life Expectancy (Years)
Neanderthal	20
Upper Paleolithic	33
Neolithic	22
Bronze Age	18
Greco-Roman Empires	28
Dark Ages	24
Middle Ages	33
1800	38
1900	47*
1950	68*
2000	78*

*In the United States

What's responsible for this windfall? Higher standards of living (diminished poverty, better hygiene, dramatic improvements in the quality of food and water) and startling medical advances (vaccines, treatments, cures). With the promise of genetic engineering and stem-cell research on the horizon, the Social Security Administration projects that people born in 2080 may average 95 years.

The longer we live, the more time we have to get sick and complain about it. Not to mention issues of overpopulation and overcrowding (today there are 6 billion of us, with 12 billion projected by 2050), an environment that is growing ever warmer and more toxic (even if we adopt strict pollution standards today), and potentially scarce food and water—all leading to wars between the haves and the have-nots.

More ominous are viruses and bacteria that evolve at lightning speeds. With higher numbers of people in closer contact, deadly plagues caused by viruses like Ebola and HIV are all but inevitable. Or, you could just get hit by a bus. Even with all our incredible advances, nature still has her own built-in methods of population control.

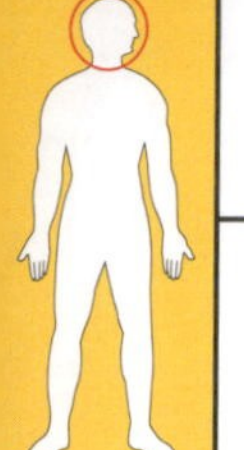

TREATMENT: Removal from contaminated environment. Antifungals.

CONTAGION: **1** 2 3 4

PAIN: 1 **2** 3 4

SUFFERING: 1 2 **3** 4

FATAL: Yes **No** Maybe

If you're restless...

...you might have
WERNICKE'S ENCEPHALOPATHY

WHAT IT IS: Serious disorder causing encephalitis (inflammation of brain). Stems from thiamine (vitamin B1) deficiency. Can arise from alcoholism, malnutrition, self-imposed starvation, or prolonged vomiting. Often undiagnosed until neurological examination reveals damage to nervous and muscle systems.

SPECIALIST TO SEE: Neurologist

OTHER SYMPTOMS:

- Abnormal eye or leg movement
- Irritability
- Loss of short-term memory
- Delirium
- Drowsiness
- Cold or clammy skin

PROGRESSION: Starts with altered mental state, agitation, and mobility problems. Without treatment, further deterioration and permanent nerve damage occur. Can lead to coma or chronic and ultimately fatal Korsakoff's psychosis. Irreversible amnesia and neurological disturbances possible.

TREATMENT: Thiamine injections to ease symptoms. Rehydration and intravenous glucose to treat malnutrition.

CONTAGION: **1** 2 3 4

PAIN: 1 2 **3** 4

SUFFERING: 1 2 3 **4**

FATAL: Yes No **Maybe**

If you lose your memory...

...you might have
ALZHEIMER'S DISEASE

WHAT IT IS: Fatal, degenerative type of dementia, marked by memory loss. Caused by progressive destruction of neurons. Results in long-term impairment of cognitive abilities. Fourth most common cause of death in American adults over age 65.

SPECIALIST TO SEE: Neurologist

OTHER SYMPTOMS:

- Incontinence
- Muscle weakness
- Seizures
- Mood swings

PROGRESSION: First, slight memory loss occurs, then becomes persistent. Followed by difficulties with abstract thinking and words. Eventually, personality change and inability to perform daily functions. Inability to speak, walk, or sit up follows, then death.

TREATMENT: Cholinesterase inhibitors to improve neurotransmitter levels. Palliative care to increase comfort. In late stages, full-time care necessary.

CONTAGION: **1** 2 3 4

PAIN: 1 2 **3** 4

SUFFERING: 1 2 3 **4**

FATAL: **Yes** No Maybe

...or you might have
TRANSIENT GLOBAL AMNESIA

WHAT IT IS: Sudden and sporadic form of short-term memory loss marked by inability to retain new information or remember recent events. Malfunction in memory-controlling temporal lobe triggered by physical trauma or emotional stress. Attacks flare and resolve abruptly, usually lasting from 3 to 6 hours. More common after age 50.

SPECIALIST TO SEE: Neurologist

OTHER SYMPTOMS:

- Anxiety
- Dizziness

- Disorientation
- Nausea

PROGRESSION: Rapid onset of memory loss. Rarely lasts more than several hours. Appears after vigorous physical exertion, sexual intercourse, or major stress. Recurs infrequently and few physical or mental side effects.

TREATMENT: No known cure.

CONTAGION:	**1**	2	3	4
PAIN:	**1**	2	3	4
SUFFERING:	1	2	**3**	4
FATAL:	Yes	**No**	Maybe	

If you have speech difficulty...

...you might have
AMYOTROPHIC LATERAL SCLEROSIS

WHAT IT IS: Debilitating neurological disease that aggressively attacks muscles, affecting ability to move, speak, eat, and breathe. Motor neurons connecting brain, spinal cord, and muscles die, impairing muscle control. Complete paralysis likely, but intellect and senses remain unaffected. Also known as Lou Gehrig's disease.

SPECIALIST TO SEE: Neurologist

OTHER SYMPTOMS:
- Difficulty lifting feet
- Muscle spasms
- Cramping in arms, shoulders, or tongue
- Slurred speech

PROGRESSION: Diagnosis may not be confirmed until 3 to 5 years after symptoms first arise. Entire muscle system eventually affected. 100 percent fatality rate; nearly 80 percent die within 5 years of diagnosis.

TREATMENT: No known cure. Constant care, respirators, catheters, and feeding tubes.

CONTAGION:	**1**	2	3	4
PAIN:	1	2	3	**4**
SUFFERING:	1	2	3	**4**
FATAL:	**Yes**	No	Maybe	

...or you might have
APHASIA

WHAT IT IS: Cognitive dysfunction caused by stroke, brain tumor, infection, head injury, dementia, or arterial thrombosis (blood clot in artery). Results in inability to communicate. Less common causes include epilepsy, drug intoxication, and tertiary syphilis. Affects approximately 1 million people. Rare primary progressive form can be mistaken for Alzheimer's.

SPECIALIST TO SEE: Neurologist

OTHER SYMPTOMS:
- Difficulty reading or writing
- Stuttering
- Inability to repeat language

PROGRESSION: In receptive form, ability to speak is preserved, but comprehension and name recollection are compromised. Expressive form causes stuttering, speech errors, and poor repetition skills. Primary progressive form leads to loss of speech and comprehension of written or spoken word. Eventually affects other mental skills.

TREATMENT: Speech and language therapy.

CONTAGION:	**1**	2	3	4
PAIN:	1	**2**	3	4
SUFFERING:	1	2	3	**4**
FATAL:	Yes	**No**	Maybe	

...or you might have
ATAXIA TELANGIECTASIA

WHAT IT IS: Inherited neurological disease that affects brain, blood, and bodily functions. Neural degeneration may lead to partial paralysis. Often diagnosed in childhood, but adult onset possible. Telangiectasias (small spider veins) may appear on ears, cheeks, and in corners of eyes. Increased risk for cancer.

SPECIALIST TO SEE: Neurologist

OTHER SYMPTOMS:
- Chronic bronchial infections
- Pneumonia
- Decreased mobility
- Seizures

FACT | 49 percent of Americans don't wash their hands after sneezing and coughing.

Alzheimer's Disease

[Fig. 119]

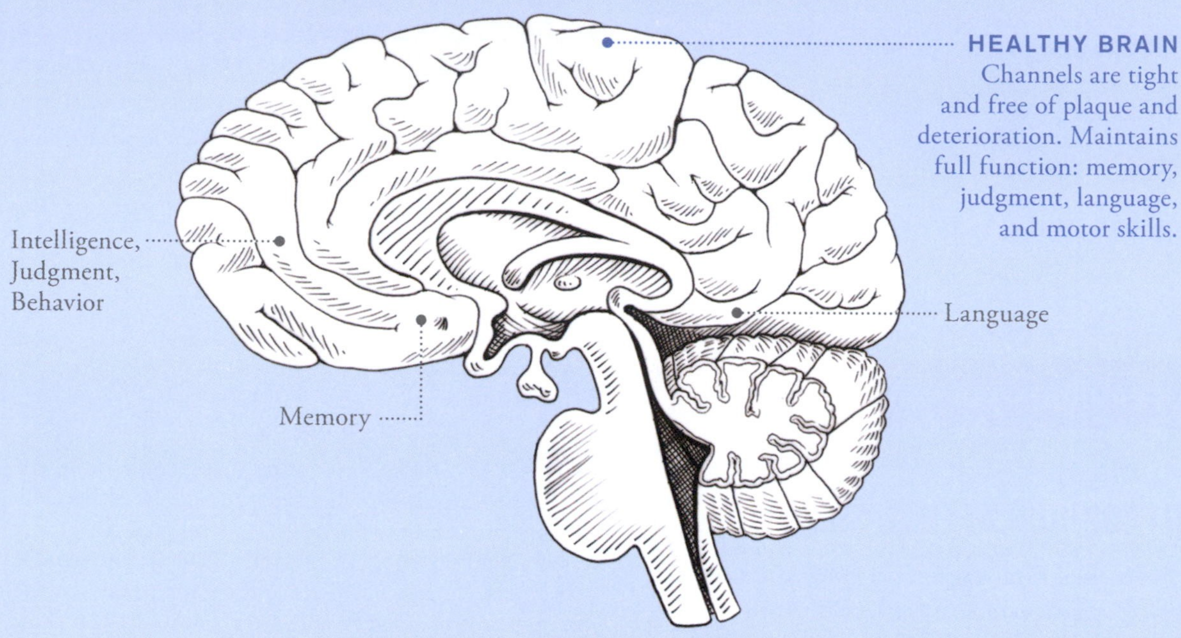

HEALTHY BRAIN
Channels are tight and free of plaque and deterioration. Maintains full function: memory, judgment, language, and motor skills.

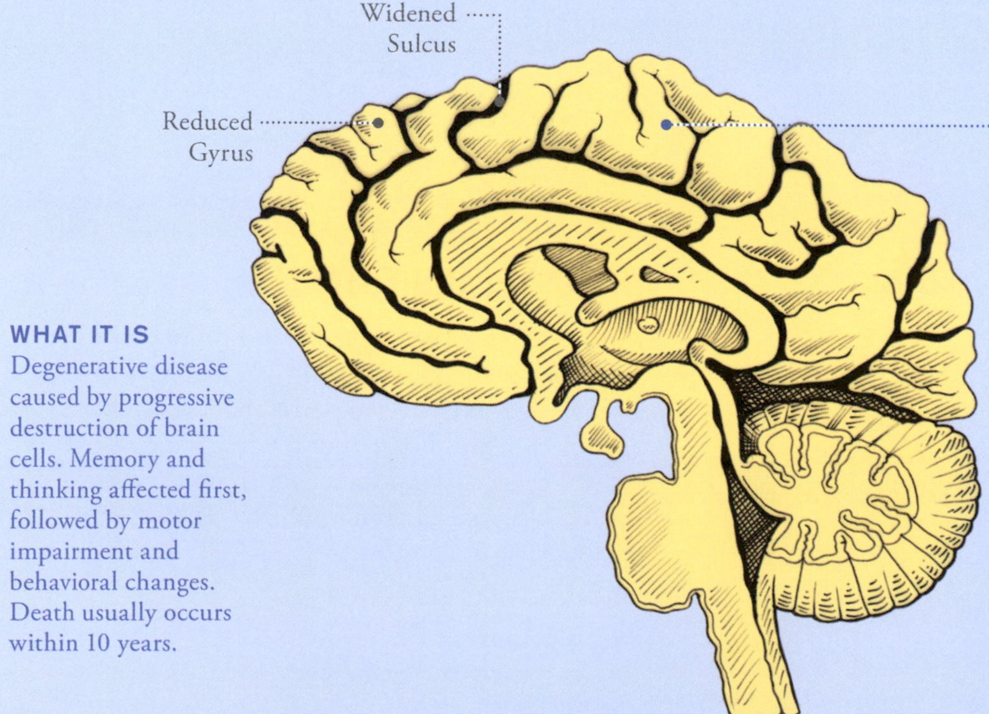

DISEASED BRAIN
Overall brain shrinkage occurs, especially of gyri (folds of brain's outer layer). Sulci (furrows in brain) widen. Microscopic protein plaques and tangles proliferate.

WHAT IT IS
Degenerative disease caused by progressive destruction of brain cells. Memory and thinking affected first, followed by motor impairment and behavioral changes. Death usually occurs within 10 years.

For disease description, see page 172.

PROGRESSION: First, impaired balance and slurred speech progress to loss of muscle control. Full-body degeneration ensues, leaving most wheelchair-bound. Immune system compromised, causing chronic pneumonia. Finally, opportunistic infections may result in death.

TREATMENT: No known cure. Physical, occupational, and speech therapy to reduce symptoms. Gamma globulin (antibodies) injections to boost immune system.

CONTAGION: 1 **2** 3 4

PAIN: 1 2 **3** 4

SUFFERING: 1 2 3 **4**

FATAL: **Yes** No Maybe

...or you might have

TAY-SACHS DISEASE

WHAT IT IS: Genetic disorder that results in insufficient amounts of enzyme that breaks down fatty compounds in cells. Compounds accumulate in brain and nerve cells, inhibiting normal function. In adult-onset form, presents between ages 20 and 40. Common among those of Ashkenazi Jewish, French-Canadian, and Cajun descent.

SPECIALIST TO SEE: Neurologist

OTHER SYMPTOMS:

- Red spots in retinas
- Hearing loss
- Blindness
- Manic depression
- Muscle atrophy
- Difficulty swallowing

PROGRESSION: Commonly starts with slurred speech, muscle cramps, and loss of coordination. Then, as motor and muscle functions degenerate, deafness and blindness follow. Manic-depressive and psychotic episodes may develop.

TREATMENT: No known cure. Antispasmodics to relieve convulsions. Enzyme therapy targeted at nerve cells. Antidepressants.

CONTAGION: 1 **2** 3 4

PAIN: 1 2 **3** 4

SUFFERING: 1 2 3 **4**

FATAL: Yes No **Maybe**

QUOTE | "The art of medicine consists in amusing the patient while nature cures the disease." —Voltaire

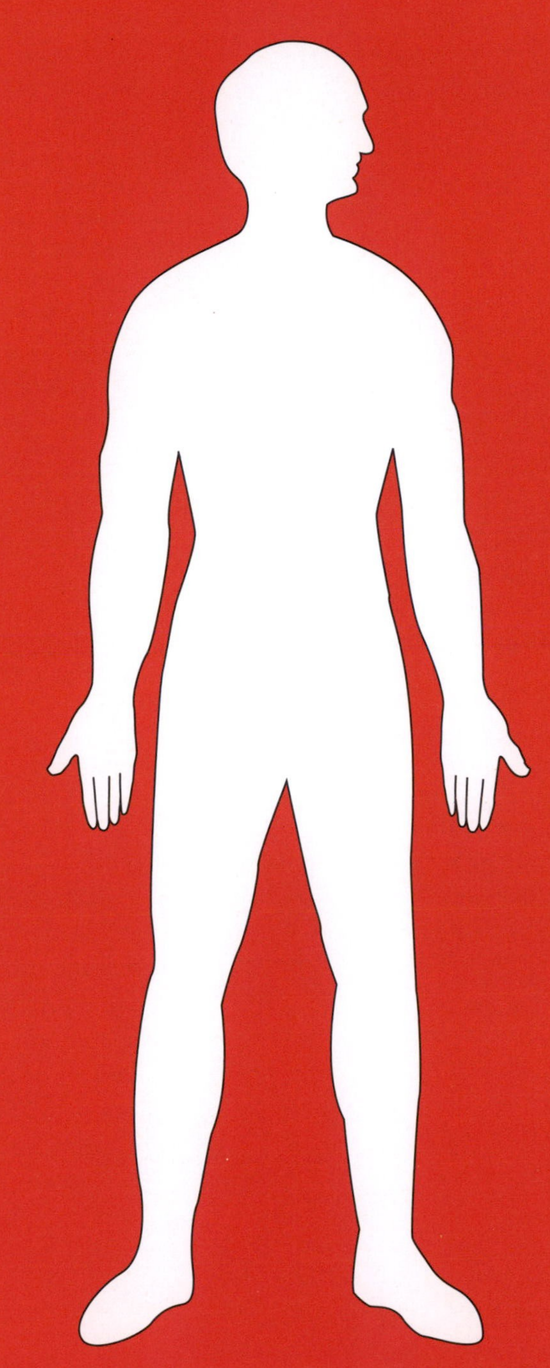

Glossary of Medical Terminology

LOOK UP A MALADY

Between the Latin, the Greek, and the bad handwriting, it can seem like there's an overabundance of mumbo-jumbo in medicine. Once you crack the code, however, it couldn't be easier to syllabize with the white coats. All you have to do is break a word into its constituent parts (see below, under "Actual"), then look up the prefix, suffix, and everything in between.

MAKE UP A MALADY

If you've run the gamut of potential illnesses and nothing suits your symptoms, why not invent a new disease? Simply combine your desired characteristics, then practice pronunciation. If you'd like it to be curable, remove the malady suffix and tack on a treatment. If you want to see a specialist, add an "-iatrist" or an "-ologist" and make an appointment.

ACTUAL CONSTRUCTIONS

- **Hematemesis**: *hemat-* (blood) + *-emesis* (vomiting) = vomiting blood.
- **Leukopenia:** *leuko-* (white blood cell) + *-penia* (deficiency) = low white blood cell count.
- **Cholecystitis:** *cholecyst-* (gallbladder) + *-itis* (inflammation) = inflammation of the gallbladder. The fix? Add *-ectomy* (surgical removal) and have a cholecystectomy.
- **Hydrocephalus:** *hydro-* (water, fluid) + *-cephalus* (head) = fluid in the cranial cavity.

INVENTED CONSTRUCTIONS

- **Bradycraniomalacia:** *brady-* (slow) + *cranio-* (skull) + *-malacia* (softening) = slow softening of the skull.
- **Tachyopthalmorhinomegaly:** *tachy-* (rapid) + *opthalmo-* (eye) + *rhino-* (nose) + *-megaly* (enlargement) = rapid enlargement of the eyes and nose.
- **Dystrichospasm:** *dys-* (diseased, disturbed) + *tricho-* (hair) + *-spasm* (sudden muscle contraction) = unhealthy hair spasm.
- **Cerebrosclerosis:** *cerebro-* (brain) + *-sclerosis* (hardening) = hardening of the brain.

Medical to English

a-, an-: without, not

ab-: away from

-ac: pertaining to

acou/o-: hearing

acr/o-: extremities

ad-: toward

aden/o-: gland

adip/o-: fat

-agra: intense pain

-al: pertaining to

alb-: white

-algia: pain

ana-: upward

andr/o-: man

angi/o-: vessel (blood, lymph)

ankyl/o-: bent, crooked

ant/i-, anth-: against

ante-: before

antero-: front, anterior

-ar/y: pertaining to

arteri/o-: artery

arthr/o-: joint

-ase: enzyme

asthen/o-: weakness, lack

aud/i/o-: hearing

aur/i-: ear

aut/o-: self

bi-: both, two

blephar/o-: eyelid

brachi/o-: arm

brachy-: short

brady-: slow

bronch/o-, bronchi/o-: air passage

bucc/o-: cheek

cac/o-: bad, ill

-capnia: carbon dioxide

carcin/o-: cancer

cardi/a/o-: heart

carp/o-: wrist

cav-: hollow

-cele: hernia, protrusion

-centesis: surgical puncture

cephal/o-: head

cerat/o-: horn

cerebr/i/o-: cerebrum (brain)

cervic/i/o-: neck

cheir/o-: hand

chlor/o-: green

chol/e/o-: bile, gall

cholecyst/o-: gallbladder

chondr/i/o-: cartilage

-cide: killing

circum-: around

cirrh/o-: red-yellow

-clasia: breaking

-clast: break

co/l/m/n/r-: with, together

-coccus: berry-shaped

coel/o-: hollow

col/i/o-, colon/o-: colon

contra-: against

NOTE ON USAGE: Slashes indicate different formations the combining words can take when constructing terms. For example, *hem/o-*, meaning blood, would be *hem-* before a vowel (as in *hemarthrosis*) or *hemo-* before a consonant (as in *hemorrhage*). *Col/i/o-*, meaning colon, could be *col-*, *coli-*, or *colo-*. Don't worry about whether your combination is correctly assembled; instead, just focus on whether it sounds right.

cor/e/o-: pupil

cornu-: horn

cort-: covering

cost/i/o-: ribs

cox-: hip

crani/o-: cranium (skull)

-crine: secretion

cry/o-: cold

cubito-: elbow

cutaneo-: skin

cyan/o-: blue

cyst/i/o-: bladder, sac

cyt/o-: cell

-cyte: cell

dent/i/o-: tooth

derm/a/o-, dermat/o-: skin

-desis: surgical binding, fusion

dexi/o-, dextr/o-: right

di/a-: through

dipl/o-: double

dist/i/o-: far, farthest, away from

dors/i/o-: back

dys-: diseased, disturbed

-eal: pertaining to

ect/o-: outside

-ectasis: expansion

-ectomy: excision, removal (surgical)

-ectopia: displacement

edem-: swelling (fluid)

-emesis: vomiting

-emia: blood condition

encephal/o-: brain

end/o-: within, inner

enter/o-: intestine

ep/i-: above, upon

erythr/o-: red

eso-: inner

-esthesia: sensation, feeling

eu-: good, well

eury-: broad, wide

ex/o-: out of, away from

faci/o-: face

gastr/i/o-: stomach

-gen: producing, generating

-genesis: origin, cause

genu-: knee

gingiv/o-: gums

gloss/o-: tongue

gluc/o-, glyc/o-: sugar, glucose

gnath/o-: jaw

-gram: record, drawing

-graphy: recording

grav-, gravis-: heavy

gravid-: pregnant

gyn/e/o-: woman

hem/i/o-: half

hem/o-, hemat/o-: blood

hemangi/o-: blood vessel

hepat/o-: liver

hidr/o-: sweat

hist/o-: tissue

hom/o-: same, like

humer/o-: shoulder

hydr/o-: water, fluid

hyper-: excessive

hyp/o-: deficient

hyster/o-: uterus, womb

-ia/l: pertaining to

-iasis: condition

-iatrist: doctor, physician, healer

-iatry: treatment

-ic: pertaining to

-ician: specialist

-ictal: seizure, attack

infra-: below

inter-: between

intra-: within

irid/o-: iris (eye)

is/o-: equal

-ism: condition

-itis: inflammation

jaun-: yellow

kerat/o-: cornea, horny tissue

labio-: lip

lact/i/o-: milk

lapar/o-: abdomen

laryng/o-: larynx (voice box)

later/i/o-: lateral, one side

-lepsia, -lepsis, -lepsy: seizure

leuc/o-, leuk/o-: white, white blood cell

lingu/a/i/o-: tongue

lip/o-: fat

-logist: specialist in the study of

-logy: study of

lymph/o-: fluid

-lysis, -lytic: decomposition, destruction

macr/o-: large

mal/o-: bad

-malacia: softening

mamm/o-, mast/o-: breast

maxi-: extra-large

medi/o-: middle

meg/a-: large

megal/o-: enlargement

-megaly: enlargement

melano-: black

mes/o-: middle

meta-: later, after, behind

-meter: instrument for measuring

-metry: measurement

micr/o-: small

mini-: extra-small

mon/o-: one, single

-morph: form, shape

muc/i/o-: mucus

my/o-: muscle

myc/o-: fungus

myel/o-: spinal cord, bone marrow

nas/i/o-: nose

nat/o-: birth

ne/o-: new

necr/o-: death

nephr/o-: kidney

neur/o-: nerve

noct/i/o-: night

ocul/o-: eye

-odynia: pain

-oid: resembling

olig/o-: few

om/o-: shoulder

-oma: tumor

onych/o-: nail

ophthalm/o-: eye

-opia, -opy: vision

-opsy: examination

ori-: mouth

orchi/o-: testes

orth/o-: straight, correct

-osis: condition

oste/o-: bone

ot/o-: ear

-ous: pertaining to

ovar/i/o-: ovary

oxy-: sharp

pachy-: thick

paleo-: old

pan/o-: all

papill/o-: nipple-shaped, projecting

par/a-: near, beside

part-: birth, labor

patell/o-: kneecap

-pathy: disease

ped-: child

ped/i/o-, pod/o-: foot

pelv/i/o-: pelvis

-penia: decrease, deficiency

-pepsia: digestion

peri-: around

-pexy: surgical fixation

-phagia, -phagy: eating, swallowing

pharyng/o-: throat (upper)

-phasia: speech

phleb/o-: vein

-phobia: fear

-phonia, -phony: sound or voice

-phoria: feeling

phren/i/o-: diaphragm

physi/o-: body

-plasia, -plasy: development

-plasm: formed material

-plasty: plastic surgery

platy-: flat

-plegia: paralysis

pleur/i/o-: rib

pluri-: several, more

-pnea: breathing

pneum/o-: lung

-poiesis: formation

poikil/o-: varied, various

poli/o-: gray

poly-: many, multiple

-porosis: passage

porphyr/o-: purple

post-: after, behind

postero-: back, behind

-praxia: movement, performance

pre-: before

presby/o-: old age

proct/o-: anus, rectum

prur-, prurit-: itching

pseud/o-: false

psych/o-: mind

-ptosis: dropping, sagging,

-ptysis: spitting

pulmo-: lung

py/o-: pus

ren/i/o-: kidney

retro-: backward

rhin/o-: nose

rhod/o-: red

-rrhagia: blood flow (rapid)

-rrhaphy: suturing, sewing

-rrhea: flow, discharge (excessive)

-rrhexis: rupture

sarc/o-: flesh

-schisis: split, fissure

scler/o-: hardening

-sclerosis: hardening

-scope: instrument for viewing

-scopy: visual examination

semi-: half, partial

-sepsis, -septic: infection

sial/o-: saliva, salivary glands

-sis: condition

som/a-: body

-spasm: sudden muscle contraction, spasm

spin/i/o-: spine

splen/o-: spleen

spondyl/o-: vertebrae

-stasis: stoppage, stability

sten/o-: narrowing, constricting

-stenosis: narrowing, constriction

stomat/o-: mouth

-stomy: creation of an opening

sub-: below, inferior

super-, supra-: above, in excess

sym-, syn-: with, together

tachy-: fast, rapid

tend/o-, teno-: tendon

therm/o-: heat

thorac/i/o-: chest

thromb/o-: clot

-tocia: birth, labor

-tome: instrument for cutting

-tomy: incision

tox/i/o-, toxic/o-: poison

trache/o-, trachel/o-: trachea, neck

trans-: across

trich/o-: hair

-tripsy: crushing (surgical)

-trophy: nourishment

-ule: small, diminutive

uni-: one

ur/o-: urine

urethr/o-: urethra

vascul/o-, vas/i/o-: blood vessel

ven/i/o-: vein

vertebr/o-: vertebrae

vesico-: bladder

viscer/a/i/o-: organ

xanth/o-: yellow

xer/o-: dry

English to Medical

abdomen: lapar/o-

above, upon: ep/i-, super-, supra-

across: trans-

after, behind: meta-, post-

against: ant/i-, contra-

air passage: bronch/o-, bronchi/o-

all: pan/o-

arm: brachi/o-

around, surrounding: circum-, peri-

artery: arteri/o-

away from: ab-, dist/i/o-

back: dors/i/o-

bad, incorrect: cac/o-, mal/o-

before: ante-, pre-

below, inferior: infra-, sub-

bent, crooked: ankyl/o-

berry-shaped: -coccus

between: inter-

bile, gall: chol/e/o-

binding, fusion (surgical): -desis

birth, labor: nat/o-, part-, -tocia

black: melano-

bladder: cyst/i/o-, vesico-

blood: hem/o-, hemat/o-

blood condition: -emia

blood flow (rapid): -rrhagia

blue: cyan/o-

body: physi/o-, som/a-

bone: oste/o-

bone marrow: myel/o-

both, two: bi-

brain: cerebr/i/o-, encephal/o-

break: -clast, -clasia

breast: mamm/o-, mast/o-

breathing: -pnea

broad, wide: eury-

cancer: carcin/o-

cartilage: chondr/i/o-

cell: cyt/o-

cheek: bucc/o-

chest: thorac/i/o-

child: ped-

clot: thromb/o-

cold: cry/o-

colon: col/i/o-, colon/o-

condition: -iasis, -ism, -osis

cornea: kerat/o-

covering: cort-

crushing (surgical): -tripsy

death: necr/o-

decrease, deficiency: hyp/o-, -penia

destroy, reduce: -cide, -lysis, -lytic

diaphragm: phren/i/o-

digestion: -pepsia

disease: -pathy

diseased, disturbed: dys-

displacement: -ectopia

NOTE ON USAGE: Slashes indicate different formations the combining words can take when constructing terms. For example, *hem/o-*, meaning blood, would be *hem-* before a vowel (as in *hemarthrosis*) or *hemo-* before a consonant (as in *hemorrhage*). *Col/i/o-*, meaning colon, could be *col-*, *coli-*, or *colo-*. Don't worry about whether your combination is correctly assembled; instead, just focus on whether it sounds right.

doctor, physician, healer: -iatrist

double, twice: dipl/o-

dropping, sagging: -ptosis

dry: xer/o-

ear: aur/i-, ot/i/o-

eating, swallowing: -phagia, -phagy

elbow: cubito-

enlargement: megal/o-

equal: is/o-

examination: -opsy

excessive: hyper-, supra-

excision, removal (surgical): -ectomy

expansion: -ectasis

extremities: acr/o-

eye: ocul/o-, ophthalm/o-

eyelid: blephar/o-

face: faci/o-

false: pseud/o-

far, farthest: dist/i/o-

fast, rapid: tachy-

fat: adip/o-, lip/o-

fear: -phobia

feeling, sensation: -phoria, -esthesia

few: olig/o-

fixation (surgical): -pexy

flat: platy-

flesh: sarc/o-

flow, discharge (excessive): -rrhea

fluid: lymph/o-

foot: ped/i/o-, pod/o-

form, shape: -morph

formation, growth: -plasia, -plasm, -poiesis

front, anterior: antero-

fungus: myc/o-

gallbladder: cholecyst/o-

gland: aden/o-

good, well: eu-

gray: poli/o-

green: chlor/o-

gums: gingiv/o-

hair: trich/o-

half: hem/i/o-, semi-

hand: cheir/o-

hardening: scler/o-

head: cephal/o-

hearing: acou/o-, aud/i/o-

heart: cardi/a/o-

heat: therm/o-

heavy: grav-, gravis-

hernia, protrusion: -cele

hip: cox-

hollow: coel/o-, cav-

horn: cerat/o-, cornu-

horny tissue: kerat/o-

incision: -tomy

infection: -sepsis, -septic

inflammation: -itis

inner: eso-

instrument for cutting: -tome

instrument for measuring: -meter

instrument for viewing: -scope

intestine: enter/o-

iris (eye): irid/o-

itching: prur-, prurit-

jaw: gnath/o-

joint: arthr/o-

kidney: nephr/o-, ren/i/o-

kill: -cide

knee: genu-

kneecap: patell/o-

large: macr/o-, maxi-, meg/a-

larynx (voice box): laryng/o-

later, after, behind: meta-

lateral, one side: later/i/o-

lip: labio-

liver: hepat/o-

lungs: pneum/o-

man: andr/o-

many, several, multiple: poly-, pluri-

measurement: -metry

middle: mes/o-, medi/o-

milk: lact/i/o-

mind: psych/o-

mouth: ori-, stomat/o-

mucus: muc/i/o-

muscle: my/o-

nail: onych/o-

narrowing, constricting: sten/o-

near, beside: par/a-

neck: cervic/i/o-, trache/o-, trachel/o-

nerve: neur/o-

new: ne/o-

nipple-shaped, projecting: papill/o-

nose: nas/i/o-, rhin/o-

nourishment: -trophy

old: paleo-

one, single: mon/o-, uni-

opening (creation of): -stomy

organ: viscer/a/i/o-

origin, cause: -genesis

out of: ex/o-

outside: ect/o-

ovary: ovar/i/o-

pain: -agra, -algia, -odynia,

paralysis: -plegia

pelvis: pelv/i/o-

pertaining to: -ac, -al, -ar/y, -eal, -ia/l, -ic, -ous

plastic surgery: -plasty

poison: tox/i/o-, toxic/o-

pregnant: gravid-

producing, forming: -gen

puncture (surgical): -centesis

pupil: cor/e/o-

purple: porphyr/o-

pus: py/o-

record: -gram

recording: -graphy

rectum: proct/o-

red: erythr/o-, rhod/o-

red-yellow: cirrh/o-

rib: cost/i/o-, pleur/i/o-,

right: dexi/o-, dextr/o-

rupture: -rrhexis

saliva: sial/o-

same, like, resembling: hom/o-, -oid

secretion: -crine

seizure, attack: -ictal, -lepsy

self: aut/o-

sharp: oxy-

short: brachy-

shoulder: om/o-, humer/o-

skin: cutaneo-, derm/a/o-, dermat/o-

skull: crani/o-

slow: brady-

small: micr/o-, mini-, -ule

softening: -malacia

sound or voice: -phonia, -phony

spasm: -spasm

specialist: -ician

specialist in the study of: -logist

speech: -phasia

spine: spin/i/o-

spitting: -ptysis

spleen: splen/o-

split, fissure: -schisis

stomach: gastr/i/o-

stoppage, stability: -stasis

straight, correct: orth/o-

study of: -logy

sugar, glucose: gluc/o-, glyc/o-

suturing, sewing: -rrhaphy

sweat: hidr/o-

swelling: edem-

tendon: tend/o-, teno-

testes: orchi/o-

thick: pachy-

throat (upper): pharyng/o-

throat (voice box): laryng/o-

through: di/a-

tissue: hist/o-

tongue: gloss/o-, lingu/a/i/o-

tooth: dent/i/o-

toward: ad-

treatment: -iatry

tumor: -oma

upward: ana-

urethra: urethr/o-

urine: ur/o-

uterus: hyster/o-

varied, various: poikil/o-

vein: phleb/o-, ven/i/o-

vertebrae: spondyl/o-, vertebr/o-

vessel: angi/o-, hemangi/o-, vascul/o-, vas/i/o-

vision (condition): -opia, -opy

visual examination: -scopy

vomiting: -emesis

water, fluid: hydr/o-

weakness, lack: asthen/o-

white: alb-, leuc/o-, leuk/o-

white blood cell: leuc/o-, leuk/o-

with, together: co/l/m/n/r-, sym-, syn-

within, inner: end/o-, intra-

without, not: a-, an-

woman: gyn/e/o-

wrist: carp/o-

yellow: xanth/o-, jaun-

Disease Index

M

N

O

P

R

S

T

V

W

X

Y

Z